2107

The Creative Enterprise

The Creative Enterprise
Managing Innovative Organizations and People

CULTURE
VOLUME 2

Edited by
Tony Davila
Marc J. Epstein
and
Robert Shelton

Praeger Perspectives

Westport, Connecticut
London

Library of Congress Cataloging-in-Publication Data

The creative enterprise : managing innovative organizations and people / edited by
Tony Davila, Marc J. Epstein, and Robert Shelton.
    p. cm.
  Includes bibliographical references and index.
    ISBN 0-275-98685-3 (set : alk. paper) — ISBN 0-275-98686-1 (vol. 1 : alk. paper) —
ISBN 0-275-98687-X (vol. 2 : alk. paper) — ISBN 0-275-98688-8 (vol. 3 : alk. paper)
    1. Organizational change—Management. 2. Technological innovations—Management.
3. Creative ability in business—Management. 4. Industrial management. I. Davila, Tony.
II. Epstein, Marc J. III. Shelton, Robert D.
HD58.8.C727   2007
658.4′063—dc22   2006030628

British Library Cataloguing in Publication Data is available.

Library of Congress Catalog Card Number: 2006030628
ISBN: 0-275-98685-3 (set)
      0-275-98686-1 (vol. 1)
      0-275-98687-X (vol. 2)
      0-275-98688-8 (vol. 3)

First published in 2007

Praeger Publishers, 88 Post Road West, Westport, CT 06881
An imprint of Greenwood Publishing Group, Inc.
www.praeger.com

Printed in the United States of America

The paper used in this book complies with the
Permanent Paper Standard issued by the National
Information Standards Organization (Z39.48-1984).

10 9 8 7 6 5 4 3 2 1

Contents

Introduction

Business forces are eroding static competitive advantages faster than ever. And this is not only true for technology markets, where the pace has just accelerated. It is also true in industries that were considered "mature." Mittal, the steel company, is revolutionizing its industry. And its advantage does not come from amazing new technology, but from a relentless focus on doing business differently. Procter & Gamble has made explicit its compromise with innovation as the only way to remain profitable. This compromise with new technologies and business practices has already meant the resignation of one CEO, but not because he was too slow. Rather, he went too fast.

Innovation has emerged as the only way to sustain competitive advantage over time. Success is not to be found in a technology, in a market position, or in a business model; success resides in an organization's ability to innovate and be ahead of its competitors. This three-volume set is designed to provide the reader with the most up-to-date knowledge on how to be innovative. It addresses this issue from the various perspectives that are needed to have a well-rounded understanding of how to drive innovation in an organization.

The first volume takes a strategy perspective to answer the question of how to design an organization to be competitive in its market space. Innovation is not something that a manager can turn on only when needed. It is not a faucet that can be shut off when we don't need innovation and turned on when we do. Innovation is both a state of mind and a way of life. The first volume explores this idea from different perspectives on strategy.

The second volume looks at innovation from the perspective of the individual. It addresses the question of how to design organizations to enhance creativity. This volume focuses on drivers of creativity at the individual and team levels. Then it moves up a level of analysis and looks at organizational forces that shape this creativity—culture and rewards.

The third volume is about execution. It answers the question of how to get innovation done. The focus of this volume is how to design the management infrastructure to encourage innovation. Using a car race metaphor, the second volume is about the driver; this third one is about the car. The chapters address different tools to enhance innovation, from organizational structures to processes and measures.

The three volumes combine the perspective of large companies and small start-ups. Innovation is not the exclusive territory of one set of organizations. It happens in large companies as well as young ones; it happens in for-profit companies as well as not-for-profit organizations—under the umbrella of social innovation. The three volumes combine these various sources of innovation.

VOLUME 1: DEFINING INNOVATION STRATEGIES

Innovation starts at the top of an organization. It is top management's compromise with innovation that drives it. The first chapter in this volume shows how companies following an innovation strategy have outperformed more conservative ones. The chapter presents evidence from research studies and company stories to illustrate the importance of innovation to success.

Top management's commitment to innovation shows up in many different aspects. The chapters in Volume 1 address the aspects that make an innovative enterprise. The first aspect is the design of the *organization's interfaces with the environment.*

A key finding in both academic research and managerial practice is that innovation is not an individual activity—the popular image of the lone genius coming up with the most amazing ideas in a garage is a gross and dangerous simplification. Innovation—moving ideas into value—is a team effort. Ideas emerge and improve through exposure. The not-invented-here syndrome, where anything from the outside of a limited group is seen as inferior, is one of the most dangerous organizational pathologies. Top management is in charge of encouraging the interaction among people from different departments, bringing in people with different backgrounds, and ensuring the fluidity of ideas from outside the organization. One of the chapters in the first volume provides an interesting story on how innovation has happened in history. After reading this chapter, the reader will see innovation in a different light and understand how personalities, groups, and the environment interacted to deliver some of the most important innovations of the twentieth century.

In this first volume, three chapters cover the importance of the environment to innovation. One of them examines how Silicon Valley is redefining itself to maintain its undisputed leadership as the world's innovation hub. The chapter delineates the dynamism linked to people with different trainings interacting to create. Innovation in Silicon Valley is a team sport, with constant fluidity of ideas and backgrounds. Isolated companies have no room in the Valley. The second chapter takes the perspective of a university—one of the main sources of technological innovation—and its experiences with the corporate world. The chapter provides an interesting discussion on how technology-transfer offices work and the challenges they are facing to become more effective in moving technology breakthroughs to society. The third chapter also looks at the interface of the university and industry—a key link in leveraging the knowledge generated in universities. It presents a study on Engineering Research Centers: an organizational form that the National Science Foundation developed to improve technology commercialization at universities. The chapter details what makes some of these centers more successful.

Another aspect of innovation management that top management is in charge of is *defining the organization's innovation strategy.* Innovation is often confused with freedom. Providing direction and guidelines, setting criteria, and telling people what not to do are seen as ingredients to kill innovation. Much like the lone innovator, the need for unrestricted freedom to innovate is a myth. If top management wants innovation, it needs to set the strategy—decide what not to do and where the company needs to go. The CEO of Logitech—the leading company in computer devices such as mice and keyboards—provides a good example of giving directions and defining what is not within the company's strategy. He describes his company's strategy as "dominating the last inch," the inch that puts a person in contact with technology. So the company is not interested in technology products or in software products; it is interested in technology and software that facilitate the person-machine interaction. Logitech's CEO believes that this is a large enough space.

Three chapters in this first volume address the strategic dimension of innovation management. One of them provides a framework on how to think about innovation strategies. It describes the various levers that top management use to shape strategy. A second one addresses the important distinction between incremental and radical innovations. Incentives, risk aversion, and organizational antibodies lead to an emphasis on incremental innovation—more visible and profitable over the short term, but with the risk of jeopardizing the long term. The need for radical innovation and how to manage radical innovations are issues addressed in these chapters. While too much incremental innovation is dangerous, the opposite is also true. The right amount of innovation and the right mix are unique to every organization and where they are in their development. The third chapter addresses different ways in which management knowledge has thought about innovation strategy—how it has evolved from the idea of strategy as a plan designed by top management and implemented by the organization to the idea of innovation happening throughout the organization with top management being in charge of guiding and structuring these efforts. The evolution of the concept of strategy has led to changes in the way strategy implementation is executed.

Two chapters in the first volume address two important topics related to innovation. The first one presents the idea of social innovation—innovation in social settings, often through not-for-profit organizations. The advances in this topic of innovation have been amazing over the last few years. The world of social organizations has seen a management revolution as donors with deep managerial experience have adopted best practices in commercial companies as well as social organizations. In the academic world, a topic that was hardly taught has become one of the most popular courses in business schools. Stanford Graduate School of Business has launched a Social Innovation Center that publishes a magazine focused on the topic; it also offers several electives to MBAs and executive programs for non-profit organizations' leaders. The chapter addresses this important topic and examines how to adapt what we know about innovation in for-profit companies to social innovation.

The second important topic covered in this initial volume is innovation in start-up firms. The paradox here is that when talking about innovation, some people only think about how to make large firms more innovative, while others believe that only start-ups are innovative. The truth is that innovation happens in both types of organizations. This chapter discusses the evolution of start-up firms. A key transition point for these companies happens when their size is such that professional management tools are needed to implement strategy. The company is not a group of friends who can be managed as a group; it becomes an organization. Entrepreneurs often have a difficult time making this transition, and often they are replaced to bring in a manager. This chapter focuses on this transition point and how successful start-ups make this transition.

VOLUME 2: IMPROVING INNOVATION THROUGH PEOPLE AND CULTURE

The innovation lever addressed in the second volume is the internal environment. The amount of innovation within an organization depends, to a large extent, on top management's ability *to create the right culture and the right setting for people's creativity to thrive.* The volume starts by looking at what makes people creative. The first chapters describe in detail what we know about creativity and how to fully use the creative potential of people.

Creativity at the individual level has been the focus of much recent research. The conclusions from this research provide a complex picture, even more when creativity happens in an organization with different forces acting upon it. The need to transform ideas into useful solutions creates additional tensions in organizations. These tensions require balancing acts and a commitment from top management to let people run with ideas with a fuzzy future. The more novel an idea, the harder it is to visualize where it leads and the more fragile it is. Ideas need a runway to develop and an encouraging environment without premature judgments or negative feelings. They need experiments and prototypes to manage uncertainty. The planning is about how to resolve uncertainty, rather than visualizing the future, which is the practice with which we commonly associate planning.

Creativity is not about creating a perfect state; it is about balancing different forces over time. Positive and negative affective states, extrinsic and intrinsic motivation, autonomy, and guidance are required.

A recurring theme is the importance of the environment beyond individual creativity traits. People who could be considered less creative will outperform creative individuals if they have a supportive environment that the latter do not have. The characteristics of this environment range from leadership to co-workers. A person will be more creative when her supervisor does not micromanage and leaves space for ideas to emerge and mature, when the supervisor provides inspiration and stimulates innovation through, for instance, goals that demand creativity, when this person is fair and supportive in her evaluations. Similarly, co-workers who are creative and value creativity put together an environment where people thrive.

Contrary to common wisdom, creativity requires discipline—not the military discipline that eliminates it, but the discipline of working on it. Creativity does not just happen; people and organizations need to want it to happen. A key component of creativity is openness to experience, interacting with the outside world, with people with different experiences and points of view. Some people have a natural tendency to interact with "weird" people; but most of us prefer the safety of what we know. Discipline is required to overcome these creative blocks. Another component of creativity is to consciously think about these experiences and make the effort to translate them into ideas. Again, our natural tendency is to let these experiences go by, without considering how they can enrich the way we live and work.

Another important ingredient of creativity is self-confidence. Often, we are not creative because we do not believe we can be so. We don't even try to come up with new ways to look at the world. Several personal attitudes are blocks to new ideas, from having doubts about trying to think differently to fear of failing. Failure and creativity come together; actually, failure happens more often than success when risks are taken. In the same way that organizations that penalize failure will kill innovation, fear of failure kills the risk-taking attitude required for creativity.

The initial stage in formally tackling creativity is idea generation. At this stage, there should be no limits to what comes into the process. To do this, people involved have to forget about their self-image and their fear of saying something wrong—what other people are going to think. The richer this initial step, the better the raw material available. It is only as this process progresses that this raw material is processed into feasible ideas.

From individual creativity, the volume progresses into the topic of organizational culture and the social context of innovation. Certain organizations are more innovative than others. Strategy, as described in Volume 1, accounts for part of it. The informal norms and codes of conduct, what is broadly understood as culture, account for another important part. Finally, management infrastructure—the focus of Volume 3—accounts for the rest.

Culture has always fascinated managers and researchers in organizations. A culture that supports innovation is a culture that encourages people to interact with their networks to identify opportunities. It also provides resources and recognition to people who take risks exploring new ideas. It is a culture that recognizes effort and failure—a key ingredient of innovation. More importantly, innovative cultures tend to be strong cultures—cultures that reinforce and live very clear values and objectives. Clear values shift the attention from short-term financial performance to consistency with these values over time.

An innovative culture supports autonomy—where people can experiment—and risk taking. It has bias for action; rather than waiting for things to happen, an innovative culture will support people experimenting and prototyping their ideas. It has a winning mentality, with the objective of leading the market and achieving goals that seemed to be unreachable. It values openness to the world to enrich the idea generation process and values teamwork where ideas are bounced and refined. It is a culture that does not kill dissenting views but rather encourages the different points of view.

But culture goes beyond the organization to the level of nations. Certain nations are more innovative than others. The economic well-being, an appreciation for scientific work, a robust educational system, and the size of the nation all affect the level of innovativeness of a nation.

Finally, the second volume addresses the process of innovation—how to design such a process to enhance individual creativity—and the design of incentives—both social and economic—to support rather than hinder innovation. Creativity may be useless without adequate processes that support and nurture this creativity. Similarly, creativity and innovation can be damaged if incentives are counter-productive. Interestingly, the design of appropriate incentives varies with the type of innovation.

VOLUME 3: DESIGNING STRUCTURE AND SYSTEMS FOR SUPERIOR INNOVATION

The prior volumes deal with strategy and how to create an environment that encourages innovation. The focus of this third volume is how to design the organization and its management systems to support innovation. It addresses the third aspect that top management has to address in creating an innovative company: *designing the structures, processes, and systems that generate ideas, selecting the most promising ones, and transforming them into value.*

The volume also emphasizes the importance of cross-national interaction in getting innovation done. Three chapters address this issue from different perspectives. One of them examines the international component within product development. The second one looks at how venture capital—the money of innovation—has evolved from a regional to an international focus. Today, most venture capital firms' portfolios are diversified geographically with investments in North America, Europe, and Asia. A third chapter devotes its attention to how leading firms are managing R&D across borders. Different models are possible in addressing the need to coordinate knowledge from different parts of the world. But certain models are more adequate given the particular characteristics of the challenges at hand.

Another aspect relevant to the structure and systems of innovative organizations is the design of an appropriate measurement system. "What gets measured gets done" is frequently cited as a management principle, and it also applies to innovation management. But measures should not be used to evaluate performance, as they are sometimes used in other settings; their main role is to supply the information that guides discussion. Only in very specific types of innovation is it advisable to link measures to evaluation. Well-designed measurement systems track the entire innovation process. They provide information about the quality of the raw material for innovation—diversity of people, contact with the external world, and the quality of the ideas—all the way to the value created by innovation. In between, the system measures the balance of the innovation portfolio and the effectiveness of the innovation process.

Three chapters focus on organizing for innovation. One of them provides a balanced perspective between academic research and organizational applications on how to run product development projects. The second looks into the organization of novel ideas—usually harder to develop within an established organization—around the concept of incubators. Both chapters complement each other, providing the tools required to manage incremental and radical innovation. The third chapter presents the results of a research project on the characteristics of innovative firms. The study combines scientific rigor with enlightening examples.

An important issue in innovation management also addressed in this volume is intellectual property—in particular, how new intellectual property emerges from the combination of existing ideas. Innovation is not a blank page but the ability to combine existing ideas in novel ways.

Overall, the three volumes give a complete view of how to make an organization innovative. They balance depth in the state-of-the-art scientific knowledge with state-of-the-art managerial applications. We hope you will enjoy them!

1

Dialectics of Creativity in Complex Organizations

JENNIFER M. GEORGE

Most, if not all, innovation in organizations stems from the creative ideas of individuals and groups. In fact, innovation is typically defined as the implementation of creative ideas.[1] Thus, it is not surprising that scholarly theorizing and research, as well as management practice, have focused on understanding the factors that can foster or facilitate creativity in organizations. For example, recent literature reviews identify a variety of factors that research has found serve to encourage creativity, and also factors that inhibit or thwart creativity.[2] In considering the range of factors and processes that have been linked to creativity in organizations, and adopting a broad perspective that takes into account the nature of work and organizing in modern, complex organizations, fundamental paradoxes or contradictions can be seen. It is through the ongoing interactions of the opposing dualities of these paradoxes that creativity emerges.

In this chapter, I focus on several fundamental paradoxes surrounding creativity in complex organizations and explicate how creativity emerges from the ongoing interactions between the contradictory forces underlying the paradoxes.

THE PARADOX OF THE DEFINITION

Creativity is commonly defined as the production of new and useful ideas; both novelty and usefulness must be present for an idea to be considered creative.[3] Novelty alone (without usefulness) results in unusualness; unusualness per se is not the same thing as creativity. Usefulness (without novelty) results in practicality; practicality is, of course, a good thing, but again, not the same thing as creativity. Take the simple example of trying to come up with a creative idea for designing a new restaurant. An unusual idea would be to locate the kitchen in an open space in the center of the seating area, like a bull-pen. Though unusual, this idea is far from practical. All of the chaos that goes on in the kitchen would be on full view to diners, as would the never-ending traffic of the wait staff in and out of the kitchen (including the returning of prepared dishes that diners found inferior). A practical idea would be to have the kitchen as a closed-off area at the back of the restaurant: functional, but not creative. A creative idea might be to search for an existing, aesthetically pleasing structure initially used for another purpose (e.g., an old church or an old warehouse) and then modify the structure to be functional for a restaurant, retaining as many physical elements of the existing structure as feasible.

Requiring that ideas be both novel and useful to be considered creative seems to make perfect sense, especially in complex, modern organizations experiencing many competitive pressures. However, the paradox of joining novelty and usefulness becomes apparent when we consider how people process information and make judgments about the usefulness of creative ideas. An extensive body of theorizing and research suggests that people perceive and process information and make judgments based on cognitive schemas.[4] Schemas are abstract knowledge structures based on prior experience and stored in memory about a type of stimuli, person, situation, or event. People develop schemas for types of stimuli they encounter repeatedly, and schemas guide information processing and judgment. People tend to pay attention to information that is consistent with their schemas. Essentially, schemas are people's mental models or views of what things and people are like.

Organizational members, of course, rely on their schemas to process information and make judgments in a variety of domains such as how key processes should operate, desirable features of products, types of customers or clients, competitors, the nature of work tasks and jobs, and so forth. In judging a truly novel idea in one of these or other domains, relevant, pre-existing schemas will be brought to bear to determine if the idea is useful or practical. Often, novel ideas are likely to be inconsistent with pre-existing schemas about how a particular process should work, what a product is used for, and what clients or customers really need and want. This inconsistency is likely to lead to judgments that the idea is not useful or impractical. The more novel the idea, the more the inconsistency, and the more potential for it to be dismissed as impractical. In relying on pre-existing schemas to judge ideas, ideas are put to the consistency test in terms of prior experience and knowledge about what things are like, how they should be dealt with, and how they work. Failing the consistency test with current mental models or world views leads to the conclusion of a lack of usefulness or practicality; it just won't work. However, novel ideas are often novel because they *are* inconsistent with preconceived notions and schemas.

Yet we cannot discard usefulness as a criteria for creativity, as modern organizations do face many challenges and competitive pressures and cannot afford to expend resources pursuing novel ideas that are not useful; the usefulness criteria gives needed discipline to creative pursuits. And of course, without novelty, there is no creativity or innovation. So the paradox of requiring creative ideas to be both novel and useful is not something that can be easily resolved but rather is something that can be managed to ensure that those ideas that are truly novel and useful see the light of day and lead to innovation.

MANAGING THE NOVELTY/USEFULNESS PARADOX

There are several steps that managers and all employees can take to manage the novelty/usefulness paradox of creativity. Here, I describe five ways to effectively manage this paradox: avoid premature judgments, run with and vet ideas, focus on how ideas could be useful, not on why they won't be, encourage small experiments, and build prototypes.

Avoid Premature Judgments

Extensive research in psychology indicates that it is a basic human tendency to make very quick judgments and jump to conclusions. And how do people make these judgments? In essence, they rely on their pre-existing schemas based on prior experience.[5] So to encourage creativity, this basic human tendency needs to be temporarily suspended or put on hold.

Run with and Vet Ideas

Allowing oneself and others the luxury of running with ideas can seem just that, an unjustified luxury. However, in order for truly creative ideas to lead to innovation, organizational members need the freedom to run with ideas that might be far-fetched and might not work out, but then again might lead to a real breakthrough. It is for this reason that organizations employing scientists and researchers sometimes allow them to spend some percentage of their time (typically around 15 percent) pursuing their own projects and interests.[6] Across the board, however, employees should be encouraged to run with ideas they might have for improving processes, services, and products. When employees have the freedom to run with their ideas, they may often conclude for themselves that the ideas are not practical, but in the process of learning that, they formulate a novel idea that is useful. An important part of running with ideas is vetting them with others, which can lead to refinements and improvements along the way, as well as support for eventual implementation.

Focus on How Ideas Could Be Potentially Useful

Often, when people are presented with something that represents a change from the status quo, their initial reaction is to voice all the reasons why it won't work, based on their pre-existing schemas (essentially their roadmaps *of* the status quo and why it is the way it is). Creativity and innovation require a shift in mindset from why something novel won't or couldn't work to how it potentially might work.

Encourage Small Experiments

Sometimes, rather than debating the merits of a new idea, the idea can be tested in a small experiment. Small experiments allow organizational members to try out their ideas by making changes in a relatively risk-free manner. Such trial runs can not only serve as a good testing ground for ideas, but can also lead to a richer understanding of the phenomenon at hand, revision and improvement of ideas, or the generation of alternative, superior ideas.

Build Prototypes

Prototypes are models, sketches, blueprints, and other kinds of enactments of creative ideas. They are an action-oriented approach to determining if and how novel ideas can be potentially useful. The innovative Palo Alto design firm Ideo excels at the use of prototypes to spark innovation. As Tom Kelley, general manager of Ideo, puts it, "Quick prototyping is about acting before you've got the answers, about taking chances, stumbling a little, but then making it right."[7]

THE PARADOX OF THE PERSON

All creative ideas and innovation have their origins in people. Researchers have devoted considerable attention to determining if some people are predisposed to be more creative than others. While there do appear to be certain enduring characteristics of individuals that may make them more or less prone to creativity, relationships between these characteristics and creativity have tended to be small in magnitude. Moreover, in organizational contexts, such relationships are likely to depend on the context or situation. In certain situations (e.g., jobs entailing very algorithmic tasks with little discretion or autonomy), employees may be bound not to be creative, regardless of their natural proclivities.[8] In other situations (e.g., high autonomy and availability of creative role models and developmental feedback), employees who by nature may be less inclined toward creativity, may nonetheless come up with new and useful ideas.[9] Clearly, the potential for creativity resides in all human beings and is part and parcel of the human condition. Organizations can serve to thwart encouragement of this natural inclination.

So the paradox of the person is not really concerned with across-person differences. Rather, it is concerned with dispositions and states residing within individuals that can seem to be paradoxical on the surface yet which, operating together, result in creativity. And of course, these dispositions and states that occur within people also can operate in a collective manner when people are working together in teams and organizations.

Paradoxical Predispositions

A useful way to think about predispositions is in terms of personality, which represents the relatively enduring patterns of how a person feels, thinks, and behaves. Each individual's personality can be described in terms of his or her standing on traits that are specific dimensions of personality.[10] While hundreds of personality traits have been identified and studied, research suggests that they are structured hierarchically, with five very broad and general traits at the top of the trait hierarchy (i.e., extraversion, neuroticism, conscientiousness, openness to experience, and agreeableness). More specific personality traits are nested below the "Big Five" in a hierarchically organized structure.[11]

Research has found that two of the Big Five traits—openness to experience and conscientiousness[12]—show the most consistent relations with creativity among artists and scientists. Openness to experience reflects the degree to which people are curious, imaginative, open minded, aesthetically oriented, original, risk taking, unconventional, and independent in their thinking. People high on openness have both a broader range and depth of experience than those who are low on this trait; people without much openness to experience tend be more conventional and conservative, preferring things that are familiar and routine.[13] As one would expect, among artists and scientists, openness to experience has been found to be associated positively with creativity.[14] In organizational contexts and jobs in which creativity is not actually a part of one's day-to-day work tasks (as it is for artists and scientists), it is less clear that openness to experience will necessarily be positively associated with creativity. Whether this is actually the case likely depends upon the extent to which the work contexts allow these trait influences to manifest themselves.[15]

Conscientiousness reflects the tendency to be dependable, reliable, careful, organized, determined, and goal oriented. People who are high on conscientiousness tend to be more persevering, have more impulse control, be more conformist and rule abiding, and engage in more self-control than those low on conscientiousness.[16] While conscientiousness has been found to be positively associated with job performance in a variety of kinds of jobs, among artists and scientists, it has been found to be negatively associated with creativity.[17] Again, in work contexts, it is likely that conscientiousness may only be negatively associated with creativity when the context emphasizes conformity, following rules, and meeting predetermined goals and standards.[18]

Openness to experience and conscientiousness would seem to have paradoxical influences on creativity. Yet these are independent personality traits, so individuals could be high on both, low on both, or high on one and low on the other. In thinking about their potentially paradoxical influences, it becomes apparent that both can contribute to creativity, albeit in different ways. Clearly, being curious, open minded, risk taking, and imaginative and being open to a wide and deep range of experience would seem to foster developing novel ideas. Nonetheless, creativity that leads to innovation often entails perseverance, hard work, sustained efforts over time, and self-discipline; and high conscientiousness brings with it these kinds of tendencies. And in considering that novel ideas must also be useful for creativity and innovation, those high on conscientiousness might be especially attuned to putting effort into making novel ideas truly useful.

Managing Paradoxical Predispositions

Thus, tendencies embodied in both of these traits, which can coexist side by side, can contribute to creativity in different ways. These tendencies can be reflected within individuals or across individuals who are working in teams. Rather than thinking that certain people or groups will be more or less creative depending upon their predispositions or personalities, or that being high on both conscientiousness and openness to experience leads to a paradoxical state of affairs, managers should recognize that creativity arises from different tendencies within people and from different kinds of people and groups, and that different tendencies can promote creativity in different ways. Understanding the patterning of traits within individuals and the ways in which people differ from each other is important in terms of providing a context that supports creativity.

Paradoxical Affective States

A second seeming paradox of the person concerns the influence of affective states or moods. An extensive body of literature suggests that feeling (affect) and thinking (cognition) are highly interdependent and reciprocally related and has focused on the ways in which people's moods influence their thought processes and behaviors.[19] When people are in a positive mood, they tend to be more playful, engage in more divergent thinking, and be more integrative and flexible in terms of seeing connections between different kinds of stimuli.

These kinds of influences of positive moods would seem to foster or promote creativity, as some research has documented.[20]

However, when people are in positive moods, they are also much more likely to rely on schemas to guide their information processing and judgments. People in positive moods tend to make top-down judgments based on their schemas and heuristics, and pay less attention to the details and specifics at hand.[21] Reliance on schemas and pre-existing expectations and assumptions has the potential to discourage creativity as novel ideas necessarily reflect a break with pre-existing world views.

People in positive moods also are more likely to have a rosy view of their surroundings and current conditions. When in a positive mood, the glass is half full rather than half empty, and ambiguous information and conditions are perceived in a positive light. Research has found that when people are in positive moods, their perceptions and judgments about a wide variety of stimuli (e.g., products, people) tend to be more positive than when they are in a more neutral frame of mind.[22] Of course, these influences of positive mood occur only for perceptions and judgments that are somewhat subjective in nature.

From a creativity standpoint, the rosy view accompanying a positive mood can have seemingly paradoxical effects. On the one hand, being optimistic and having positive perceptions would seem to encourage creativity, as all creative pursuits entail the risk of failure. On the other hand, people in positive moods might be too positive and not pay enough attention to potential problems and feasibility issues. Moreover, creativity and innovation often come about because there are real problems and performance shortfalls in organizations. Problem recognition and dissatisfaction with the status quo can be important triggers for creativity and innovation. When people are in positive moods, they may be less likely to recognize problems and deficiencies with the current state of affairs, and thus have less impetus to seek ways to make changes.

Thus far, I have been contrasting positive moods to more neutral affective states rather than to negative moods. This has been deliberate. Contrary to intuition, extensive research suggests that the experience of positive and negative moods tends to be independent over time. Put differently, positive and negative moods are not opposite ends of a single continuum but instead are relatively independent continua. A high positive mood is described by terms such as excited, enthusiastic, and proud; a low positive mood is described by terms such as sleepy and sluggish. A high negative mood is described by terms such as distressed, upset, and nervous; a low negative mood is described by terms such as calm and relaxed. Not only are the mood states themselves independent, but so are their determinants.[23]

When people are in negative moods, their perceptions and judgments tend to be more critical and discerning. People in negative moods pay more attention to the facts at hand and process information in a systematic, bottom-up fashion. Rather than relying on pre-existing schemas and assumptions, they are more likely to pay attention to the facts and details at hand.[24]

As with positive moods, the effects of negative moods on creativity can seem paradoxical. On the one hand, having more negative and critical perceptions and judgments might discourage creativity, as one might be too quick to shoot down new ideas and think of why they won't work. On the other hand, people in negative moods might be more likely to recognize problems and performance shortfalls in need of creative solutions. And when working on problems and creative solutions, they may be more demanding of themselves, pushing themselves to come up with ideas that are really novel and useful. Focusing on the details and facts of the current situation rather than relying on pre-existing assumptions and schemas also can be advantageous when change is needed.[25]

Importantly, while people differ in their proneness to experiencing positive moods and negative moods, people experience both mood states at different points in their day-to-day experience, and both mood states can facilitate or encourage creativity. Positive moods can give one a sense of enthusiasm and optimism that real improvements can be made and be a source of positive energy and divergent ideas. Negative moods can help ensure that systematic attention is paid to the details and facts at hand regarding the realities of the current situation and that concerted and sustained effort is directed at developing ideas that really are novel and useful and will result in real innovation and improvements.[26] Paradoxical effects of moods parallel, in some sense, the paradoxical nature of creativity, and thus serve to encourage it.

These effects of mood states likely play out both within individuals and across individuals, as much creativity that takes place in organizations occurs in groups or teams. For example, the varying mood states of team members seeking to creatively solve a problem or take advantage of an opportunity likely complement each other and contribute, in different ways, to the creative process.

Managing Paradoxical Affective States

Clearly, both positive and negative mood states can contribute to creativity in different ways. So rather than trying to put people or oneself in a certain kind of mood to encourage creativity, it makes much more sense to take advantage of the naturally occurring fluctuations in mood states that do take place. Moreover, it is advantageous to revisit issues, judgments, ideas, and potential courses of action in differing mood states to have a more flexible, realistic approach.[27] What might seem like an insurmountable problem when in a negative mood might appear more tractable when in a positive mood. A creative idea developed when in a positive mood might seem like a sure winner. When revisited in a negative mood, it might become apparent that certain critical contingencies have been overlooked, or that the idea needs more refinement and effort, or that it just won't work. By revisiting ideas in varying moods and from varying perspectives, it is more likely that really creative ideas will be developed that lead to innovation.

Similarly, in work teams, it is important to recognize that the differing moods and perspectives of team members likely enhance creativity and should be embraced, not minimized. Suppose a team is working on a creative idea. While the majority of team members enthusiastically support it, a minority of the team does not. Research suggests that listening to this minority may enhance creativity.[28] Perhaps the minority is right on target in their critical stance; perhaps the majority has overlooked certain facts at hand; or perhaps not enough effort has been devoted to generating, refining, and evaluating ideas. Even if the majority *is* right on target, listening to and taking into account the perspectives of the minority can lead to improvements, increased commitment, and successful innovation.

Paradoxical Processes

While some creativity has its origins in serendipity, the pursuit of creative ideas, even those that come about by chance, is through a motivational process. Creativity is effortful behavior that often challenges the status quo; it is motivated behavior. Motivation is typically defined as the psychological forces within a person that determine his or her direction of behavior (what behaviors or actions he or she chooses to initiate and engage in), levels of effort, and levels of persistence in the face of obstacles or difficulties.[29] In terms of creativity, the distinction is often made between intrinsic motivation and extrinsic motivation. Intrinsically motivated behavior is behavior that is performed for its own sake; the motivation comes from performing the behavior itself. In this case, behaviors are chosen and effort and persistence accompany them because engaging in the behavior itself is of value to the individual.[30] A research scientist who loves the thrill of discovery, a computer programmer who enjoys developing new programs, and a product designer who relishes the challenges of blending form and function are all intrinsically motivated, and the act of performing the work itself can serve as its own reward.

Extrinsically motivated behavior is behavior that is performed for its consequences (e.g., to achieve some end, to obtain social or material rewards, or to avoid negative consequences).[31] Clearly, there is an element of extrinsic motivation to most work that is performed in complex organizations, as employees are paid for their efforts and contributions and in the absence of material rewards for their efforts, the efforts would often cease.

Researchers have suggested that intrinsic motivation facilitates creativity, as it entails the kind of involvement in work tasks that should lead to the development of new and useful ideas—total immersion, flexibility and curiosity, willingness to try out new things and take risks, and persistent self-determined engagement in the work itself.[32] And extrinsic motivation, particularly when outside forces are seen as controlling and limiting autonomy, has been viewed as a potential detriment to creativity.[33]

Considering that complex organizations often engage in creativity to improve a problematic state of affairs or take advantage of a potential opportunity, and that the very definition of creativity includes "usefulness" as a fundamental aspect of creativity, clearly, there is an extrinsic motivational element to most forms of creativity and innovation in organizations. That is, employees are trying to come up with new and better ideas for a reason, and not just for the sake of the activity itself. And, of course, the more pressing the reason, the more the need for creative ideas.

So a potential paradox here is that creativity benefits from a motivational process that is internally initiated, driven, and sustained rather than from a process that is initiated and controlled by outside forces. Yet these outside forces exist and are ever present in many organizations. Clearly, managers and organizations cannot afford to ignore them for very long.

An additional potential paradox of motivation relates to the potential toll of sustained intrinsic motivation over time. While most people would likely indicate they would prefer to be actively engaged and fully involved in their work for its own sake, this kind of engagement can become all-consuming.[34] In an era of ever-increasing work demands and working hours, time "off" from work and actual leisure time that is not consumed with household chores and all the complexities of living seems to be getting scarcer, at least for significant portions of the population. The kind of work that is intrinsically motivating is the kind of work that prompts people to put in long working hours and makes them hesitant to let go of the work, even when not working.[35] While enjoyable, stimulating, and exciting, it is still work that is being performed for financial and other consequences by people who have multidimensional lives and interests and responsibilities outside of the workplace.

Managing Paradoxical Processes

The intrinsic/extrinsic motivation paradox, in some sense, centers on the relative importance of the engagement in creative activities versus the consequences of those activities for individuals (and organizations). If the consequences become all important, the engagement suffers, as the creative pursuit is seen as a means to a predetermined end; once the end is seen as predetermined, creativity is stifled because something truly new cannot be determined in advance. Yet consequences cannot be completely ignored, as there are extrinsic reasons for engagement, even intrinsic engagement in creative activities. Just as a composer or an actor can be both intrinsically motivated by, and really enjoy, composing or acting while at the same time hoping his or her compositions or performances strike a chord in audiences, so too can employees be intrinsically engaged in their work while at the same time be aware of the consequences of that work, the need for usefulness, and the need to solve problems, make improvements, or seize potential opportunities.

Managing this seeming paradox entails keeping a dynamic balance between distal and proximal origins of behaviors.[36] Distal origins—the need to solve problems, make improvements, develop and take advantage of opportunities, and create value—relate to extrinsic motivation and the need for creative ideas to be useful. In a sense, these distal origins put boundary conditions on creative pursuits. Proximal origins—the actual engagement in thinking and doing that can yield creative ideas and innovation—relate to intrinsic motivation and the sense of excitement, enthusiasm, and enjoyment from the thinking and doing itself. This balance between the distal and the proximal is dynamic in the sense that proximal engagement can lead to revisions, and changes to distal criteria—such as when, through proximal engagement, a problem to be solved is no longer seen as a problem at all but rather an opportunity, or when a new distal criteria is discovered. Recognition of distal consequences can help mitigate against the potential for too much immersion in intrinsically motivated work that leaves little to no time or energy for other life pursuits and responsibilities. Interestingly, many factors that research has found to facilitate creativity, such as autonomy, developmental feedback, support, and job complexity,[37] can support both intrinsically motivated proximal engagement as well as the channeling of creative endeavors in the direction of distal, extrinsic outcomes that yield real benefits for organizations and their members in terms of successful innovation.

THE PARADOX OF THE CONTEXT

Multiple aspects of organizational contexts can serve to promote or inhibit creativity. The ways that jobs are designed, the nature of supervision, how performance is evaluated and rewarded, how employees are grouped in teams and units, how decisions are made and implemented, how coworkers interact with each other, and the organizational culture are some of the many contextual influences on creativity and innovation.[38] While it is beyond the scope of this chapter to highlight paradoxes of each of these contextual elements, there are certain paradoxical themes that emerge from their consideration.

Take, for example, the administration of the nursing staff in a large hospital. Multiple aspects of the work context for nurses would seem to constrain creativity on the job, such as the need to provide high quality patient care while meeting the latest standards and guidelines and minimizing errors as much as possible. Yet nurses are potentially a valuable source of creative ideas for how the work they do can be organized and how the context can be structured to yield high quality care and minimize errors. They are the ones closest to the work process, the ones who can see the pitfalls of current approaches and may have valuable insights on how to improve things. As it stands, there is an ongoing nursing shortage, and nurses tend to be relatively dissatisfied with their jobs and have high turnover rates.[39] And yet, nurses might be the ones most likely to have creative ideas for improving the conditions of the work for which they received specialized training and which they now find dissatisfying.

The challenge for hospitals, and for many other kinds of organizations, is both ensuring that certain tasks are reliably performed according to predetermined standards while at the same time allowing and encouraging creativity in the interests of real improvements and innovation. This challenge revolves around at least two paradoxes—the paradox of autonomy and the paradox of invention.

The Paradox of Autonomy

Research has found that contexts in which there are high levels of autonomy, an absence of close supervision, and high levels of employee discretion facilitate creativity.[40] Such contexts provide workers with the freedom to pursue novel ideas without the imposition of external constraints. High autonomy gives workers closest to critical processes and tasks the freedom to spontaneously address problems, explore opportunities, and make improvements. It also instills in workers a sense of ownership over their work that motivates them to want to be creative to improve things.

Yet complex organizations also require predictability and control. Certain tasks must be accomplished reliably, work needs to be coordinated across individuals, groups, and units, and organizations need to efficiently and effectively produce goods and services to remain competitive and provide secure employment for their members. Of course, when predictability and control become ends in and of themselves, competitiveness is lost. Organizations lose touch with their environments, fail to make needed changes, and become the victims of their own routines, which once may have been sensible but now are no longer appropriate.

The Paradox of Invention

Organizations develop routines and standardized responses to recurring problems and opportunities in the interests of efficiency and effectiveness.[41] When the nature of problems and opportunities changes, routines and standardized responses must change and creative ideas are needed. When change occurs rapidly and unpredictably, creativity is all the more important. Yet a certain level of routine and standardization is also necessary to avoid "reinventing the wheel" on a day-to-day basis.

The paradox of invention reflects this tension between being creatively responsive to ongoing activities and challenges, while at the same time having a level of collective learning in an organization whereby solutions that work are not being repeatedly reinvented, albeit in slightly different forms.

Managing the Paradox of Context

Creativity can be both facilitated and constrained by the context. In many organizations, context serves more as a constraint than a facilitator in that typically, employees do not have the autonomy and the freedom to break from routines to develop new and useful ideas. Yet autonomy is necessarily constrained in practically all organizations and routines, though at some level it needs to be developed and relied on (and, of course, abandoned when no longer useful or relevant). Managers and organizations essentially need to provide employees with autonomy and support invention while at the same time exerting enough control and having certain levels of standardization to support ongoing operations. Importantly, control and standardization should be adopted with the recognition that current routines are temporary, can, will, and need to be improved upon or changed over time, and are necessarily provisional means to evolving ends.

CONCLUSION

Recognizing these and other paradoxes surrounding creativity, allowing their seemingly opposing forces to play out, and managing the process so that they do play out in balanced ways is no easy task, yet it is critical for creativity and innovation in organizations. Creativity is fun and exhilarating; it is also a labor of love that entails high levels of effort, persistence, commitment, and time. By recognizing and embracing creativity's contradictions, managers and all members of an organization are better suited to the challenge of allowing it to flourish.

NOTES

1. T. M. Amabile, "A Model of Creativity and Innovation in Organizations," in *Research in Organizational Behavior* (volume 10), edited by B. M. Staw and L. L. Cummings, 123–167 (Greenwich, CT: JAI Press, 1988).

2. C. E. Shalley et al., "The Effects of Personal and Contextual Characteristics on Creativity: Where Should We Go From Here," *Journal of Management* 30 (2004): 933–958; C. E. Shalley and J. Zhou, "Research on Employee Creativity: A Critical Review and Directions for Future Research," in *Research in Personnel and Human Resource Management*, edited by J. Martoccio, 165–217 (Oxford, England: Elsevier, 2003).

3. Amabile, 1988; T. M. Amabile, *Creativity in Context* (Boulder, CO: Westview Press, 1996); G. R. Oldham and A. Cummings, "Employee Creativity: Personal and Contextual Factors at Work," *Academy of Management Journal* 39 (1996): 607–634.

4. S. T. Fiske and S. E. Taylor, *Social Cognition*, 2nd ed. (New York: McGraw-Hill, 1991); J. M. George and G. R. Jones, "Towards a Process Model of Individual Change in Organizations," *Human Relations* 54 (2001): 419–444; J. M. George and G. R. Jones, *Understanding and Managing Organizational Behavior*, 4th ed. (Upper Saddle River, NJ: Pearson Prentice Hall, 2005); S. E. Taylor and J. Crocker, "Schematic Bases of Social

Information Processing," in *Social Cognition: The Ontario Symposium*, edited by E. T. Higgins, C. P. Herman, and M. P. Zanna, 89–134 (Hillsdale, NJ: Erlbaum, 1981).

5. Fiske and Taylor, 1991.

6. P. R. Nayak and J. M. Ketteringham, *Breakthroughs* (San Diego: Pfeiffer & Co., 1994).

7. T. Kelley (with J. Littman), *The Art of Innovation* (New York: Doubleday, 2001).

8. J. M. George and J. Zhou, "When Openness to Experience and Conscientiousness are Related to Creative Behavior: An Interactional Approach," *Journal of Applied Psychology* 86 (2001): 513–524.

9. J. Zhou, "When the Presence of Creative Coworkers is Related to Creativity: Role of Supervisor Close Monitoring, Developmental Feedback, and Creative Personality," *Journal of Applied Psychology* 88 (2003): 413–422.

10. George and Jones, 2005.

11. O. P. John and S. Srivastava, "The Big Five Trait Taxonomy: History, Measurement, and Theoretical Perspectives," in *Handbook of Personality: Theory and Research*, edited by L. A. Pervin and O. P. John, 102–138 (New York: Guilford Press, 1999).

12. G. J. Feist, "A Meta-Analysis of Personality in Scientific and Artistic Creativity," *Personality and Social Psychology Review* 4 (1998): 290–309.

13. P. T. Costa and R. R. McCrae, *Revised NEO Personality Inventory (NEO-FFI) Professional Manual* (Odessa, FL: Psychological Assessments Resources, 1992); George and Zhou, 2001; R. R. McCrae, "Social Consequences of Experiential Openness," *Psychological Bulletin* 120 (1996): 323–337; R. R. McCrae and P. T. Costa, "Conceptions and Correlates of Openness to Experience," in *Handbook of Personality*, edited by R. Hogan, J. Johnson, and S. Briggs, 825–847 (San Diego, CA: Academic Press, 1997).

14. Feist, 1998.

15. George and Zhou, 2001.

16. Costa and McCrae, 1992; L. R. Goldberg, "The Development of Markers for the Big-Five Factor Structure," *Psychological Assessment* 4 (1992): 26–42; J. Hogan and D. S. Ones, "Conscientiousness and Integrity at Work," in *Handbook of Personality Psychology*, edited by R. Hogan, J. Johnson, and S. Briggs, 849–870 (San Diego, CA: Academic Press, 1997).

17. M. R. Barrick and M. K. Mount, "The Big Five Personality Dimensions and Job Performance: A Meta-Analysis," *Personnel Psychology* 44 (1991): 1–26; Feist, 1998; R. P. Tett, et al., "Personality Measures as Predictors of Job Performance: A Meta-Analytic Review," *Personnel Psychology* 44 (1991):703–742.

18. George and Zhou, 2001.

19. J. P. Forgas, "Mood and Judgment: The Affect Infusion Model," *Psychological Bulletin* 117 (1995): 39–66; J. P. Forgas and P. T. Vargas, "The Effects of Mood on Social Judgments and Reasoning," in *Handbook of Emotions*, 2nd ed., edited by M. Lewis and J. M. Haviland-Jones, 350–367 (New York: Guilford, 2000); N. Schwarz, "Situated Cognition and the Wisdom of Feelings: Cognitive Tuning," in *The Wisdom in Feelings*, edited by L. Feldman Barrett and P. Salovey, 144–166 (New York: Guilford, 2002); N. Schwarz and G. L. Clore, "Mood as Information: 20 Years Later," *Psychological Inquiry* 14 (2003): 296–303.

20. A. M. Isen et al., "The Influence of Positive Affect on the Unusualness of Word Associations," *Journal of Personality and Social Psychology* 48 (1985): 1413–1426; A. M. Isen et al., "Positive Affect Facilitates Creative Problem Solving," *Journal of Personality and Social Psychology* 52 (1987): 1122–1131; Schwarz, 2002.

21. K. Fiedler, "Emotional Mood, Cognitive Style, and Behavior Regulation," in *Affect, Cognition, and Social Behavior*, edited by K. Fiedler and J. Forgas, 101–119 (Toronto: J. Hogrefe, 1988); K. Fiedler, "Toward an Account of Affect and Cognition Phenomena Using the BIAS Computer Algorithm," in *Feeling and Thinking: The Role of Affect in Social Cognition*, 223–252 (Paris: Cambridge University Press, 2000); G. Kaufmann, "The Effect of Mood on Creativity in the Innovation Process," in *The International Handbook on Innovation*, 191–203 (Oxford, England: Elsevier Science, 2003).

22. Forgas, 1995.

23. D. Watson, *Mood and Temperament* (New York: Guilford Press, 2000).

24. Schwarz, 2002.

25. J. M. George and J. Zhou, "Understanding When Bad Moods Foster Creativity and Good Ones Don't: The Role of Context and Clarity of Feelings," *Journal of Applied Psychology* 87 (2002): 687–697; Kaufmann, 2003; Schwarz, 2002.

26. George and Zhou, 2002; Kaufmann, 2003.

27. J. M. George, "Emotions and Leadership: The Role of Emotional Intelligence," *Human Relations* 53 (2000): 1027–1055.

28. C. J. Nemeth, "Differential Contributions of Majority and Minority Influence," *Psychological Review* 93 (1986): 23–32.

29. George and Jones, 2005.

30. Amabile, 1996; Shalley et al., 2004.

31. Amabile, 1996; George and Jones, 2005.

32. Amabile, 1996; Shalley et al., 2004.

33. Amabile, 1996; Shalley et al., 2004.

34. A. Ross, *No-Collar: The Humane Workplace and Its Hidden Costs* (Philadelphia: Temple University Press, 2004).

35. Ross, 2004; B. M. Staw, "Why No One Really Wants Creativity," in *Creative Action in Organizations*, edited by C. M. Ford and D. A. Gioia, 161–166 (Thousand Oaks, CA: Sage, 1995).

36. R. Kanfer, "Motivation Theory and Industrial and Organizational Psychology," in *Handbook of Industrial and Organizational Psychology*, vol.1, edited by M. D. Dunnette and L. M. Hough, 75–170 (Palo Alto, CA: Consulting Psychologists Press, 1990).

37. Shalley et al., 2004.

38. Shalley et al., 2004.

39. J. Malone, "Nursing Prognosis Worsens as Caregivers Vent Frustration," *Houston Chronicle*, 12A, May 13, 2001; L. M. Sixel, "It's a Man's Job: Nursing That Is." *Houston Chronicle*, 1C, May 18, 2001.

40. Shalley et al., 2004.

41. George and Jones, 2005.

2

Leading for Creativity: An Employee-Manager Dyadic Approach

JING ZHOU

Technological advancements are accelerating. Prices for raw materials are rising. The globalization of businesses has provided unprecedented challenges as well as opportunities to business organizations. Observers have commented that we may have entered an era of a "creative economy" in which business organizations' rise or fall ultimately would depend on creativity exhibited by their rank-and-file employees.[1]

Although product innovation has always been one of the key drivers for firm growth and competitiveness, the "creative economy" is different from previous eras of economic development in that creativity is no longer the job description reserved for scientists and engineers who work in research and development (R&D) functions. Whereas traditionally theorizing and research on employee creativity has focused on scientists and engineers working on R&D jobs,[2] more recently this stream of research has expanded to examining conditions that promote creativity in employees who do not hold R&D jobs.[3] This recent shift of interests to non-R&D employees reflects the reality that in addition to creativity in product design and development, creative idea production from employees holding non-R&D jobs is also desirable and especially important in enhancing organizations' ability to improve work processes, increase efficiency and effectiveness, and consequently to gain competitive advantage.[4]

Indeed, to stay competitive in this economy, organizations are required to encourage all of their employees to be creative, not just those who hold traditionally "creative" types of jobs such as R&D and advertising. For example, a front-line employee at a manufacturing plant could suggest a new way of improving the manufacturing process so that her work can be done more efficiently. Or a nurse at a hospital could come up with a new strategy for retaining experienced nurses, thereby reducing the high turnover rate of nurses and saving costs in recruiting and training new nurses.

Scientific research in the field of management has made substantial progress in gaining an understanding of what factors promote or inhibit employee creativity in the workplace.[5] Separately, an emerging line of inquiry centers on managers' recognition of employees' creative ideas.[6] Surprisingly, although these two lines of research essentially address the same general phenomenon—employee creativity in the context of organizations—they have never been integrated.

The goal of this chapter is to integrate previous theory and research on employee creativity and on managers' recognition of employees' creative ideas, and to propose a parsimonious framework to inform researchers and business leaders on factors critical for leading and building a creative organization.

Essentially, this framework posits that to build a truly creative organization, researchers need to move their levels of analysis one level up. Specifically, they need to elevate individual level-of-analysis that either focuses on the employee engaged in generating creative ideas or the manager engaged in recognizing creative ideas to a dyadic level of analysis that involves the employee-manager dyad. As such, this line of research would inform business leaders that to promote creativity, they need to attend to two factors. First, leaders need to find ways to enhance their employees' creative idea production. Second, leaders need to understand and find ways to increase the accuracy of their managers' recognition of employees' creative ideas. As Figure 2.1 illustrates, for any given organization, employees' creative idea production can be at high versus low levels, and managers' ability to accurately recognize creative ideas produced by employees can be high versus low. As shown in Figure 2.1, crossing these two factors results in four cells. A truly creative organization is represented by the first cell, in which employees' creative idea production is at high levels and managers' ability to accurately recognize employees' creative idea is also high.

This chapter is different from previous reviews in two ways. First, its goal is not to serve as a comprehensive literature review. Instead, on the basis of a selected review of the literature, it attempts to offer fresh ideas and to integrate two sets of literatures—predictors of employee creativity and managers' recognition of creative ideas—that have been developed separately. Given that the focus of the chapter is on leading a creative organization, the literature review will select prior research that addresses behaviors that leaders can exhibit to promote creativity. Readers who are interested in a more comprehensive review of theory and research on predictors of employee creativity are referred to Shalley, Zhou, and Oldham (2004) and Zhou and Shalley (2003).[7]

Manager's Recognition of Creative Ideas

		Accurate	Not Accurate
Employee Creative Idea Production	High	Highest	Limited
	Low	Limited Creativity	Lowest Creativity

FIGURE 2.1   Degree of Creativity at the Employee-Manager Dyad

Second, the chapter is not limited to the so-called "creative employees"—employees who work on creativity-centered jobs. For a more focused review and integration on leading creative employees whose works revolve around creativity and innovation, the reader is referred to Mumford, Scott, Gaddis, and Strange (2002).[8]

PERSONAL AND ENVIRONMENTAL FACTORS INFLUENCING EMPLOYEES' PRODUCTION OF CREATIVE IDEAS

In this section, I focus on discussing what leaders should do in order to enhance employees' production of creative ideas. The literature defines creativity as new and useful or potentially useful ideas developed by employees.[9] These ideas could address any aspects of the employees' jobs, or the unit or organization in which the employees work, including products, services, and work processes.

This definition focuses on the outcome instead of the mental or cognitive processes through which an individual generates an idea. Here, outcome means that the employee has produced a tangible idea that is both novel and useful. Therefore, if someone claims that she has spent two hours engaging in creative thinking yet is unable to demonstrate any concrete ideas, we would not consider the self-reported creative thinking as creativity.

In addition, both novelty and usefulness are necessary conditions for an idea to be judged ascreative. If the employee comes up with an idea that is novel but is completely useless for the organization, we would not consider the idea to be creative. Likewise, if an idea is useful but is not new, it would not be seen as creative either.

On the basis of the creativity literature, I suggest that business leaders can enhance creativity by attending to employees' personal factors related to creativity, and by exhibiting everyday behaviors that facilitate creativity. In addition, leaders need to take an interactional approach—which emphasizes that personal and environmental factors jointly affect creativity—to nurturing employee creativity.

Personal Factors

Creative personality. Individuals may differ in their potential to generate creative ideas.[10] Early research on individuals' creative achievements focused almost exclusively on effects of individual differences, namely, their personalities or thinking and problem-solving abilities and styles. For example, Gough (1979)[11] developed the Creative Personality Scale (CPS) to measure individuals' creativity-relevant personality characteristics. In addition to Gough's own work that showed the validity of the CPS, some previous research provides support to the notion that the CPS directly and positively relates to creativity. For example, in a laboratory study, Zhou and Oldham (2001)[12] show a direct and positive link between individuals' creative personality measured by the CPS and their actual creativity.

However, more recent research on creativity in the workplace tends to take an interactional approach, taking both employees' individual differences and the characteristics of the workplace into consideration in predicting and managing creativity. This is because, although different employees have different personality configurations and these differences predispose the employees as more or less likely to exhibit actual creative behaviors, the workplace sometimes creates strong situations in which the employees' individual differences are not allowed to manifest. For example, Zhou (2003)[13] found no direct relationship between creative personalities and employees' creativity. As another example, a field study by Oldham and Cummings (1996)[14] showed that the CPS was positively correlated with just one of the three indicators of creativity—patent disclosures written. On the other hand, these researchers showed that there was an interactive relationship among creative personalities, contextual factors, and employees' creativity. Specifically, the CPS interacted with job complexity, supportive supervision, and noncontrolling supervision in such a way that employees exhibited the highest creativity (i.e., patent disclosures written and supervisor ratings of creativity) when they scored high on the CPS, worked on complex jobs, and were supervised in a supportive and noncontrolling fashion. These results were consistent with the interactional approach to understanding employee creativity.

Whereas the above two studies focused on conditions that maximize the creativity of individuals with creative personalities, Zhou (2003) wonders what leaders can do to nurture creativity in employees with less creative personalities. Results in her study show that creative personality moderates the joint condition of supervisory close monitoring and the presence of creative coworkers. More specifically, employees with relatively less creative personalities exhibited greater creativity when they were surrounded by creative co-workers and their supervisors did not closely monitor them.

Big five personality factors. Many personality researchers agree that the Five-Factor Model of personality can satisfactorily capture various configurations of individual differences in personality.[15] The five factors are conscientiousness, openness to experience, extraversion, neuroticism, and agreeableness. Conceptually, conscientiousness and openness to experience seem to be most relevant to creativity.[16] Empirically, Feist (1998)[17] found that creative artists and scientists tend to be more open to experiences and less conscientious than their less creative counterparts.

Samples included in the Feist study consisted of artists and scientists. Would this pattern of results hold for employees whose jobs do not revolve around creativity? George and Zhou (2001)[18] investigated relationships between conscientiousness and openness to experience and creativity with a sample of ordinary employees whose job descriptions did not explicitly require creativity. Contrary to results obtained from artists and scientists, results obtained by George and Zhou did not show any direct relationships between conscientiousness, openness to experience, and employee creativity. Instead, these two personality factors each interacted with contextual or environmental factors to affect creativity. More specifically, conscientiousness was related to low levels of creativity when supervisors engaged in close monitoring and coworkers were unsupportive (i.e., engaging in inaccurate communication, being unhelpful, and creating a negative work environment). In addition, employees with high levels of openness to experience exhibited greater creativity when they received positive feedback and worked on heuristics tasks (i.e., ends or means of their tasks were unclear, which provided them with the opportunity to explore new and better ways of getting their work done). These results again suggest that leaders take the interactional approach to managing employee creativity.

Self-efficacy. Employees may differ in their creative self-efficacy, which refers to the degree to which they believe they can be creative at work. Tierney and Farmer (2002)[19] found that employees with high levels of creative self-efficacy exhibited greater creativity in the workplace. In addition, these researchers found that job tenure, job self-efficacy, supervisor behavior, and job complexity contributed to employees' creative efficacy beliefs.

Summary. In this section, I have selectively reviewed research on the relations between individual differences and creativity in the workplace. This body of work, as well as a much larger body of literature that space here does not allow for a more detailed and complete review, suggests that leaders need to take an interactional approach in managing employee creativity. Individuals differ in their predisposition to be more or less creative. However, sometimes the work environment can be so strong and oppressive that even individuals who are naturally inclined to be creative cannot engage in creative activities or demonstrate creative accomplishments. On the other hand, sometimes the work environment can be strong and nurturing in such a way that even individuals with less creative potential (e.g., scoring low on the CPS) can be encouraged and taught to be creative. Informed by the interactional perspective of creativity, leaders can focus on designing the right environment for different employees.[20] Moreover, because leaders themselves constitute an important aspect of the work environment, leaders can encourage employee creativity by engaging in everyday leadership behaviors that facilitate creativity.

Environment—Everyday Creativity-Facilitative Leadership Behaviors

In this section, I review and discuss several everyday behaviors that leaders can engage in to promote employee creativity. The behaviors reviewed below are by no means exhaustive—I do not intend to suggest that they are the only behaviors leaders should exhibit in their efforts to promote creativity. Instead, they are reviewed here for illustrative purposes.

Transformational leadership. Research has shown that leaders can encourage their employees to exhibit creativity by being transformational leaders. Management scholars[21] consider transformational leadership as a multidimensional concept that includes four dimensions: intellectual stimulation, individualized consideration, charisma, and inspirational motivation. One of the most frequently used measurement instruments that measure the extent to which managers and leaders in the workplace exhibit transformational leadership has been the Multifactor Leadership Questionnaire (MLQ) developed by Bernard Bass and Bruce Avolio.[22]

Leaders who score high on the intellectual stimulation dimension frequently stimulate their employees by questioning assumptions, challenging the status quo, inspiring the employees to reformulate problems in order to solve them more effectively, and encouraging them to use their imagination, intellectual curiosity, and novel approaches. Leaders who score high on the individualized consideration dimension treat their employees as individuals with unique abilities, needs, and aspirations. They listen to the employees, coach them, and help them to develop. The charisma dimension is also called idealized influence. Leaders who score high on this dimension serve as role models by showing values and conviction. They emphasize trust, commitment, and the importance of making ethical decisions. As such, these leaders are able to generate pride, loyalty, trust, and a shared purpose in their employees. Finally, leaders who score high on the inspirational motivation dimension articulate an appealing vision and energize their employees to work toward the vision.[23]

In an empirical study concerning the relation between transformational leadership and employee creativity, Shin and Zhou (2003)[24] showed that employees exhibited higher levels of creativity when their managers more frequently demonstrated transformational leadership behaviors than employees whose managers engaged in transformational leadership behaviors less frequently. The data used in their study were collected from 290 employees and their supervisors in forty-six companies in a variety of industries. Thus, their results had external validity.

In addition to demonstrating the positive relation between transformational leadership and creativity, Shin and Zhou sought to uncover the psychological mechanism that would explain this relation. Interestingly, their results demonstrated that the employees' intrinsic motivation partially mediated (that is, explained) the contribution of transformational leadership to creativity. These results were consistent with an intrinsic motivation theory of creativity.

According to this theory, employees may predominantly experience intrinsic or extrinsic motivation while working on a task.[25] When they experience high levels of intrinsic motivation, they are excited and energized by the task itself; when they experience high levels of extrinsic motivation, their attention is focused on rewards external to the task, which they would obtain by completing the task.

Social psychological theory and research suggest that intrinsically motivated employees are cognitively more flexible and more playful with ideas. They are also more persistent when faced with obstacles and challenges.[26] This flexibility, playfulness, and persistence would allow them to try to generate and experiment with many alternatives to solve a problem, to use nontraditional approaches, and to stay focused and undeterred until a truly novel and useful idea or solution is produced. All of these cognitive and behavioral tendencies associated with intrinsically motivated individuals suggest that they are more likely to exhibit high levels of creativity.

According to the intrinsic motivation theory, factors representing aspects of the work environment promote or inhibit creativity by influencing employees' intrinsic motivation.[27] Because transformational leadership represents the leadership aspect of the work environment, theoretically it is expected to promote creativity by affecting intrinsic motivation. The Shin and Zhou study provided some empirical support for this theoretical position.

An interesting issue concerning transformational leadership and creativity is how much transformational leaders should be directly involved in the creative process.[28] Some researchers argue that transformational leaders should only set a broad vision, and that they should not attempt to get directly involved in or micromanage the creative process itself. If these leaders micromanage, they may actually stifle creativity because their charisma and strong presence would limit employees' initiative and imagination. The employees may be too busy following the leaders instead of thinking out of the box independently, and searching for the less traveled path.

Close monitoring. Related to the foregoing discussion on transformational leaders' not micromanaging the creative process, previous research suggests that to promote creativity in their employees, leaders should not engage in close monitoring. George and Zhou (2001)[29] defined close monitoring as a form of supervisory behavior in which supervisors keep close tabs on their employees to ensure that the employees not only do what they are told, but also complete their tasks in expected ways. These supervisors create fear and restriction in their employees so that these employees would be excessively careful and hesitate not to do anything that their supervisors might disapprove of. The focus of the study was testing interactive effects of employees' personality, task heuristicness, and supervisory and coworker behaviors instead of the simple relationship between close monitoring and creativity. Nevertheless, their data yielded a negative correlation between supervisory close monitoring and employee creativity, suggesting that supervisory close monitoring had detrimental effects on employee creativity.

Separately, using data collected from staff members and their supervisors in two professional units at a large university, Zhou (2003)[30] showed that when supervisors engage in close monitoring, their employees exhibited low levels of creativity. These results were later replicated with data collected from a sample of employees at a different organization in a different industry—hospital employees and their supervisors.

Leader-member-exchange (LMX). Research has also shown that the quality of the dyadic relationship a leader develops with each of his or her subordinates could influence the subordinates' creativity or innovative behavior. According to the Leader-Member-Exchange (LMX) theory of leadership, leaders develop different kinds of relationships with different subordinates under their supervision.[31] Gradually, leaders develop high-quality relationships with some of their subordinates. Those subordinates are often called the leaders' "in-group." Once they become members of the "in-group," the subordinates tend to enjoy their leaders' trust and be granted high levels of autonomy and discretion in decision making and performing their work tasks. This trust, autonomy, and discretion provide the subordinates with opportunity to be innovative and with confidence to take risks.

In contrast, leaders may develop low-quality relationships with other subordinates. Those subordinates are said to belong to the leaders' "out-group." Once in the "out-group," the subordinates do not have the leaders' trust, and the leaders tend not to like those subordinates. In addition, the leaders are not likely to grant these subordinates much autonomy or discretion in decision-making and in performing their tasks. This limited autonomy and discretion, coupled with not having the leaders' trust and not even being liked by the leaders, discourages the subordinates from taking initiatives and risks to explore new and better ways of doing things. Consequently, they exhibit relatively low levels of creativity.

On the basis of the LMX theory, Scott and Bruce (1994)[32] conducted an empirical study to test the hypothesis that the quality of leader-member exchange between an employee and his or her supervisor would be positively related to the employee's innovative behavior. Using data collected from 172 scientists, engineers, and technicians, as well as their supervisors at a R&D unit of a large company, they found support for the hypothesis.

In another study of R&D employees at a large company, Tierney, Farmer, and Graen (1999)[33] also found a positive relation between the quality of LMX and three measures of employee creativity. The creativity measures included creativity ratings provided by the employees' supervisors, number of invention disclosure forms submitted, and number of research reports published by the employees.

Previous research has shown that in addition to being transformational leaders and developing high-quality exchange relationships with their employees, leaders can either promote or inhibit creativity by displaying specific behaviors or by engaging in specific management practices. Research on these behaviors and practices are reviewed below.

Setting creativity goals. Leaders can promote creativity by setting creativity goals. When used appropriately, goal setting can be an effective motivational strategy in boosting individuals' productivity.[34] For example, numerous studies have demonstrated that when they had a difficult and specific goal, individuals performed better (e.g., completed more task units) than individuals who had an easy or "do your best" goal.

The body of work concerning effects of goal setting on productivity is truly impressive for both its volume and its depth. For example, over four decades of research have been devoted to an understanding of effects of goal setting on productivity.[35] Moreover, in addition to demonstrating the robust and direct impact of goal setting on productivity, this literature has also documented studies probing mechanisms or psychological processes through which effects of goal setting occur. According to this literature, goal setting affects productivity via both cognitive and motivational forces. Cognitively, it directs individuals' attention and cognitive resources toward certain tasks. Motivationally, it pushes the individuals to put forth more effort, devise suitable strategies to meet the challenges of the task, and persist longer on the task.

In contrast, effects of goal setting on creativity did not attract a great deal of research attention until the mid- to late '80s. This research started with an interesting question: if goal setting can push individuals with a difficult and specific goal to devote their cognitive and motivational resources to work hard toward accomplishing the difficult goal, what effects would it exert on creativity?

To answer this question, Shalley (1991)[36] examined the effects of these two types of goals—a creativity goal and a productivity goal—on creativity. Each of these two types of goals was examined at three levels: difficult, do-your-best, or no goal. Results showed that individuals who were assigned a do-your-best or difficult productivity goal and who were not assigned a creativity goal exhibited low levels of creativity. In contrast, individuals who were assigned a do-your-best or difficult creativity goal and a difficult productivity goal exhibited high levels of creativity and productivity.

Later, Shalley (1995)[37] conducted more studies to further untangle the complexity of effects of goal setting on creativity. Results showed that individuals who were assigned a creativity goal exhibited greater creativity. Interestingly, these individuals were less productive than those who did not have a creativity goal.

Taken together, the results obtained in the studies in which effects of goal setting on creativity were examined suggest that setting a creativity goal would facilitate creativity. However, a creativity goal may be so effective in directing individuals' attention and energy toward being creative that these individuals' productivity may suffer. This pattern of results suggests that there is a trade off faced by business leaders: they may not be able to enhance creativity and at the same time obtain high levels of productivity. Employees' cognitive resources and energy are limited, and they may experience great difficulty in delivering high levels of creativity and productivity simultaneously. These results inform the leaders that they would have to make tough choices between enhancing creativity versus routine productivity.

Feedback. Zhou (forthcoming)[38] has developed a model describing how and why feedback can be used to promote employee creativity. She argues that when used appropriately, feedback can serve three functions that are essential for producing creative ideas. First, feedback may boost its recipient's intrinsic motivation. Second, it may clarify standards of creative ideas for the feedback recipient. Knowing the standards concerning what kinds of ideas are considered creative can help the recipient to generate, judge, and refine ideas. Third, feedback may facilitate its recipient in learning and acquiring creativity-relevant skills and strategies.

According to Zhou (forthcoming), although feedback may serve the above three functions that would lead to high levels of creativity, there is no guarantee that these positive effects of feedback would occur. Indeed, three sets of factors need to be considered in predicting whether the delivery of feedback would achieve the goal of facilitating creativity. These three sets of factors are concerned with the nature and components of feedback, characteristics of the feedback recipient, and characteristics of the feedback provider.

The first set, the nature and components of feedback, includes a differentiation between feedback valence and feedback style, the developmental orientation of feedback, and the person-versus-task-focused nature of feedback. Feedback valence refers to the positive or negative outcome of a comparison between an individual's creativity and normative or situational criteria.[39] If the comparison shows that the individual has produced more creative ideas than the criteria, the feedback valence would be positive. On the other hand, if the comparison shows that the individual's ideas are less creative than the criteria, then feedback valence would be negative.

Feedback valence works in combination with feedback style to influence creativity. Feedback style refers to the manner in which feedback is delivered.

Feedback can be delivered in either an informational or a controlling style. When receiving feedback delivered in an informational style, the feedback recipient would not feel restricted or controlled. Instead, the recipient would feel that he is still in control of his own actions and behaviors, and the external feedback would be helpful to learn and develop his creative capabilities and, ultimately, his creativity. In contrast, when receiving feedback delivered in a controlling style, the feedback recipient would feel that she is being controlled by external forces and that she is not in charge of her own actions and behaviors. Consequently, she would feel that she is the pawn of the feedback provider, losing control of her own behavior. Thus, according to this model, to promote creativity, the best combination of feedback valence and style is positive feedback delivered in an informational style.

In addition, Zhou (forthcoming) maintains that feedback may vary on its developmental orientation. Feedback that is high on this dimension would provide individuals with valuable information that would help the individuals to learn, develop, and make improvements on the job. Feedback with high levels of developmental orientation should create a favorable context for creative idea production.

Moreover, Zhou argues that while delivering creativity-relevant feedback, leaders need to give task-focused instead of person-focused feedback. Person-focused feedback primes ego involvement, a psychological state in which individuals feel the pressure to prove themselves. This focus on proving themselves tends to distract individuals' attention away from the task, resulting in less involvement in the task and less creativity. In contrast, task-focused feedback can elicit or deepen task involvement, which could result in creative responses to task requirements.

In addition to the above reviewed three components of feedback, Zhou's model also posits that the characteristics of the feedback recipient influence the way in which he or she responds to the feedback. In particular, individuals differ in achievement motivation. Those high on achievement motivation would strive to deliver high performance compared with standards of excellence.[40] Additionally, individuals also differ in power motivation. Those high on power motivation have a greater need to exert influences on others and to experience recognition for power-oriented activities.[41]

Zhou argues that individuals' achievement motivation and power motivation affect the manner in which they respond to positive versus negative feedback. Previous research provides suggestive support to her arguments. For example, Foder and Carver (2000)[42] showed that compared with individuals who did not receive any feedback, individuals high on achievement motivation produced more creative solutions after receiving negative feedback. However, individuals high on power motivation did not have such improvement in creativity after receiving negative feedback. In addition, these researchers showed that after receiving positive feedback, individuals high on achievement motivation exhibited great creativity, and so did individuals high on power motivation.

Another characteristic associated with the feedback recipient is emotional intelligence. It is defined by Mayer and Salovey (1997)[43] as one's ability to (a) accurately perceive, appraise, and express emotion; (b) understand emotion; (c) use emotion to facilitate one's thought processes; and (d) regulate and manage emotion.

It is conceivable that one's emotional intelligence influences one's response to feedback. For example, when an employee with high emotional intelligence receives negative feedback delivered in an informational style, he can accurately perceive any negative emotions that arise from the negative feedback. His high emotional intelligence also allows him to understand that although the feedback appears to be negative, it does contain useful informational that will help him to learn and improve. He can then manage his negative emotion and turn it into something functional—to use it to push himself to work harder to produce creative ideas.

Finally, the feedback and creativity model maintains that the characteristics of the feedback provider also influence the manner in which the feedback recipient responds to the feedback. In essence, the recipient will respond more strongly and positively to feedback given by those with more knowledge and expertise, and higher seniority and status.

In sum, the model formulated by Zhou (forthcoming) suggests that feedback can be an effective tool for promoting employees' creativity. To use it effectively, however, leaders are advised to consider all three sets of factors (i.e., the nature and components of feedback, and the characteristics of the feedback provider and of the recipient) that determine whether feedback is effective in enhancing employees' creativity.

Finally, knowing when to exhibit what kind of leadership behavior may not be sufficient in building a creative organization. In addition to the aforementioned everyday leadership behaviors, leaders need to pay attention to creativity training in order to build a creative organization.

Training programs. Although most organizations find employee creativity to be desirable, few of them have exerted systematic efforts to invest in creativity training programs. Amabile (1988)[44] posits that creativity-relevant skills and strategies are key components for creativity. Indeed, creativity is not the result of a random act. It is often a thoughtful process that involves finding the right problems or defining an existing problem appropriately, collecting data and information, producing many alternative ideas or solutions, and refining these ideas to arrive at a solution that is truly new and useful. From problem definition to the final solution, one needs to have appropriate skills to generate creative ideas and to have proper standards in deciding how to refine the ideas. All these support Amabile's (1988) assertion that creativity-relevant skills and strategies are critical for successfully producing creative ideas.

Unfortunately, most employees are not able to systematically acquire those skills and strategies at school. Indeed, other than schools and programs in the fields of arts, architecture, advertising, creative writing, and so forth, very few schools' curriculums incorporate creativity training. Thus, business leaders are often faced with the reality that most of their employees have not received much creativity training. To foster creativity, leaders need to make the investment and provide opportunities so that their employees can receive systematic training on creativity skills and strategies.

Basadur (2004)[45] points out that training can serve several functions critical for creative idea production. First, training can encourage employees to be more willing to engage in divergent instead of convergent thinking. Second, training can teach employees to focus on idea generation first and idea evaluation later. By not judging too early, the employees can have a better chance of producing a large quantity of novel ideas. Third, training may teach the employees to use better standards to evaluate ideas. Basadur's research has shown that individuals' creativity-relevant skills were improved after they had participated in creativity training.

Summary. In this section, I have reviewed several everyday behaviors that leaders should engage in (i.e., transformational leadership, non-close monitoring, LMX, goal setting, and feedback) to facilitate employee creativity. Each of these behaviors has been examined in multiple empirical studies that were based on sound theory, and results demonstrated that each of these behaviors could be used to enhance creativity.

Note, however, that in engaging in these behaviors leaders should exercise great care because the relations between these behaviors and creativity are complex. This complexity dictates that only when used appropriately will these behaviors truly facilitate creativity. For example, the effectiveness of feedback in promoting creativity is determined by a host of factors, including nature and components of the feedback message, and characteristics of the feedback provider and recipient. As another example, setting creativity goals could come at the expense of achieving high levels of productivity. This complexity also once again conforms to the notion that leadership is not a simple prescription of a "to do" list. Instead, leaders need to exercise prudent judgment on when, how, and with which employee certain leadership behaviors would be most effective to nurture creativity in that employee.

Last, I have suggested that leaders provide their employees with creativity training so that the employees have the opportunity to systematically acquire creativity-relevant skills and strategies. Such training would help the employees learn how to think creatively, and how to interact with others to discover synergy and cross-fertilization that would lead to greater creativity.

MANAGERS' RECOGNITION OF EMPLOYEES' CREATIVE IDEAS

In this section, I focus on the second aspect of leading a creative organization. I emphasize that in order to build a truly creative organization—in addition to enhancing employees' production of creative ideas—business leaders need to take a dyadic approach and understand how managers recognize employees' creative ideas. An understanding of this issue provides important implications on training managers to be creativity enablers instead of inhibitors. To this end, I introduce a theoretical model developed by Zhou (1998), and Zhou and Woodman (2003).[46]

More specifically, Zhou (1998) initially developed a social-cognitive model concerning factors that predict managers' recognition of employees' creative ideas. This model was later refined by Zhou and Woodman (2003). They note that much of the contemporary research has been focused on factors that facilitate or inhibit employee creativity. One significant gap in the workplace creativity literature is that we know little about factors that predict managers' recognition of creative ideas. This state of the literature is surprising, because to a great extent whether a manager can recognize a creative idea would determine whether the manager will continue to support the employee's endeavor to refine and eventually implement the idea.

Zhou and Woodman contend that whether an idea is judged as creative (i.e., both new and useful) is not completely objective. Instead, this judgment includes certain subjective elements. In the behavioral laboratory, novelty has been operationalized as statistically infrequent events.[47] For example, one could ask 100 research participants to each generate one new and useful idea for the use of a brick. The novelty of each participant's idea can be operationalized as the frequency that this idea is produced by these 100 participants. The more frequently an idea is mentioned, the less novel the idea is considered to be. In contrast, the less frequently an idea is mentioned, the more novel the idea is.

Such precise operationalization of novelty cannot be directly applied to the workplace. Thus, managers often have to use some subjective judgment instead of relying on precise statistical procedures to "calculate" the extent to which an idea is novel.

Zhou and Woodman maintain that the usefulness of an idea is even harder to judge in the workplace. According to the definition of creativity, the usefulness dimension of creativity requires that the idea add value, or have the potential to add value, to the effectiveness of the focal employee's work or to the effectiveness of the employee's work unit or the entire organization. Thus, we can say that a redesigned new manufacturing process is useful if it is more efficient than a process that existed prior to the redesign. And we can say that a new product is useful if customers want to buy it and if the company is profitable by selling this product to the customers.

However, when the idea for redesigning the manufacturing process or the idea for making the product is initially conceived, it usually is not clear whether the idea can indeed make the manufacturing process more efficient or whether it will lead to profitable products. It often takes a long process, from initially generating the raw idea to eventually benefiting from the implementation of this idea. Therefore, the judgment of usefulness is crucial at the idea stage of the creative process, and this judgment is often made under a great deal of uncertainty.

On the basis of research in social and cognitive psychology, Zhou and Woodman argue that creativity schema is a useful concept in understanding what factors influence managers' recognition of creative ideas. According to social cognitive psychology, a schema is a simplified mental representation of a type of external object, target, or event. It helps an individual to organize incoming information and make sense of external objects, targets, and events that are perceived by the individual.

Zhou and Woodman theorize that a creativity schema includes three aspects: causality, valence, and inferences. They define causality as the aspect of a creativity schema that details sequential relations among events. That is, it would allow a manager to make sense of where an idea has come from and why it has been produced. The second aspect, valence, refers to the significance of the target idea. It would allow the manager to gauge whether the idea is meaningful and significant. The third aspect, inferences, would allow the manager to predict whether the target idea can be successfully implemented, and what the consequences of implementing this idea are.

Zhou and Woodman then identify a set of antecedents that would lead to each of the three aspects of the creativity schema. They group these antecedents into three categories: (a) manager's personal characteristics; (b) manager's relationship with the employee who has produced and proposed the idea; and (c) organizational influences. While a full and complete review of their theoretical model is beyond the scope of this chapter, for purposes of illustration, I will list a few factors that they have identified. For example, they theorize that openness to experience, one of the Big Five personality factors, is positively related to valence. As another example, the manager's cognitive complexity is theorized to be positively related to the causality and inferences components of the manager's creativity schema. Finally, the manager's liking of the focal employees is theorized to be positively related to the valence and inferences aspects of the manager's creativity schema.

Although a fuller review and appraisal of the manager's recognition of creative ideas model developed by Zhou (1998) and Zhou and Woodman (2003) is beyond the scope of the present chapter, this model provides important suggestions. What is particularly relevant here is their notion that the manager's recognition of creative ideas is not completely objective. Rather, the extent to which a manager can accurately recognize a creative idea is influenced by the manager's personal characteristics, the relationship that this manager has with the employee who has produced the idea, and organizational level influences. In essence, the Zhou and Woodman model suggests that some managers are more capable of accurately recognizing creative ideas than others, managers are more likely to recognize creative ideas produced by certain employees than other employees, and in certain organizational contexts managers are more likely to accurately recognize creative ideas than in other organizational contexts.

DISCUSSION AND IMPLICATIONS FOR LEADING
A CREATIVE ORGANIZATION

In this chapter, I have attempted to integrate two separate streams of creativity research: one focusing on antecedents of employee creativity and the other centering on an understanding of managers' recognition of employees' creative ideas. I suggest that from the organization's perspective, only when both aspects bear fruit—that employees produce many creative ideas and managers are able to recognize such ideas—can truly creative ideas be produced by individual employees and organizations ultimately benefit from creativity. If only one of these two aspects is present, the organization will not be as creative as when both of these aspects are at high levels.

More specifically, if an employee produces a lot of potentially creative ideas and yet his manager fails to recognize them as such, those ideas would not have the chance to be further developed and refined into something that is truly new and useful, and would not be ultimately implemented in the organization. On the other hand, if a manager can accurately recognize creative ideas but her employees seldom produce creative ideas, there is not much raw material that the manager can work with to help the employees to fine-tune the ideas so that they can eventually be tangible ideas that would lead to the introduction of new and better ways of doing things in her unit or the organization as a whole. If the employees supervised by a manager rarely come up with potentially creative ideas, and the manager is unable or unwilling to recognize creative ideas, the overall level of creativity in his unit would obviously be low.

Therefore, it would be desirable for researchers and business leaders alike to move up to the dyadic level-of-analysis from the individual level-of-analysis that has been predominantly used in previous research. Taking this dyadic approach would allow creativity research to truly capture the critical moments of creative idea production, and the key factors affecting whether creative ideas can be successfully produced. It is important to note that this dyadic approach complements, instead of replaces, research on antecedents of employees' production of creative ideas and research on managers' recognition of creative ideas. As Shalley et al. (2004)[48] concluded, there is still a great deal to be learned about what antecedents facilitate or inhibit employees' production of creative ideas. Theorizing and research on managers' recognition of creative ideas are still at their infancy with much discovery to be made. Thus, research along those two lines of inquiry would still be quite valuable in advancing our knowledge of employee creativity.

This dyadic approach suggests that in addition to provide employees with creativity training, leaders and managers can benefit substantially from creativity training as well. First, leaders themselves should be trained to be producers of creative ideas. Second, leaders should be trained to be creativity enablers by displaying everyday leadership behaviors that promote creativity.

Third, leaders should be trained to be customers of creative ideas. That is, they need to develop the ability to "see" the creative ideas produced by their employees, even if the ideas are still premature and at an early stage of development. Such ability on the part of the leaders may encourage and nurture employees' creative idea production at critical moments in the creative process, and are likely to be the key factors that enable the organizations to harvest the benefits of employees' creative ideas. In conclusion, taking this dyadic approach would allow leaders to build their organizations into truly creative enterprises.

NOTES

1. Nussbaum, B. Get Creative! How to build innovative companies. *BusinessWeek,* August 1, 2005.

2. Pelz, D. C., & Andrews, F. M. (1966). *Scientists in organizations: Productive climates for research and development.* New York: Wiley.

3. Zhou, J., & George, J. M. (2001). When job dissatisfaction leads to creativity: Encouraging the expression of voice. *Academy of Management Journal, 44,* 682–696.

4. Zhou, J., & George, J. M. (2003). Awakening employee creativity: The role of leader emotional intelligence. *Leadership Quarterly, 14,* 545–568.

5. See Note 4.

6. Zhou, J. (1998). *Managers' recognition of employee creative ideas: A social-cognitive approach.* Paper presented at "The 21st Century Change Imperative: Evolving Organizations & Emerging Networks" Conference, Center for the Study of Organizational Change, University of Missouri-Columbia, June 12–14; Zhou, J., & Woodman, R. W. (2003). Managers' recognition of employees' creative ideas. In L. V. Shavinina (Ed.), *International handbook on innovation.* Hillsdale, NJ: Lawrence Erlbaum.

7. Shalley, C. E., Zhou, J., & Oldham, G. R. (2004). The effects of personal and contextual characteristics on creativity: Where should we go from here? *Journal of Management, 30,* 933–958; Zhou, J., & Shalley, C. E. (2003). Research on employee creativity: A critical review and directions for future research. In J. J. Martocchio & G. R. Ferris (Eds.), *Research in personnel and human resource management* (Vol. 22, pp. 165–217). Oxford, England: Elsevier Science.

8. Mumford, M. D., Scott, G. M., Gaddis, B., & Strange, J. M. (2002). Leading creative people: Orchestrating expertise and relationships. *Leadership Quarterly, 13,* 705–750.

9. Amabile, T. M. (1988). A model of creativity and innovation in organizations. In B. M. Staw & L. L. Cummings (Eds.), Research in organizational behavior (Vol. 10, pp. 123–167). Greenwich, CT: JAI Press; Oldham, G. R., & Cummings, A. (1996). Employee creativity: Personal and contextual factors at work. *Academy of Management Journal,* 39, 607–634; Shalley, C. E. (1991). Effects of productivity goals, creativity goals, and personal discretion on individual creativity. *Journal of Applied Psychology, 76,* 179–185; Zhou, J. (1998). Feedback valence, feedback style, task autonomy, and

achievement orientation: Interactive effects on creative performance. *Journal of Applied Psychology, 83*, 261–276.

10. Barron, F. (1965). The psychology of creativity. In T. Newcombe (Ed.), *New directions in psychology, 2*, 1–34. New York: Holt, Rinehart & Winston; Mackinnon, D.W. (1965). Personality and the realization of creative potential. *American Psychologist, 20*, 273–281.

11. Gough, H. G. (1979). A creative personality scale for the Adjective Check List. *Journal of Personality and Social Psychology, 37*, 1398–1405.

12. Zhou, J., & Oldham, G. R. (2001). Enhancing creative performance: Effects of expected developmental assessment strategies and creative personality. *Journal of Creative Behavior, 35*, 151–167.

13. Zhou, J. (2003). When the presence of creative coworkers is related to creativity: Role of supervisor close monitoring, developmental feedback, and creative personality. *Journal of Applied Psychology, 88*, 413–422.

14. Oldham, G. R., & Cummings, A. (1996). Employee creativity: Personal and contextual factors at work. *Academy of Management Journal, 39*, 607–634.

15. See Note 10.

16. Costa, P. T., & McCrae, R. R. (1992). *Revised NEO Personality Inventory (NEO PI-R) and NEO Five-Factor Inventory (NEO-FFI) Professional Manual*. Odessa, FL: Psychological Assessment Resources; McCrae, R. R. (1987). Creativity, divergent thinking, and openness to experience. *Journal of Personality and Social Psychology, 52*, 1258–1265.

17. Feist, G. J. (1998). A meta-analysis of personality in scientific and artistic creativity. *Personality and Social Psychology Review, 4*, 290–309.

18. George, J. M., & Zhou, J. (2001). When openness to experience and conscientiousness are related to creative behavior: An interactional approach. *Journal of Applied Psychology, 86*, 513–524.

19. Tierney, P., & Farmer, S. M. (2002). Creative self-efficacy: Potential antecedents and relationship to creative performance. *Academy of Management Journal, 45*, 1137–1148.

20. Shalley, C. E., Zhou, J., & Oldham, G. R. (2004). The effects of personal and contextual characteristics on creativity: Where should we go from here? *Journal of Management, 30*, 933–958.

21. For example, Bass, B. M. (1985). *Leadership and performance beyond expectation*. New York: Free Press.

22. See, for example, Bass, B. M., & Avolio, B. J. (1995). *MLQ multifactor leadership questionnaire (2nd Ed.)*. Redwood City, CA: Mind Garden.

23. Avolio, B. J., Bass, B. M., & Jung, D. I. (1999). Re-examining the components of transformational and transactional leadership using the multifactor leadership questionnaire. *Journal of Occupational and Organizational Psychology, 72*, 441–462; Sosik, J. J., Avolio, B. J., & Kahai, S. S. (1998). Inspiring group creativity: comparing anonymous and identified electronic brainstorming. *Small Group Research, 29*, 3–31.

24. Shin, S., & Zhou, J. (2003). Transformational leadership, conservation, and creativity: Evidence from Korea. *Academy of Management Journal, 46*, 703–714.

25. Deci, E. L., & Ryan, R. M. (1985). *Intrinsic motivation and self-determination in human behavior*. New York: Plenum.

26. McGraw, K. O., & Fiala, J. (1982). Undermining the Zeigarnik effect: Another hidden cost of reward. *Journal of Personality, 50,* 58–66; McGraw, K. O., & McCullers, J. C. (1979). Evidence of a detrimental effect of extrinsic incentives on breaking a mental set. *Journal of Experimental Social Psychology, 15,* 285–294.

27. Amabile, T. M. (1988). A model of creativity and innovation in organizations. In B. M. Staw & L. L. Cummings (Eds.), *Research in organizational behavior* (Vol. 10, pp. 123–167). Greenwich, CT: JAI Press; Oldham, G. R., & Cummings, A. (1996). Employee creativity: Personal and contextual factors at work. *Academy of Management Journal, 39,* 607–634.

28. Mumford, M., D., & Licuanan, B. (2004). Leading for innovation: Conclusions, issues, and directions. *Leadership Quarterly, 15,* 163–171.

29. George, J. M., & Zhou, J. (2001). When openness to experience and conscientiousness are related to creative behavior: An interactional approach. *Journal of Applied Psychology, 86,* 513–524.

30. See Note 13.

31. Dansereau, F., Graen, G., & Haga, W. (1975). A vertical dyad linkage approach to leadership within formal organizations: A longitudinal investigation of the rolemaking process. *Organizational Behavior and Human Performance, 13,* 46–78; Graen, G. B., & Scandura, T. A. (1987). Toward a psychology of dyadic organizing. In B. M. Staw & L. L. Cummings (Eds.), *Research in organizational behavior* (Vol. 9, pp. 175–208).

32. Scott, S. G., & Bruce, R. A. (1994). Determinants of innovative behavior: A path model of individual innovation in the workplace. *Academy of Management Journal, 37,* 580–607.

33. Tierney, P., Farmer, S. M., & Graen, G. B. (1999). An examination of leadership and employee creativity: The relevance of traits and relationships. *Personnel Psychology, 52,* 591–620.

34. Locke, E.A., & Latham, G. P. (1990). *A theory of goal setting and task performance.* Englewood Cliffs, NJ: Prentice-Hall.

35. For reviews of this body of work, see Locke, E.A., & Latham, G. P. (1990). *A theory of goal setting and task performance.* Englewood Cliffs, NJ: Prentice-Hall; Locke, E. A., Shaw, K. N., Saari, L., & Latham, G.P. (1981). Goal setting and task performance: 1969–1980. *Psychological Bulletin, 90,* 125–152.

36. Shalley, C. E. (1991). Effects of productivity goals, creativity goals, and personal discretion on individual creativity. *Journal of Applied Psychology, 76,* 179–185.

37. Shalley, C. E. (1995). Effects of coaction, expected evaluation, and goal setting on creativity and productivity. *Academy of Management Journal, 38,* 483–503.

38. Zhou, J. (forthcoming). Promoting creativity through feedback. In C. Ford (Ed.), *Handbook of organizational creativity.* Hillsdale, NJ: Lawrence Erlbaum.

39. Zhou, J. (1998a). Feedback valence, feedback style, task autonomy, and achievement orientation: Interactive effects on creative performance. *Journal of Applied Psychology, 83,* 261–276.

40. McClelland, D. C. (1985). *Human motivation.* Glenview, IL: Scott, Foresman.

41. Winter, D. G. (1973). *The power motive.* New York: Free Press.

42. Fodor, E. M., & Carver, R. A. (2000). Achievement and power motives, performance feedback, and creativity. *Journal of Research in Personality, 34:* 380–396.

43. Mayer, J. D., & Salovey, P. (1997). What is emotional intelligence? In P. Salovey & D. Sluyter (Eds.), *Emotional development and emotional intelligence: Educational implications* (pp. 3–34). New York: Basic Books.

44. Amabile, T. M. (1988). A model of creativity and innovation in organizations. In B. M. Staw & L. L. Cummings (Eds.), *Research in organizational behavior* (Vol. 10, pp. 123–167). Greenwich, CT: JAI Press.

45. Basadur, M. (2004). Leading others to think creatively together: Creative leadership. *Leadership Quarterly, 15,* 103–121.

46. Zhou, J. (1998). *Managers' recognition of employee creative ideas: A social-cognitive approach.* Paper presented at "The 21st Century Change Imperative: Evolving Organizations & Emerging Networks" Conference, Center for the Study of Organizational Change, University of Missouri-Columbia, June 12-14; Zhou, J., & Woodman, R. W. (2003). Managers' recognition of employees' creative ideas: A social-cognitive model. In L. V. Shavinina (Ed.), *International handbook on innovation.* Hillsdale, NJ: Lawrence Erlbaum.

47. Carson, P. P., & Carson, K. D. (1993). Managing creativity enhancement through goal setting and feedback. *Journal of Creative Behavior, 27,* 36–45.

48. See Note 20.

3-D Creativity in Organizations: Discipline, Discipline, Discipline

NANCY K. NAPIER

D rawing on case studies of three organizations—a regional theater, a software firm, and an American football program—this chapter discusses three types of discipline that enhance organizational creativity. Out-of-discipline thinking involves looking beyond a discipline or field for ideas that may benefit an organization. Within-discipline thinking and acting refers to how organizational members seek to be the best in their fields, through internal friendly competition, quicker learning, and going beyond discipline basics to become more creative. Finally, having a disciplined process suggests that routine and structure can actually free participants to experiment and be more creative.

What do football, software, and theater have in common? Certainly not the setting—stadium, cubicles, and stage. And not the participants—one football player can overpower several actors or software engineers. What about environment? Live regional theater may have few direct competitors, and football has one opponent per game, but software has many in a volatile environment. Surprisingly, though, such diverse organizations may indeed have some common approaches to creativity. This chapter focuses on characteristics that three sample organizations exhibit in the way they approach creative activities.

Many thanks to the Idaho Shakespeare Festival, the Boise State University Football program, and ProClarity, Inc. for supporting this project.

Creativity research and practice has a long history.[1] Many researchers have defined it as the development of new or novel ideas, appropriate for their context, that have value.[2] Da Vinci's idea for a flying machine was novel, but inappropriate for the context. Since it could not be made, or even imagined by most people, it lacked value. A child's Lego model may be appropriate for her time and place, but it has relatively little value, except to the parents and child. Creative ideas that have the three components—new, appropriate for the context, and valuable—often move to an innovation stage, where they become marketable outcomes with economic value.[3]

Both creativity and innovation are increasingly seen as potential critical resources for countries, communities, and organizations,[4] and interest at all levels has grown rapidly in the last decade, in both the academic world and the general press alike.[5] Since the 1950s, much research has emphasized individual-focused creativity issues, such as motivation, creative problem solving and thinking, and the characteristics of creative persons.[6] More recently, researchers and practitioners have explored how to improve organizational creativity, including what enhances or inhibits group creativity, how workplace and environmental conditions may influence creative processes and outcomes, and what role leaders and members of groups play in generating creative results.[7]

This chapter builds on and applies ideas about creativity in three organizational settings. In particular, the chapter examines three medium-sized, project-based organizations in three industry sectors in the U.S. (regional theater, business analysis software, and university sports—American football).[8] The organizations met three criteria: (1) each is recognized nationally or globally in its industry as a consistently high performer, with a high-quality product or service; (2) each is small or medium sized (less than 200 members); and (3) each has a reputation in its field for being creative or "different." The case studies revealed that the organizations have more in common than what might appear on the surface. In particular, they exhibited the 3 D's of creativity: discipline, discipline, and discipline.

The chapter has three major sections. The first part describes briefly the three types of discipline. The next part illustrates the disciplines within three organizations. Finally, the chapter closes with several observations.

3-D CREATIVITY

For this discussion, "3-D creativity" has two meanings. First, it refers to three types of discipline that organizations and groups can pursue to enhance opportunities for generating creative outputs. Second, the 3-D idea also seeks to convey the notion that creativity is multidimensional—in other words, organizations and their members need to shift across dimensions or disciplines to remain nimble and competitive.

This section of the chapter reviews three types of disciplines that emerged from literature and case studies: (1) out-of-discipline thinking; (2) within-discipline expertise; and (3) a disciplined process.

Out-of-Discipline Thinking

When people talk of being creative, many (Americans) use the phrase "out-of-the-box thinking." For most, this means thinking in ways that are not traditional, linear, or expected in their given fields. Similarly, out-of-discipline thinking means taking risks, by accepting or seeking ideas that fall outside of disciplinary, expertise, or knowledge boundaries and then finding ways to use those ideas.[9]

To develop such out-of-discipline thinking, one needs the ability, time, and motivation to scan the environment in an almost promiscuous way. Out-of-discipline thinkers absorb information from sources beyond their normal fields and then seek to understand how the ideas might apply in their situations.[10] For example, Steven Jobs' recognition (nearly too late, according to him) of the trend toward downloading music onto computers helped the company come up with the worldwide phenomenon of the iPod.[11]

Even though finding uses for ideas can be critical, out-of-discipline creative groups and people also accept that not all ideas will be usable—right away or ever. In fact, there seems to be an implicit classification of ideas. "Big" ideas, such as the iPod, may change or shake an organization's—or industry's—way of operating. Incremental or "tweaking" ideas may focus more on improvement and slight adjustments.[12] Toyota's lean manufacturing processes exemplify such improvement ideas. Other ideas may need to simmer or bake for a while; these are the "hmmm" or back burner ideas that may come to the fore eventually—or may not.

Within-Discipline Expertise

A second aspect of 3-D creativity is a focus on building depth of discipline, or expertise.[13] Organizations may hire people with deep technical skill, yet the notion of "within-discipline" expertise takes the concept further. Specifically, within-discipline thinking has at least three components and purposes: (1) being (with) the best; (2) speeding learning; and (3) moving "beyond the fundamentals."

Being (with) the best. Highly creative organizations seem to have people who are among the best in their fields, which brings a sense of pride at being part of such a group.[14] Thus, organizational or group members who want to remain the best and with the best continually increase their discipline knowledge. As a result, informal competition may exist among participants in some highly creative, high-performing organizations, where members monitor what their colleagues are learning, what experiences they may have, or how well they are performing.

Speeding learning. Another benefit of having strong within-discipline thinking and skills is that they speed learning when people who do not know each other come together to work on projects. This form of fast learning differs from the notion of continuous organizational learning.[15] Rather, this type of within-discipline expertise focuses on the language and concepts that people gain within their fields and how they can use that to interact more efficiently.

All fields have jargon to facilitate describing and implementing tasks. When organizational members are highly competent within their disciplines, they can work with counterparts without needing to explain concepts, assumptions, and techniques. In time-constrained organizations seeking creative output, such within-discipline expertise becomes especially important where teams form and reform regularly, such as in project-based organizations. Such experts sometimes resent people who lack knowledge or language expertise because it requires them to educate new or unknowledgeable team members. So, while a team may still need to build psychological knowledge and trust of members, within-discipline thinking provides a common starting point.

On the other hand, within-discipline thinking may limit creativity. In particular, assuming that participants know a discipline and language well may inhibit questioning and idea forming that comes from out-of-discipline thinking. In other words, organizational members must balance the depth they bring to a creative endeavor with the need for the first creative D—out-of-discipline thinking.[16] Balancing out-of- and within-discipline thinking is something successful creative groups appear to do well. Cross-functional teams, for instance, tend to break down the initial benefits of within-discipline thinking because they explicitly bring out-of-discipline thinking into the team equation.[17]

Moving beyond the fundamentals. A final aspect of within-discipline thinking is being so grounded and competent in a discipline that one can move beyond it. In any discipline, learning the basic concepts, techniques, and ways of approaching problems is crucial for going into more creative ground. Examples of inventors illustrate the importance of knowing the fundamentals before they "move beyond." Louis Pasteur (1822–1895), French chemist and bacteriologist, said in 1854 that "In the field of observation, chance favors the prepared mind."[18] Depth of knowledge, preparation, and expertise that is solid and substantial, then, provide a foundation from which one can test ideas and develop new ones.

Disciplined Process

The third discipline in 3-D creativity is having a systematic, disciplined process or approach for carrying out creative endeavors.[19] This suggests that organizations or groups have a set of behaviors, steps, or routines that can form the basic structure for creativity. An interesting paradox for many people is the idea that structure, rather than being a constraint, can actually enhance creativity and freedom.

Such a process starts with recognizing the need for time to be creative,[20] which includes iteration, testing, and retesting, before an idea is usable.[21] In addition, especially in temporary project-oriented organizations, the time and process for group formations are critical.[22]

APPLICATION OF 3-D CREATIVITY

This section describes organizations from different sectors that use the disciplines of creativity. The section starts with a description of each organization and then applies the notions of the 3-Ds within each.

ORGANIZATIONS

As mentioned, three case study organizations provided the basis for this chapter. All are headquartered in Boise, Idaho, a medium-sized western U.S. city, which has received attention for attracting entrepreneurs and creative people.[23]

Regional Theater

Similar to many arts organizations, American regional theater faces significant financial and market challenges.[24] In the last decade, several theaters have closed, scaled back, tried to merge, or run deficits. They compete for customers with arts endeavors that include dance, classical and club music, and experiences outside of the arts, like participative and spectator sports, family activities (e.g., children's sports), and even Internet-driven activities, like video gaming. Thus, theaters that succeed have had to find competitive niches and manage themselves in an exemplary manner.

The present case is a regional theater located in Boise, Idaho. The group comprises a relatively stable acting company (about 80 percent of actors return annually), as well as regularly returning directors, designers, and technicians who come from larger cities (e.g., New York, Los Angeles, and Chicago). Many artists know one another from graduate programs or from earlier acting, directing, or designing assignments in other cities. The administrative, and a few of the artistic, staff of about thirty people stay on site year round. The artistic and technical staffs who work during the season raise the total number of employees to about 150.

The outdoor theater is the same size as the Globe Theatre in England, with attendance at 90–100 percent capacity throughout its four-month summer season. This means 50,000 attendees annually in a city of 200,000, typically

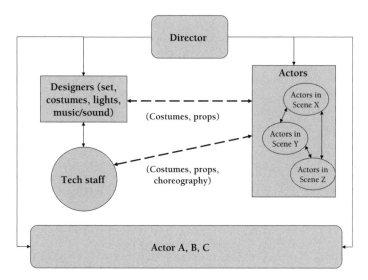

FIGURE 3.1. Theater Participants

unheard of in the U.S. regional theater world. Thus, financially, the theater is strong, with no long-term debt in the last decade.

The theater's producing artistic director hires external directors for most of its plays, who in turn hire most of the designers (e.g., set, lighting, music/sound, costume) for a given play. The producing artistic director also hires the actors and technicians who work with the designers (e.g., in building sets, sewing costumes). The teams of artistic and technical staff are, by their very nature, temporary. They work on a given play, which is constrained by time, budget, and place.[25] Thus, the director, actors, designers, and technicians remain in the city for the life of their respective responsibilities.

Theaters tend to have similar types of participants during the production of a play (Figure 3.1). Three general categories of participants include (1) the director, in charge of overall creative and technical quality and direction; (2) designers and technicians related to their expertise areas; and (3) actors. The theater also comprises the administrative staff who run operations, but they were not the focus of the creative process for this case study.

Football

Unlike much of regional theater in the U.S., American university football appears to be thriving and popular with a wide audience.[26] In 2004, for example, the National Collegiate Athletic Association (NCAA) reported that revenues for Division I football programs, which make up the 115 teams in the top level of university programs, were $1.6 billion, ranging from less than

$1 million (University of Akron, Ohio) to over $47 million (University of Texas). The industry is competitive—with "rankings" of top teams done before, during, and at the close of the five-month season, which runs from August until the end of December.[27] In addition to revenues from games and souvenirs, winning teams may receive major donations—usually to the athletic programs, but sometimes to academic programs and student scholarships. Finally, discouraging as it may be for faculty members, the recognition that a winning team brings to a university can be a major draw for students and donors. Thus, high performance is critical for football programs.

The present case study is a university football program in the Division I group. In 2004, its revenues were $4 million, and it was not ranked in the top twenty-five U.S. teams until 2002 (when it was #23). Each year since, it finished in the top twenty-five and was rated #12 in the U.S. in 2004, against universities with much better funding and resources. Partly because of this, the head coach has had to be innovative with limited resources in building his program. The program comprises approximately 130 people, including about twenty coaches and staff members and about 110 players.

Until recently, the program has been relatively unknown, lacking the cache of major programs like the University of Southern California, the University of Oklahoma, or the University of Michigan. As a result, it faced difficulty in recruiting highly sought-after players. Coaches, therefore, focused on recruiting players who were relatively smaller in size and weight, removing bulk and power as a competitive advantage, compared to opposing teams. The head coach has thus sought other ways to build competitive advantage, such as using creativity in how he prepares players, the types of plays the team uses, and the ideas he draws from other disciplines. Indeed, the team and its coach have been profiled in the news because of the coach's willingness to take risks, devotion to Zen Buddhism, and commitment to finding new ideas.[28]

University football programs have three main groups of participants: coaches, players, and support personnel (e.g., strength conditioning coaches who help players become stronger and trainers who work with injured players). The first two are the focus of the discussion here (Figure 3.2). In addition to the head coach, who is like the COO and CEO, managing both inside and outside, three other groups of coaches exist. The offensive coaches focus on moving the football downfield when their team has control. The movement comes from a series of plays, where the ball moves (usually) down the field through a run or pass/throw by one or more players. The defensive team's goal is to stop the opposing team's forward movement of the ball. The defensive coaches and players try to anticipate the opposing team's play and seek to prevent its success. In the lucky situation where the defensive side gains control of the ball, its players must be prepared to run toward their own goal. The special teams group comprises players who kick the ball at various points in the game, such as at the beginning of significant plays, and those who receive and run with the ball when it has been kicked by the opposing team.

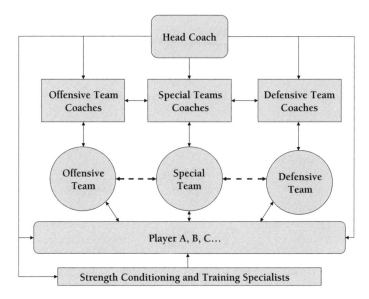

FIGURE 3.2. Football Participants

Each group of coaches oversees players within those clusters of positions. This team is somewhat different because the head coach shuffles players across various positions during their spring training to see if an offensive player could also play in a defensive position, for example. His goal, and one of the creative features in his tactics, is to have several players able to play many positions. As a result, the opposing team never knows whom to expect on the field in certain positions. Thus, unlike most teams that use one or two players in critical positions, like catching and running with the ball, the present team may have five or six players who are able to do the task. It not only gives players more chance to play, it reduces reliance on any one or two. If one is injured, there are more in reserve.

Software

The third organization develops business intelligence software for analyzing and presenting huge amounts of data for decision support to managers. The firm claims to offer "out-of-the box business intelligence software and a leading analytic application platform." It operates in the global, fast-changing, somewhat struggling software industry, which has revenues of $75 billion. However, some industry segments appear to be growing, including business intelligence software, open source software, and virus/spam protection software.

The privately held case study firm has consistently received accolades and awards. It is frequently listed as one of the fastest growing or best firms in

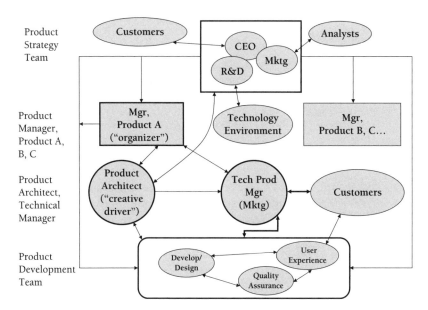

Product
Strategy
Team

Product
Manager,
Product A,
B, C

Product
Architect,
Technical
Manager

Product
Development
Team

FIGURE 3.3. Software Participants

class in the world by publications such as Deloitte Technology Fast 500, Inc., 500, Software 500, Teched 2005, and Intelligent Enterprise. So it is highly competitive, despite its remote location in Idaho and small size (about 150 employees worldwide).

Partly because of its small size, relative isolation, and competition from much larger and better known firms, the CEO claims that the firm must compete on creativity and innovation. As he puts it, "We need 1.0 thinking, not 2.0." The firm cannot be "as good as" a competitor; it must be 30–100 percent better than any competitor.

The firm has four main levels of participants involved in new product development: (1) the product strategy team; (2) the product manager; (3) the product architect and technical product manager; and (4) the product development team. The product strategy team sets the overall vision and taps three areas of the environment for creative ideas: the CEO, who interacts with key customers and partners, the senior vice president of marketing and investment, who maintains contact with financial analysts, and the senior vice president of research and development, who monitors technology changes (Figure 3.3). They convey an overall vision to a product manager, product architect, and technical product manager. The product manager's main role is logistical planning/management throughout the course of a project, including deadlines and budget goals. The product architect translates the product strategy team's vision into product features with the product development team, which does development/programming, quality assurance, and user experience. Once the product is ready for launch, it goes to the technical product manager.

SO HOW DOES 3-D CREATIVITY WORK?

This section of the paper examines the three disciplines in the example organizations, comparing and contrasting different approaches.

Out-of-Discipline Thinking

The leaders of the three organizations exemplify out-of-discipline thinking, as creative agents who model and encourage creativity. Several aspects come into play, including simply being open to new ideas, becoming known as someone who will consider unusual ideas, and, finally, actively pursuing out-of-discipline ideas.

Being open to new ideas. The producing artistic director of the theater has an acting and directing background, but grew up with a father who was a finance professor. His ability to combine artistic and business skills is unprecedented, according to theater board members. One theater that conducted a nationwide search for a new artistic director found that, out of over sixty applicants, this manager was far above other candidates because of his combination of artistic and business skills. He reads widely, networks unmercifully, and learns constantly.

One example of out-of-discipline thinking includes looking to sports for marketing ideas, as in how theaters get endorsements for actors. One doesn't want to imagine Julius Caesar with a Nike endorsement on his costume and, of course, the director is not advocating that. What he does envision, though, is finding ways for sponsors to support individual actors, in addition to the ongoing sponsorship of productions as a whole, which in turn could supplement the low pay that actors typically receive. Whether such an idea will take hold is unknown; nonetheless, his willingness to consider it reveals openness to out-of-discipline thinking.

In addition to being open to ideas from others, one actor noted that being open to unexpected ideas from oneself is also important:

> Let me tell you the best way [creativity and ideas] come—if I sit down at a desk with a pencil, looking at the script and try to come up with something, it's [bad.] What has to happen is that it doesn't happen in a waking state. I'm not going to talk with you and then something will happen. It usually happens when [I'm] meditating, in a nap phase or driving. Essentially, there's something that's turned on that is working on the problem … The trick is for me to be open and available to what is presented [from within].

Being a target for unusual ideas. Like the producing artistic director, the football head coach looks outside his discipline for creative ideas that will strengthen his organizational management style—planning, practices/drilling methods, management of the organization and its stakeholders. He quotes Sun Tzu, for example, on how to approach competitors on the playing field, he reads business books on management, but he also goes further. He has become known in his field as someone who is a willing target for "wacky" ideas.

Recently, a retired Hollywood producer contacted him about a 360-degree camera that might have application for training football quarterbacks. Following his Hollywood career, the producer bought a farm in Iowa. One day, after swatting at flies and having no luck hitting them, he began thinking about, and then learning about, fly eyes. He learned that flies' compound eyes can sense rapid motion and have a wide range. He then invented a wearable camera, shaped somewhat like the goggles in the movie *The Matrix*. By wearing the goggle camera, a quarterback can "practice" a full game, such as snapping, throwing, and learning how to read the field and position of other players— by himself, alone, in a room. As the coach said, "No one else would talk to the guy—too wacky—so he came to me."

Actively seeking new ideas. Finally, out-of-discipline thinkers often proactively seek ideas, rather than waiting passively for them to appear. For example, the software CEO has studied the U.S. Army Rangers and filmmaking to learn about how to form "rapid response" teams that can develop, test, and release a new product on a tight schedule. Both Army Rangers and film ventures tend to bring together people who may not know one another, who have not worked together before, and who have time, budget and quality constraints that require speed.[29]

The CEO also studies the film industry to enhance software products. As he puts it, "When you rent a movie, how long will you watch it before you decide not to continue?" He claims that the software and movie industries are similar in the willingness of potential customers to continue. The movie industry has found individuals tend to watch a movie for about 10 percent of the time that the movie would last (e.g., ten minutes of a 100-minute movie). The CEO claims that potential software customers have even more rigorous expectations: customers will spend one or two minutes on a new piece of software before they decide whether it is "worth" the effort of buying, installing, and learning how to use it. The CEO is implicitly suggesting that software, like a film, needs to reach customers at an emotional level so they will continue with the product or movie. So his out-of-discipline idea is to learn from the film industry about how to tell a story, grab and hold an audience by the neck, and make people want to continue.

Encourage and expect out-of-discipline thinking. In each of the three organizations, the leaders model and expect others to be open to or pursue-out-of-discipline thinking and ideas, including building and using outside networks.[30] In the football training area, one coach looks to other sports for ideas to increase speed, flexibility, or agility of football players. Software engineers mine history and warfare for ideas about anticipating trends and confronting competition.

Interestingly, the notion of having a diverse group of people within a team as a spark to encourage out-of-discipline thinking seems constrained in these three groups. Observable diversity in the regional theater, for instance, seems relatively limited. Among directors, designers, and actors, there is a good mix of men and women as actors, depending upon the play and parts, but until the summer of 2004, all directors were men. Further, most of the artists in this company are highly educated, white, and in their mid-twenties to early forties, and at least eight of the resident company of about thirty attended the same graduate program.

While surface diversity seems thin, artists are diverse in other ways, such as their sexual preference, educational backgrounds, or in their acting/direct-ing/designing experiences. Most have worked throughout the U.S., some have extensive experience in Europe, and one actor spent over a month performing Shakespeare in Hanoi, Vietnam. Further, within theater, team members' move-ment from production to production creates diversity. Members bring experi-ences and ideas from recent work, from other directors, designers, and actors, and from the way other audiences react to the productions. Thus, there is a form of "built-in" or forced diversity simply because the mix of team members changes regularly.

In football, diversity is also hard to see and to expect, for at least two rea-sons. Coaches have similar characteristics and backgrounds, and they tend to remain together as a group for several years. Specifically, the football coaches in this case are all male, only two of twenty are not white, and several were trained or worked at the same program in Southern California. Further, coaches tend to join and stay with a program if they "fit." Thus, visible diver-sity as a way to generate out-of-discipline thinking is not apparent.

Because the head coach values out-of-discipline thinking, though, he explicitly seeks ways to encourage diverse views by bringing in outsiders, sending coaches to other programs, encouraging reading or learning in non-discipline-specific areas, and seeking ideas from stakeholders that one might not initially see as valuable. For example, he frequently draws upon academic partners doing research on topics that may be of use to the program. One is an engineering professor who is studying the mechanics of quarterback throwing techniques, as a way to enhance their efficiency and effectiveness. Another has offered to apply chaos theory to the team, assisting the coaches in deciding which players and plays to use at various points in the game. The coach also regularly sends clusters of coaches to other professional and uni-versity teams for tips on how they conduct practice and drill sessions, how they generate ideas for plays, or how they motivate players. After playing against (and losing to) one particular team that is very similar to his, he invited its coaches for a debriefing exchange, figuring that the chances of playing that team again soon were limited. Finally, he encourages his coaches to reach to other sports or fields for ideas. One of the strength conditioning coaches, for instance, has used techniques from women's volleyball and tennis for training ideas in football.

Likewise, the software firm faces similar challenges in terms of diversity. The research and development group is overwhelmingly male (two women out of over twenty), similar in age (mid-twenties to late thirties), very similar in education (i.e., engineering, with a few in design or writing), with long-term tenures within the firm. As the vice president for research says, "If people can make it here, they tend to like it and stay." This creates a problem: if employee turnover normally brings new ideas, then a longstanding workforce means that new ideas do not naturally enter the firm.

Thus, the company has had to force diversity of ideas and out-of-discipline thinking more explicitly, through such means as encouraging interaction with key stakeholders by people at all levels, bringing ideas from the outside into the organization, and openly testing new ways of operating. For instance, the firm's leaders claim they seek to be "bottom-centric," encouraging people at all levels to bring new ideas into the firm, especially from lower levels; they comment that there are more "touch points" at the bottom levels, simply because there are more people. Those engineers, developers, and user interface and quality assurance people will be more likely to interact with more and a wider range of people and thus capture and bring back new knowledge and ideas.

Further, the firm brings in new ideas through other means, including, for example, a monthly book discussion group. Whoever wishes can read the same book, discuss it, and mine it for ideas for the firm. If there are good ideas, the company tests them within certain units. After six weeks, the unit evaluates the idea and recommends whether it is something for the entire firm to incorporate. Finally, the company regularly invites outsiders from disciplines other than software to talk about their industries, management approaches, or other ideas. For example, given the CEO's interest in filmmaking, he invited an Academy Award-winning documentary film maker to talk about the business, artistic, logistical, and technological aspects of making an OMNIMAX film.[31]

Within-Discipline Thinking

This section discusses each organization's approach to within-discipline thinking and acting and covers three aspects: (1) being (with) the best; (2) speeding learning; and (3) moving beyond the fundamentals.

In these creative organizations, key participants, whether long-term members, like the software engineers or football players and coaches, or temporary members, such as the actors, designers, and directors, recognize the need to "sell" their abilities and themselves. Thus, commitment to building and maintaining strong within-discipline expertise, knowledge, and skill is crucial.

Being (with) the best. In all three organizations, participants valued being part of high-performing, highly creative organizations. This generates a sort of undercurrent internal competition: to remain (with) the best, each participant must continually learn and improve. Football players, actors, and software engineers know that others can do their jobs, so they need to be at their peak. For example, since this football team shuffles players into several positions, a player knows that to have an opportunity to play, he must be in top physical and mental shape in order to learn new moves and plays and develop his physical and mental memory.

Similarly, competition among actors is fierce. Actors who compete in national and international markets continually take classes to expand their range of abilities, hone their skills as professionals, and develop characteristics beyond talent, like being easy to work with:

> The moral of the story is that every job you do, you behave in a way that you'll continue to get work (or not). [But it's] sometimes based on other things than your talent ... Everyone wants to work with people who are open to new ideas and who perform with integrity—and [who] are pleasant to be around. That's a good calling card to getting more work.[32]

Likewise, software R&D participants work in a field of relentless change and competition with other firms. Their knowledge quickly becomes obsolete, thus demanding vigilant and continuous learning. In a firm that has a reputation as a good place to work and that values creativity and top-level performance, being with and one of the best demands commitment and an unspoken internal willingness to remain in top form.

Within the software firm, a product development team oversees three tasks—product design/development, quality assurance, and user experience. A team may lack extensive expertise in all three areas, requiring members to trade skills and expertise within the team or across teams. For this to work, of course, members must trust that colleagues working within the firm are among the best in the industry to ensure that the skills and expertise that are exchanged are high quality.

With the organizations, then, the spoken and unspoken competition to be noticed, to perform, and to remain part of a successful creative organization is constant.

Speeding learning. In addition to being at the top of their fields, within-discipline language and depth of expertise permits participants to come up to speed quickly with one another. This appears in at least two ways. An accepted language allows members and groups to move quickly into a task they want to achieve. In addition, the use of "backups" or understudies also allows newly added team members to join and come up to speed faster.

First, an accepted and known language allows participants to become a team and move faster in understanding the tasks at hand. Actors know the meaning of "going deeper into a character" or "building the concept" when it comes to producing a play. Interestingly, in football, many ideas are common across teams, but each program develops its own language or code for plays, drills, or patterns. As coaches or players move from one team to the next, they learn that a play called "Wild Bill Two" in one program may be "Slight Swing 55" on another team. This happens in part because teams play in front of their opponents. To foil the opponent, coaches and players refer to plays using their own codes. For example, to convey a play to a quarterback, two players send hand signals from the sideline. One is the real play, the other is a fake. Thus, even if opposing coaches and players could decode the hand signals, they still do not know which signal conveys the upcoming play.

In addition, speeding learning occurs when organizations use understudies or extra players for a given task. In acting, understudies can step in when needed because they are always "up to speed." The football team, similar to the New England Patriots, develops players to step into several positions. As mentioned earlier, while most teams may have one or two players for a position, this one typically develops up to four or five as backups. This tactic offers two benefits—when injuries occur, alternative players are ready to step in and are up to speed. In addition, players with that wider expertise may have more chance to play, again because they are ready. Rather than relying on the same ten or twelve players as its first string, this team has several who could play, as one coach explained:

> ... any time you have an injury to a specific or key player, you have to start becoming creative on how you put your personnel on the field ... I think we are a little bit different. A lot of teams will have ten players that are going to play ball ... For us, [in one game] the free safety got hurt ... nothing against him, but I don't think anybody batted an eye. We said, we'll just take another guy and throw him in there.

Having more players as backups increases players' depth and range of abilities makes them more flexible physically and mentally, and widens the options open to coaches. Finally, it confuses the opposing team, since its coaches can never be sure who will play what position.

Moving beyond the fundamentals. Several organization members commented that staying on top of their fields and learning quickly allows them to "move beyond the fundamentals" to become more creative. Specifically, as members know their fields, they can go beyond thinking mostly of the basic tasks to become more creative. This happens by (1) allowing people to move outside of expected performance boundaries; and (2) adding (often unseen) depth to their outputs or performances.

Within-discipline expertise appears to liberate individuals and groups to move outside of normal expectations and performance boundaries to develop new approaches that fit their situations or personalities. In the football team, for example, coaches insist that players have basic skills and plays committed to physical and mental memory before they may play multiple positions. The coaches then overdrill or overprepare players. According to the coaches, such overpreparation allows players to move to more creative plays because they know and are relaxed about the fundamental ones. For example, an offensive lineman commented that as his expertise grows, he understands better how his position and actions fit the broader scheme of the plays and game plan. Specifically, he has learned to look beyond his immediate job—blocking the men crouched in front of him—to read the field and identify ways to move and block more effectively other players beyond that first line. The players say that as they improve and move beyond the fundamentals, they improvise, become more flexible, and achieve their goals in different ways.

In theater, having deep knowledge and skill allows actors to move beyond fundamentals in other ways. One actor talks about the challenge and importance of making the lines her own:

> I don't think most people understand how creative theater work is. Most think the hard part is learning the lines. But it's really "making those lines human." Making them sound like they're your lines. Because when we do it well, it's invisible. That part is effortless. Our job is to erase the track.

Actors also talk about learning more than they need to, which in turn improves and deepens a performance. In theater, the audience sees only what appears on the stage. What makes a performance stronger, though, is the attitude of directors and actors toward preparation and pushing beyond the fundamentals. In a particular play, two or more actors may work on the back story in a scene to decide what it means for their characters, especially as they interact. For instance, *King Lear* revolves around the relationship of a father (Lear) and his three daughters. At no point is there mention of the daughters' mother. In this case, however, the director asked the actresses playing the daughters to discuss—and agree on— what had happened to "Mrs. Lear." Each had likely had a different relationship with the mother, and that may have affected their relationships with their father and with each other. For this play, the actresses agreed that the mother had died in childbirth when the third daughter (Cordelia) was born, many years after the first two daughters. This helped to clarify for the actresses the bitterness in Shakespeare's language that is evident among the daughters and between the daughters and their father. While none of this appears in the play itself, it clearly added to the depth of knowledge the actresses felt and, according to one of them, allowed her to be more creative in how she played the character.

Disciplined Process

This section focuses on the third discipline, a clear, albeit often unwritten, process for generating a creative output and aspects related to process. The section covers (1) context or environment that may influence creativity and the creative process; (2) the creative process itself; and (3) creative collaboration forms.

Context. The three organizations' contexts stem largely from their different industry sectors.[33] Football and theater participants have more control over their environments than do those in software. Football teams face one direct opponent per game, and both theater and football members face competition from alternative entertainment activities. For example, potential customers may choose to take a mountain bike ride, go to a hockey game, or watch a movie instead of going to live theater or to a football game. In the software industry, the environment is rapidly changing, with often unpredictable challenges from customers, suppliers, competitors, and technological trends. While audiences in football and theater provide immediate feedback, neither coaches nor a play's director are likely to make major creative decisions based upon likely audience reaction; software firms, however, must take customer responses and needs into account as they adjust to their environment.

Context may in turn influence the nature of the creative process, communication, and collaboration. Football teams typically have one week between games to set a game plan against the next opponent, thus limiting time for lengthy communication. Idea generation is fast, practice time is short, and the creative process is quite structured. Communication with the players, many of them immature young men, tends to be direct and directive, with little request for input until they prove themselves able to offer good feedback. Finally, communication among coaches and players is almost always face-to-face.

Theater comprises highly trained, very independent people who expect to be treated as professionals. The director, designers, and actors face time constraints and an unchangeable deadline—opening night. As one actor said, "Opening night happens whether you are ready or not. There is no such thing as 'sliding' the deadline, like in business or other fields." The director and designers meet at least once but then work from their respective bases, using virtual communication—mostly e-mail and phone—until they arrive at the theater location late in the process. The designers and director exchange visual output, like set designs or costume drawing, but most of their communication is not face-to-face. With actors, conversely, communication and collaboration are done *in situ*. Because the industry depends on upon language and emotion, many actors expect in-depth communication and interaction with each other as well as with the director. Thus, communication during rehearsals is nearly all face-to-face, rather than through e-mail or other virtual means.

Software firms include highly educated participants, many with high levels of energy and low thresholds for personal interaction. The case study firm does no outsourcing, which means that employment costs are relatively high, thus reinforcing the need for members to be the best they can, to improve and learn constantly, and to be able to shift quickly among tasks and focus areas. Many software engineers often prefer to communicate virtually, even within the same building. Also, because some key managers who participate in creative collaboration travel, the communication is forced to be something other than face-to-face. Nevertheless, daily progress review of a set of product features does provide short face-to-face interaction with team members.

Creative process. This section discusses the process and areas of similarity and difference across the organizations. First, the three leaders consistently exhibit positive attitudes and expectations about creativity, including recognizing the need for time[34] dedicated to it and the acceptance of failure.[35] The organizations' creative processes also have roughly similar stages of identifying, testing, and experimenting with ideas before implementing them.[36]

The basic creative outcome in theater is production of a play. Typically, American regional theaters allow six to eight months for the process. The first step is development of a concept or scheme for the play, a job primarily done by the director and designers. As one director puts it, "we have to answer the question: why this play, at this time, for this audience." The director and designers then create the "world" for the play, including time period, set, music and sound, style of delivery, and type of costumes. Typically, the director guides concept development, but may ask for extensive input from the designers. Individual designers then work independently and in parallel (Figure 3.4). They interact mostly with the director, who is the intercept point for exchanging ideas. Following the director's approval of the design elements, technicians begin to construct the physical world of set, props, and costumes. The sound, music, and lighting usually come later in the process.

Actors know which role they will play several months before rehearsals begin; as the director and designers are developing the concept, actors also prepare. Some think the directors may not recognize the extent to which they have prepared, which links back to the within-discipline aspect:

> What [directors] don't always know is that we've been working as well. We work a lot. I am usually off book [know my lines], I've looked at other productions, read reviews, actors' biographies about them. There is a lot written about some of these parts. Contemporary parts not so much, but Shakespeare, my God, there is lots to read about [a given role]. I talk to people, I think about it, I read Shakespeare scholars.

Rehearsals begin five to six weeks before opening night. Some directors start rehearsals with activities to build camaraderie, provide actors with new experiences, or encourage them to experiment. For instance, one director uses short exercises that have nothing to do with the specific play but are intended to build a cohesive team. On the King Lear production, the director and many actors did not know one another, so the director felt it was important for actors to become comfortable and open with one another and with her.

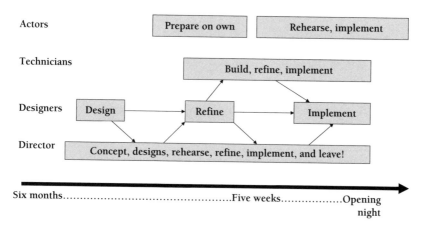

FIGURE 3.4. Play Production

She recognized the time pressure but felt that taking some time initially to build a team would save time later during rehearsal.

Once rehearsals begin, the director and actors typically work six days a week, on specific scenes, on choreography, and on voice and accents, if needed. Rehearsals also involve experimenting—with how actors say lines, move on stage, or show emotions. The director in the case study insists her role is not to "tell" an actor how to say a line, "because then it is my line, not his. I want him to own it, to be the character." So this director gives broad, more emotional suggestions, like "make someone uncomfortable" rather than telling an actor what movements to make or how to say a line.

During the final phase of rehearsal is "tech week," when the director, designers, technicians, and actors integrate the entire play. The production is done at the theater site, in this case outdoors. Actors wear costumes, the lighting and sound/music appear, and actors use the set and props. During tech week, the artists and technicians work an average of six hours per night, during which time the actors work through each scene of the play. Depending upon the director, the focus may be primarily on technical aspects of the play, such as how to move a prop or piece of scenery, how to be sure a microphone stays put, or how to deal with lighting changes, especially in an outdoor theater. But often, some new ideas may emerge, such as the need for a different way to use a prop or editing of lines.

Finally, the play previews before a live audience for one or two nights before it opens officially. This is a form of beta testing, during which the director watches the audience for its reaction to decide whether to make additional changes. If the audience does not laugh as expected, or if the laughter takes longer than anticipated, the timing may need to change. If the audience becomes bored—and people shift in their seats, yawn, or, worse, fall asleep—the director may change the pacing. This is the final time for experimenting in the creative process, because once the play opens, nothing may change. The director and members have delivered the play, in the way they see fit. The director and designers leave town and the actors and stage manager are responsible for keeping the play as it is, intact.

Even though the play timing, use of set or props, entrances, or exits may not change, creativity can continue. Interestingly, some actors claim that once the play opens, their creativity heightens, as they go "deeper" into a character, or move beyond the fundamentals. The acceptance of and reliance on the structure of the play allow freedom in actors' ability to making the character more emotionally viable. As one actor commented:

> Some people may say creativity starts to end ... once the performance begins, because you have to agree on a final product and then it needs to be set every night so everyone knows what will happen. But I think it continues ... As an actor ... you achieve your greatest amount of freedom after you've agreed on a set way that something is to go.

Further, the beauty and challenge of live theater is that even though the play is set, the audience is not. It becomes a resource for actors to draw upon—that nightly interaction with the audience can change the feel of the play as a result.

> Every night you have an unmarshalled variable in the audience and you have to do your show as you've agreed on [by] taking it [a new] audience, sometimes attentive and sometimes not. You can't radically adjust—you have to pull them in, play to them more, be aware of their listening. That's a creative element every night.

In football, the creative product is a game plan that, presumably, leads to a winning game. The creative process also includes preparation, rehearsal—or practice—and implementation or execution of a game (Figure 3.5). In contrast to theater's five to six months of lead time, football coaches typically have one

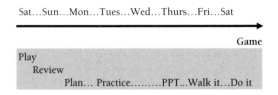

Sat...Sun...Mon...Tues...Wed...Thurs...Fri...Sat

Game

Play
   Review
       Plan... Practice.........PPT...Walk it...Do it

ONE WEEK

FIGURE 3.5. Game Plan Preparation

week to prepare for their next game. This is somewhat misleading, of course, as coaches admit they start preparing months ahead for various opponents by watching tapes, but the specific development of a game plan and the experimenting and practice that occur happen during the week immediately preceding a game. Part of this happens because the coaches have more recent information, such as videotapes of opponents' games, during the ongoing season. Thus, preparing game plans too far in advance makes little sense.

College football teams usually play games on Saturdays, which gives them six days to prepare for the next game. The preparation and planning process is very structured. This team built in as much structure as possible to allow more time for experimenting and practice later in the week. In fact, the head coach feels that a clear structure enhances creativity:

> I know the structure and I know the parameters. Then it allows you to not think about that part ... To give you an example, we used to, in the old days, we'd sit down on a Sunday and we'd come up with our practice plans for the week. [Now, the overall timing and general practice plan is set.] We will monkey with them a little bit but they're pretty much cast in stone. You don't have to waste a bunch of brain time thinking about "Let's see, what are we going to practice." Things are based on mathematical correlation as to the percentages of what we're going to do in a game. Those time parameters are based on 20 percent for special teams, 5 percent for goal line, and so on. So we don't have to think about that. [We practice plays based upon those percentages of how much times we'll devote to those areas.] The template is there and here are the ideas, so [we make our practice time] fit the category.

The coaches follow a predictable and rigid schedule during the week. On Sunday, the head coach, position coaches from offense, defense, and special teams, and the quarterbacks review segments of videotapes of the previous day's game to find what worked and what did not. On Monday and Tuesday, position coaches identify a range of options for plays they may use in the upcoming game. The defensive and offensive groups work independently, with little integration since their respective groups of players are not on the field at the same time. The special teams coaches and players, in contrast, interact with both offensive and defensive groups, because the players' role is to kick or run with the ball in both offensive and defensive situations. The head coach moves among the groups, participating more in the offensive running game development because that is his expertise.

By Tuesday afternoon's practice at 2 P.M., coaches have set the bulk of the upcoming game plan. For the game plan, each position coach identifies four to six options for each play. For example, when a team is at second down, with eight yards to go to make a first down, the offensive coaches could well have four different play options. Thus, the game plan is well underway by the time the players start their weekly practice. In fact, coaches claim that they have developed 70–80 percent of the upcoming game plan by then. They argue that the players need as much practice or drilling time as possible to memorize plays, to test out execution of plays, and to find flaws and correct them, so the coaches must decide most of the game plan early in the week.

Football's equivalent of rehearsal is practice, which begins Tuesday afternoon. Practices on Tuesday and Wednesday focus on experimenting, testing, and seeing if and how players can complete plays. By the end of Wednesday's practice, coaches say their game plan is 95 percent complete. During those two days of practice, coaches may remove plays that are too hard for the players to implement or fail to achieve what coaches hoped for. While they typically do not add new plays, once in a while they do. Part of the reason this team can do so, according to the coaches, is because they overprepare players. The argument is that if players learn and practice many plays, they will be less rattled should the coaches include a new one during the week. Also, having more options of plays ready for use gives the team an edge over competitors, who may have fewer options in the game plan. Finally, the coaches mix up the practices as a way of building player flexibility and ability to deal with change.

During practice on Thursday, the team uses a form of beta testing called "Practice Perfect Thursday" (PPT). The players go through the game plan, play by play. They must complete each play without mistakes before moving to another. For example, if there are six plays in a given option, the players may complete the first play perfectly, then move to the next and complete it flawlessly. If they bungle the third play, they have to start again from the first play and repeat their drill until each in the set of six is flawless. Thus, no player wants to cause a mistake, which reinforces one of the elements of within-discipline thinking—working hard to be "the best." Football players have their equivalent of a "preview" on Friday, with a walk-through of the game plan and a written test on plays.

The software firm's creative output is a new program or solution for users, who may be customers, programmers, or partners. The creative process normally takes about six months. Like theater and football, the general creative process for software includes developing an overall vision or concept for the product, developing a list of product features, and then creating and testing those features before integrating them into a final product for testing and release. Once the product is ready for release, it moves from the product architect and product development team to the technical product manager, who works with customers and users after release (Figure 3.6).

Whereas football coaches seek to speed up the creative idea generation part of their process so they can allocate more time for testing or practicing, this software firm seeks the reverse. Its members want to increase time available for creativity and idea development and reduce time needed for testing features. Software firms have typically needed almost one-third of the product development time for integration and beta testing at the end of the process.

IDEAS, TURNING INTO PRODUCT FEATURES.............MOVING TO MARKET

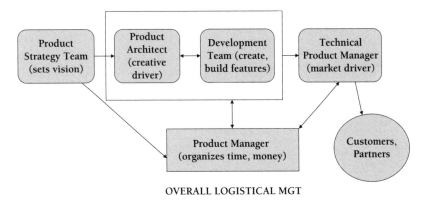

FIGURE 3.6. New Product Development

This firm seeks ways to build in testing throughout the process, thus reducing the long time frame needed for final integration and testing. In addition, the firm wants to encourage creativity throughout the firm and remove obstacles that might inhibit it. Thus, part of the firm's challenge is having a structure that supports outcomes but does not hamper creativity. The vice president of research explained:

> Every Tuesday morning we have a staff meeting and our big discussion today was around how do you manage process. What do you mandate, what do you allow people to choose [to do] because it's critical that we don't constrain. What we were going through was the roles and responsibility for an individual contributor in the lab. We were trying to articulate it as much as we could as an outcome and not ... say "here are the responsibilities." You don't want to say what [people] are supposed to do when they come to work ... we're trying to create a culture where you've got a minimum amount of mandated process and it's articulated in terms of desired outcomes.

Given such goals, the firm constantly seeks ways to enhance its creative process and stages. For example, the firm uses an approach developed by Microsoft called agile software development with scrum.[37] In essence, the process allows designers to choose a limited number of features to work on, usually two to four per month; they experiment and test, identify, and remove obstacles throughout the development process, rather than waiting until the product is fully designed. This reduces time spent on integration and beta testing products.

To remove obstacles from the creative process, the firm separates logistics and project management from the creative product development part of the process. A product manager sets and monitors the schedule and budgets for a particular product, while a product architect acts as the creative driver, translating and implementing the broad vision for a product from the top manager team to the product development team. The separation of project management from product development allows creativity within product development to be relatively uninhibited; by not focusing on money and deadlines, it allows the team to take risks and try ideas that it might otherwise think twice before doing. The separation also infuses into the process what the vice president of research calls "acceptable tension." If, for example, the product development team has an idea that will enrich a product feature, but it will take more time than originally allocated to develop, there is a conflict—finishing on time versus adding a new creative piece. The resolution of such a conflict, then, moves up the organization to level of the senior vice president, who decides whether to "finish now" or "slip the deadline." This way the creative team is not hindered by concern with deadlines, at the outset.

Creative collaboration. Creative interaction and creative collaboration sound interchangeable, but for this chapter, they differ. Creative interaction is the typically informal and casual exchange that occurs as part of the process of discovering new ideas or knowledge, as well as solving existing problems. It may happen spontaneously, without any specific creative outcome or goal in mind. Creative collaboration, on the other hand, refers to a more in-depth joint interest or partnership that focuses on seeking a particular creative outcome or solution to a problem. In a sense, it is a step beyond interaction, since collaboration usually has a goal of achieving some result, such as a new piece of software or costume designs for a play. Thus, creative interaction may, or may not, lead to creative collaboration and a specific outcome. Conversely, for creative collaboration to occur, it requires interaction among individuals or groups. Creative collaboration within organizations can vary widely, as these organizations illustrate.[38] Their approaches differ in part because of their environments, as well as the nature of their tasks. This section discusses their approaches.

Throughout the creative process in the theater, the development of new ideas appears to come from two types of collaboration—(1) between director and designers and (2) between director and actors or groups of actors. The director acts as a coordinator among designers and among actors. For example, actors may have ideas of how to change their own approach to a character and will discuss that with the director, not with other actors. Likewise, they do not give suggestions to other actors. Instead, if they have ideas for others, they go to the director, who may choose to pass along a suggestion or not.

Technicians tend to focus more on problem solving. They receive designs for sets or costumes, for example, and then must figure out how to construct them. While there is creativity in the problem solving, they are unlikely to be involved in the generation of the main creative ideas driving the production,

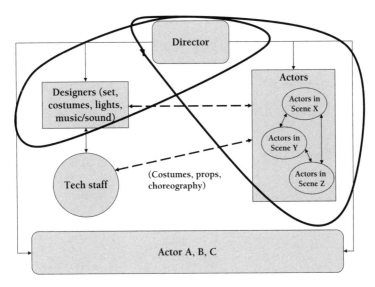

FIGURE 3.7.   Creative Collaboration in Theater

which is why they are not included in the creative collaboration process in this discussion.

Collaboration between director-designers and director-actors, then, is bi-directional and hierarchical. The director is the only person who must have complete oversight and understanding of the entire project (Figure 3.7). As the coordinator of creative collaboration, the director is the central point for decision making as well. All design and acting decisions should feed into the overall vision held by the director.

In football, most creative collaboration appears to be within the coaching groups and among the coaching groups and the head coach (Figure 3.8). Other interaction—between coaches and players, among players, between strength conditioning coaches, trainers, and players—tends to focus more on problem solving than on generating new ideas and may have no specific goal. As mentioned above, offensive and defensive coaches collaborate on developing play options within their position groups, but not across position groups, because their tasks are quite separate. The special teams coaching staff interacts—and must creatively collaborate—with the other position groups, since their players act on both sides, offensive and defensive. The head coach does not direct or coordinate the creative collaboration, although he gives input to the running offensive coordinator since he has some expertise in that area. Instead, the head coach's role as a creative agent emerges in two ways: (1) he overtly encourages and models "thinking creatively" and (2) he does an overview of the entire game plan to assess "balance" of plays. Thus, he says he oversees the entire game plan, rather than specific plays.

FIGURE 3.8. Creative Collaboration in Football

Creative collaboration among coaches appears very symmetrical, organized, and inclusive at the top of the organization, with little input coming from the bottom—the players. This stems in part from the belief that most players, other than the quarterbacks, have little to offer in developing the specific game plan and from the time pressure coaches face during a week.

In the software firm, managers urge and encourage creativity at all levels. In fact, their creative collaboration, in contrast to the other case studies, suggests there is much interaction and overlap at several levels (Figure 3.9). Compared to theater and football, the software firm's creative collaboration is more dispersed, spanning several levels, with no single coordinator or overseer of the process.

In addition, ideas seem to filter down and up. Overall vision comes from the top; product feature ideas come from the bottom. As mentioned, the vice president of R&D wants the organization to become a more "bottom-centric" organization, with most idea generation coming from the lower levels, not the top. He argues that product development team members are likely to have more "touch points" within and outside the firm where they will receive ideas, such as from customers, other programmers/developers, technical journals, or blogs. Further, more than the other two groups, communication seems to be a goal in itself, with an assumption that ideas come from all levels and multiple groups.

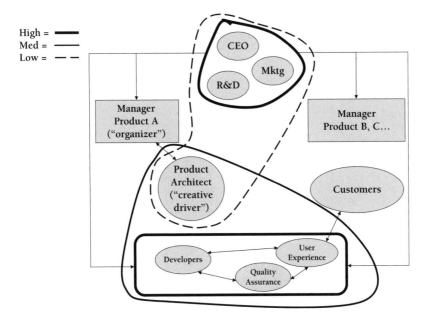

High = ▬▬
Med = ——
Low = – –

FIGURE 3.9. Creative Collaboration in Software

CONCLUSIONS AND IMPLICATIONS

Robert Sternberg, Yale University psychology professor and creativity sage, trumps other writers on creativity by volume of publications alone. In his many books and articles, he almost always uses a "triarchic," or three-part, framework to explain his latest ideas. He has a three-part theory of intelligence, a triangular theory of love, and a three-facet model of creativity. When asked why all of his theories had three parts, he responded by saying there were three good reasons for it.[39] Even creativity researchers fall into ruts.

This has also been a chapter of threes—three disciplines, three sectors, three organizations. So, to break the pattern, the chapter concludes with five observations. First, creativity emerges in all sorts of industry sectors. Arts organizations are supposed to be creative, given the nature of their output. But the relentless drive for innovation and creativity in football is surprising. As coaches say, football has little that is new—most plays exist and the rules are set. Yet this team repeatedly confounds opponents with small—and large—creative tactics.

In fact, during the course of collecting information about this team, it was difficult to find information about other teams that so aggressively seek to be creative. An oft-cited one, however, is the New England Patriots, to which this case study team has been compared. A danger, of course, is that opponents may seek to unravel a team's mode of risk taking and creative ploys. That, in turn, may affect future success, as happened during the first game of the 2005 season: the team faltered and lost dramatically. In fact, the opposing coaches admitted they had studied tapes of the present team for six months before the game. Thus, being creative and innovative intensifies expectations for even more creativity over time as opponents adapt to the new ideas.[40]

Second, pursuing and reaping benefits from creativity—in an individual, a group, or an organization—is like being a parent, requiring repetition and patience. Leaders in each organization were relentless in their pursuit of good ideas and encouraging others to be creative. They were dogged in their insistence that organization members be open to ideas, take risks and fail, and learn to adjust to changes. Like parents, they also realized that becoming a creative organization takes time, to build trust and the ability to think and act differently.

Third, the 3-Ds are obvious yet elusive, even for people with the best intentions. The software senior leaders have long talked of the importance of creativity at all levels. Yet even they thwarted their own wishes. Until about a year ago, the leaders felt they understood what would be critical in new products and thus suggested features for the development team to design. As a result, they lost ideas that development team members could have offered; they have since changed their approach, offering only broad visions for products and pushing the design—and responsibility—to the development team.

Fourth, the three disciplines may be comparable across organizations but must be distinctive for each. What is idiosyncratic about these organizations is their instinctive scrutinizing of all aspects of the disciplines to find ways to improve that fit their conditions and context. Further, while they are analytical in their use of the 3-Ds, even though they do not use those words explicitly, they do so almost without realizing it. The disciplines are so ingrained that organization members hardly notice they are following them. As one actor said, "When it looks effortless, we've done the job."

Finally, perhaps location plays a larger role in creativity than suggested here. Interestingly, leaders in the case study organizations mentioned the remoteness of Boise, Idaho—which is five hours by car from the nearest metropolitan area, Salt Lake City—as having benefits. They commented that being in the remote west encourages a pioneer or entrepreneurial spirit. Further, they feel forced to find ways to excel in their national and global fields, simply to be noticed. So maybe the 3-Ds could use a fourth: distance.

As a concept, 3-D creativity is simple, yet like many obvious ideas, it can be challenging to pursue. Nevertheless, it may offer ideas for managers seeking to enhance organizational creative output.

NOTES

1. Some key research work began with and built on Mary Parker Follett's ideas, including Mary Parker Follett, *Dynamic Administration*; Mark E. Mendenhall, John H.

Macomber, and M. Cutright, "Mary Parker Follett: Prophet of Chaos and Complexity,"; and Milorad Novicevic et al., "Communities of Creative Practice: Follett's Original Conceptualization." In addition, Guilford's seminal article called for an increase in research on the field of creativity: J. P. Guilford, "Creativity."

2. Herbert Simon, "Understanding Creativity and Creative Management."

3. Joseph Schumpeter, *The Theory of Economic Development*.

4. Examples of reports, books, and articles include the following: The Global Competitiveness Report, 2005–2006; Alan Cowell, "Nokia Falters, and the Finns Take Stock of Their Future;" Richard Florida, The *Flight of the Creative Class*; Richard Florida, *The Rise of the Creative Class*; Richard Florida and Irene Tinagli, *Europe in the Creative Age*; John Howkins, *The Creative Economy*; Charles Landry, *The Creative City*.

5. See, for example, the following research: Teresa M. Amabile, *Creativity in Context*; Teresa Amabile, "How to Kill Creativity"; Robert Drazin, Mary Ann Glynn, and Robert K. Kazanjian, "Multilevel Theorizing about Creativity in Organizations"; Bernard A. Nijstad and Paul B. Paulus, "Group Creativity: Common Themes and Future Directions"; practitioner work, informed by research, includes examples such as Tony Davila, Marc J. Epstein, and Robert Shelton, *Making Innovation Work*; Jeff DeGraff and Katherine A. Lawrence, *Creativity and Work*; Thomas L. Friedman, *The World Is Flat*; Frans Johansson, *The Medici Effect*.

6. Mark A. Runco, "Creativity"; Mark A. Runco, ed., *The Creative Research Handbook*; Robert J. Sternberg, ed., *Handbook of Creativity*; Todd Lubart, "Models of the Creative Process."

7. Jeff Degraff and Katherine A. Lawrence, *Creativity and Work*; Paul B. Paulus and Bernard A. Nijstad, eds., *Group Creativity*; Kerrie Unsworth, "Unpacking Creativity"; Wendy M. Williams and Lana T. Yang, "Organisational Creativity."

8. Information sources for these case studies included interviews with key participants (twenty-seven with the theater, thirteen with the software firm, and twenty-seven with the football program), news articles, internal documents and reports, formal studies on the community and the role of the arts, and observation.

9. Glenn M. Parker, *Cross-functional Teams*.

10. Frans Johansson, *The Medici Effect*.

11. Brent Schlender, "Interview with Steve Jobs."

12. Jeff Degraff and Katherine A. Lawrence, *Creativity and Work*.

13. Jeff Mauzy and Richard Harriman, *Creativity, Inc.*

14. Warren Bennis and Patricia Biederman, *Organizing Genius*.

15. Tony Davila, Marc J. Epstein, and Robert Shelton, *Making Innovation Work*.

16. Another way that creativity scholars talk about this is in terms of divergent and convergent thinking: when generating new ideas, a group needs divergent thinking because it reaches beyond existing methods, modes of operating, or ways of thinking. When trying to reach a consensus about direction, a group needs convergent thinking to come to an agreed-upon approach. Both are important and draw on different types of skills.

17. Glenn M. Parker, *Cross-functional Teams*.

18. For more examples, see Vera John-Steiner's *Notebooks of the Mind* for illustrations of a range of artists, writers, scientists, and inventors and their methods of encouraging creativity.

19. Peter F. Drucker, "The Discipline of Innovation."

20. J. Andrews, "Creative Ideas Take Time."

21. Bernard Ghiselin, *The Creative Process*.

22. J. Richard Hackman, ed., *Groups That Work (and Those That Don't)*.

23. In recent years, magazines like *Forbes, Fortune, Time, INC., Money*, and newspapers ranging from *The Wall Street Journal* to *The New York Times* have profiled the city as a fast-growing, high quality of life site, attractive for entrepreneurs and retirees alike. Richard Florida's first book, *The Rise of the Creative Class*, ranked Boise ninth in the U.S., controlling for city size, on his creativity index.

24. *American Theater*, the Theater Communications Group's professional journal, has had numerous stories over the last decade about the challenges facing regional theaters in particular. Like many professions, this one is relatively small, the key principals (including artistic directors, directors, and designers) know one another—or about one another—well, so information about activity throughout the U.S. was readily available; also see Heidi Waleson, "The Arts get Down to Business Tackling Shrinking Audiences."

25. Lawrence P. Goodman and Richard A. Goodman, "Theater as a Temporary System."

26. A number of books and articles have sought to explain the game to laypeople, including, for example, George Plimpton's *Paper Lion* and, more recently, Michael Lewis's profile of quarterback Eli Manning, "The Eli Experiment."

27. The NCAA provides and tracks statistics for college athletics and also monitors fairly strict regulations about sports, ranging from expectations about academic performance to recruiting. As an industry sector, then, this one faces much regulation and structure about internal operations. The theater sector also faces regulation, when it comes to equity for actors (the union) and payments/benefits for particular types of theater, but beyond that, internal operations of theaters or play production are left to theater managers and directors. Software, on the other hand, faces little external regulation about internal operations, since the context and competition create a form of industry self-monitoring.

28. See, for example, Pete Thamel, "Grass Stays Greener on Boise State Coach's Side of Fence." http://www.nytimes.com/2005/08/26/sports/ncaafootball/26hawkins.html.

29. See, for example, Charles E. Grantham, "Hollywood: A Business Model for the Future?"; Candace Jones and K. Walsh, "Boundaryless Careers in the U.S. Film Industry."

30. Denis Harrisson and Muriel Laberge, "Innovation, Identities, and Resistance."

31. Filmmaker Ben Shedd worked on early PBS Nova productions, has made several IMAX and OMNIMAX movies, and won an Oscar for his production of *The Flight of the Gossamer Condor*; http://members.aol.com/sheddprods/sheddproductions.html.

32. Doris Eikhof and Axel Haunschild, "Die Artbeitskraft-Unternehmer."

33. Cynthia E. Shalley, Jing Zhou, and Gary R. Oldham, "The Effects of Personal and Contextual Characteristics on Creativity."

34. J. Andrews, "Creative Ideas Take Time."

35. Bernard Ghiselin, *The Creative Process*; Jeff Mauzy and Richard Harriman, *Creativity, Inc.*

36. Mark D. Cannon and A. C. Edmondson, "Failing to Learn and Learning to Fail (Intelligently)."

37. Ken Schwaber and Mike Beedle, *Agile Software Development with Scrum*.

38. Vera John-Steiner, *Creative Collaboration*.

39. Robert J. Sternberg and Todd Lubart, *Defying the Crowd*.

40. For examples of how organizations fall into habits—and stumble—when they follow what have been proven approaches for too long, see Clayton M. Christensen, Scott D. Anthony, and Erik A. Roth, *Seeing What's Next*.

REFERENCES

Amabile, Teresa M. *Creativity in Context*. Boulder, CO: Westview, 1996.

Amabile, Teresa M. "How to Kill Creativity." In *Breakthrough Thinking*, 1–59. Boston: Harvard Business School Publishing, 1999.

Andrews, J. "Creative Ideas Take Time: Business Practices That Help Product Managers Cope with Time Pressure." *Journal of Product and Brand Management*, 5, no. 1 (1996): 6–18.

Bennis, Warren and Patricia Biederman. *Organizing Genius: The Secrets of Creative Collaboration*. Reading, MA: Addison-Wesley, 1997.

Breakthrough Thinking. Boston: Harvard Business School Publishing, 1999.

The Global Competitiveness Report, 2005–2006, www.palgrave.com/worldeconomicforum.

Cannon, Mark D. and A.C. Edmondson. "Failing to Learn and Learning to Fail (Intelligently): How Great Organizations Put Failure to Work to Innovate and Improve," *Long Range Planning*, 38 (2005): 299–319.

Christensen, Clayton M., Scott D. Anthony, and Erik A. Roth. *Seeing What's Next*. Boston: Harvard Business School Press, 2004.

Cowell, Alan. "Nokia Falters, and the Finns Take Stock of Their Future." *The New York Times*, 4 September (2004): B1, B3.

Davila, Tony, Marc J. Epstein, and Robert Shelton. *Making Innovation Work: How to Manage It, Measure It, and Profit from It*. Upper Saddle River, NJ: Wharton School Publishing, 2006.

DeGraff, Jeff and Katherine A. Lawrence. *Creativity and Work: Developing the Right Practices to Make Innovation Happen*. San Francisco: Jossey-Bass, 2002.

Drazin, Robert, Mary Ann Glynn, and Robert K. Kazanjian. "Multilevel Theorizing about Creativity in Organizations: A Sense Making Perspective." *Academy of Management Review*, 24, no. 2 (1999): 286–307.

Drucker, Peter F. "The Discipline of Innovation." *Harvard Business Review*, 80, no. 8 (2002): 95–108.

Eikhof, Doris and Axel Haunschild. "Die Artbeitskraft-Unternehmer." *Theaterheute*, March (2004): 5–17.

Florida, Richard. The *Flight of the Creative Class*. New York: HarperBusiness, 2005.

———. *The Rise of the Creative Class*. New York: Basic Books, 2002.

Florida, R. and Irene Tinagli. Europe in the Creative Age. London: Demos. (2004) http://www.creativeclass.org/acrobat/Europe_in_the_Creative_Age_2004.pdf

Follett, Mary Parker. *Dynamic Administration*. New York: Harper and Brothers, 1942.

Friedman, Thomas L. *The World Is Flat*. New York: Farrar, Straus and Giroux, 2005.

Ghiselin, Bernard. *The Creative Process.* New York: Mentor Books, 1952.

Goodman, Lawrence P. and Richard A. Goodman. "Theater as a Temporary System." *California Management Review,* XV, no. 2 (1972): 103–107.

Grantham, Charles E. "Hollywood: A Business Model for the Future?" Proceedings of the ACM SIG on Computer Personnel Research, April, Chicago, IL, (2000): 47–60.

Guilford, J. P. "Creativity." *American Psychologist,* 5 (1950): 444–454.

Hackman, J. Richard, ed. *Groups That Work (and Those That Don't).* San Francisco: Jossey-Bass, 1990.

Harrisson, Denis and Muriel Laberge. "Innovation, Identities, and Resistance: The Social Construction of an Innovation Network," *Journal of Management Studies,* 39, no. 4 (2002): 497–521.

Howkins, John. *The Creative Economy.* London: Penguin Books, 2001.

Johansson, Frans. *The Medici Effect.* Cambridge, MA: The Harvard Business School Press, 2004.

John-Steiner, Vera. *Creative Collaboration.* New York: Oxford University Press, 2000.

———. *Notebooks of the Mind.* New York: Oxford University Press, 1997.

Jones, Candace and K. Walsh. "Boundaryless Careers in the U.S. Film Industry: Understanding Labor Market Dynamics of Network Organizations." *Industrielle Beziehungen,* 4, no. 1 (1997): 58–73.

Landry, Charles. *The Creative City.* London: Earthscan, 2000.

Lewis, Michael. "The Eli Experiment." *The New York Times,* 19 December (2004): 42–49, 64, 68–71.

Lubart, Todd. "Models of the Creative Process: Past, Present and Future," *Creativity Research Journal,* 13, nos. 3, 4 (2000–2001): 295–308.

Mauzy, Jeff and Richard Harriman. *Creativity, Inc.* Boston: Harvard Business School Press, 2003.

Mendenhall, Mark E., John H. Macomber, and M. Cutright. "Mary Parker Follett: Prophet of Chaos and Complexity." *Journal of Management History,* 6, no. 4 (2000): 191–204.

Nijstad, Bernard A. and Paul B. Paulus. "Group Creativity: Common Themes and Future Directions." In *Group Creativity: Innovation through Collaboration,* edited by P. B. Paulus and B. A. Nijstad, 326–340. Oxford: Oxford University Press, 2003.

Novicevic, Milorad J., Michael G. Harvey, Michael R. Buckley, Daniel Wren, and Leticia Pena. "Communities of Creative Practice: Follett's Original Conceptualization," *Management Decision Journal.* Forthcoming.

Parker, Glenn M. *Cross-Functional Teams: Working with Allies, Enemies, and Other Strangers.* San Francisco, CA: Jossey-Bass, 2003.

Paulus, Paul B. and Bernard A. Nijstad, eds. *Group Creativity: Innovation through Collaboration.* Oxford: Oxford University Press, 2003.

Plimpton, George. *Paper Lion.* New York: Pocket Books, 1966.

Runco, Mark A. "Creativity." *Annual Review of Psychology,* 55 (2004): 657–687.

———, ed. *The Creative Research Handbook.* Cresskill, NJ: Hampton Press, Inc., 1997.

Schlender, Brent. "Interview with Steve Jobs." *Fortune,* 18 February 2005.

Schumpeter, Joseph. *The Theory of Economic Development.* Cambridge, MA: Harvard University Press, 1934.

Schwaber, Ken and Mike Beedle. *Agile Software Development with Scrum*. Upper Saddle River, NJ: Prentice Hall, 2002.

Shalley, Cynthia E., Jing Zhou, and Gary R. Oldham. "The Effects of Personal and Contextual Characteristics on Creativity: Where Should We Go from Here?" *Journal of Management*, 30, no. 6 (2004): 933–958.

Simon, Herbert. "Understanding Creativity and Creative Management." In *Handbook for Creative and Innovative Managers*, edited by Robert L. Kuhn, 11–24. New York: McGraw-Hill Book Company, 1988.

Sternberg, Robert J., ed. *Handbook of Creativity*. Cambridge, U.K.: Cambridge University Press, 1999.

Sternberg, Robert J., James C. Kaufman, and Jean E. Pretz. "A Propulsion Model of Creative Leadership." *The Leadership Quarterly*, 14 (2003): 455–473.

Sternberg, Robert J. and Todd Lubart. *Defying the Crowd*. New York: The Free Press, 1995.

Thamel, Pete. "Grass Stays Greener on Boise State Coach's Side of Fence," *The New York Times*, 26 August. http://www.nytimes.com/2005/08/26/sports/ncaafootball/26hawkins.html, 2005.

Unsworth, Kerrie. "Unpacking Creativity." *Academy of Management Review*, 26 (2001): 298–297.

Waleson, Heidi. "The Arts Get Down to Business Tackling Shrinking Audiences." *The Wall Street Journal*, 17 June (2004): D7.

Williams, Wendy M. and Lana T. Yang. "Organisational Creativity." In *Handbook of Creativity*, Edited by Robert J. Sternberg, 373–391. Cambridge, U.K.: Cambridge University Press, 1999.

Overcoming Creative Blocks

JAMES E. CARTER

WHAT IS CREATIVITY?

Overcoming barriers to creativity requires an understanding of creative behavior and its importance in business and in everyday activities.

Creativity is many things. It involves the power to look at perceived reality differently and to change the vision of that reality. Creativity is the process of making something strange seem familiar and of making the familiar strange. It involves diffusion—creating alternatives. It involves integration—selecting a pattern to alternatives. Creativity is the vision of possibilities not seen beforehand. It is a basis for invention as well as for problem solving and persuasion. Figure 4.1 illustrates the importance of using knowledge to create the future.

Collective creative thought can be extremely productive and valuable to a business enterprise. However, it is rarely fully exploited. Why? The truly creative organization is rare because it requires strong motivated leadership, a proactive effort, commitment, courage, and tenacity. When it's firing on all cylinders, it is truly an impressive and powerful force.

Everyone can be creative, but frequently they are not. Creativity in the workplace may be stimulated and structured by conscious programmatic means. It can be allowed to emerge in a passive unrestrained environment, but that leaves a lot to chance and requires certain focused and talented individuals acting as change agents, with certain immunity and implied authorization to be creative. Most often, creativity is to be stifled and turned off!

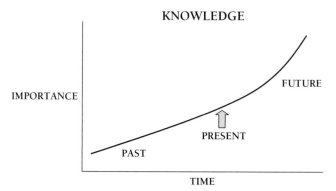

The importance of knowledge deteriorates with age. It has
value when used to formulate ideas for the future.

FIGURE 4.1   Importance of Knowledge over Time

Being creative isn't easy, especially in a business environment. When one is
in the creative mode, forgetting is often more important than learning. Knowledge and insights of the past are useful in the creative mode when such
knowledge is employed to create ideas for change and improvement. Often,
however, what we learned in the past becomes inflexible, creating a burden to
our creative capabilities in the present. The legacy of our development years
creates barriers to the creative process. We are all born with creativity talents.
Young children are curious. By their very nature, children explore their surroundings and find ways to overcome obstacles, whether physical or emotional, real or perceived. As children age, they are taught how to conform to
society's norms. Although a certain level of conformity is appropriate, the
process for channeling a child to behavioral norms frequently involves sup-
pression of creative motivation and often restricts the development of creative
skills. In the development process, children learn to be practical and to deal
with limited resources. Children are encouraged to get everything right in
school. Failure in the classroom is unacceptable. Risk taking is discouraged,
and rules are imposed as absolute. Children learn to avoid conflict, to conform to the rules, to seek the obvious path, often without a thorough consideration of alternatives. So we become conditioned to take the proverbial "path
of least resistance"—not the best path, but the easiest path that will work.

Creativity requires a mental breaking of the conformity rules. It requires
that we allow disruption of perceptions and challenges of the status quo. It
requires us to think differently than our habitual norm and ask questions like:
What if? Why not? What else? So what? Such questions were inappropriate in
school, and we are often uncomfortable raising them.

In the early years, children are noted for their imagination and their ability
to view reality in different ways, two skills that are valuable to the creative

process. Through the education and maturing processes, we are encouraged to become less imaginative and to view things in absolute black-and-white terms. Our imagination, and therefore our ability to be creative, becomes suppressed, but it is not irreversibly lost.

The notion that only certain people can be creative is simply false. It is a stumbling block that people encounter when attempting to be creative. Anyone can overcome that block by recognizing that creativity is an innate characteristic of our human behavior. Internal thought processes and environmental (workplace) considerations can be adjusted to stimulate creative behavior in individuals and in groups. It's a matter of letting go, a matter of removing the artificial constraints and proactively doing the right things to develop creative mindsets.

WHY BE CREATIVE?

Why is creative behavior important? Very fundamentally, without creativity there would be no new inventions, suboptimized solutions would dominate our world, and there would be little change from year to year. There would be no adaptation to changes in our environment. There would no improvements. In the business world, competition drives creative thinking. Tom Peters once said, "If the other guy is getting better (and he is) ... you'd better be getting better faster, or you're getting worse." This reflects the essence of business competition. Employing creative techniques can facilitate ideas for getting better faster. In fact, there can be no improvements without creative ideas. The key, in a competitive world, is which firm can be more creative than the other.

Ideas have a life cycle. They are born, they develop, they reach maturity, and they die. We need to find ways to generate new ideas or our business will become extinct. Consider a business sector of ten firms, all competing with essentially the same product. One firm develops a significant, cost-effective improvement or an alternative to that product and effectively brings it to market. What is the impact on the other nine? It's not difficult to imagine the impact of such a scenario. Look at what Ray Kroc's fast food concept for McDonald's did to the restaurant industry. Think of a problem that was recently encountered and resolved in your workplace. Was an open-minded creative process employed? Was the first solution the only solution considered? Was there a clear effort to develop alternate solutions? How certain are you that the first solution was the only solution and, more importantly, the best solution?

Adhering to the processes and the mindsets that got us all to adulthood will probably not result in the most creative solutions and ideas. More than likely, the baggage of our development and education will lead us to suboptimal decisions and will deposit a number of great ideas in the wakes of our careers, never to be developed, or perhaps available to be developed by others, our competitors. Why leave ideas on the table?

CREATIVITY BLOCKS

A number of creativity blocks act as deterrents to creative thinking. The blocks are mostly personal, dealing with psychological or emotional issues, cognition, and proactivity. However, overshadowing the personal blocks is the workplace culture block, which can be an absolute barrier to innovation and creative thinking, regardless of the creative propensities of individuals. Knowledge and proactive efforts can overcome these deterrents and lead to more creative behavior. It takes courage, trust, willingness, and often determination in order to be creative. Perhaps the biggest challenge, however, is for managers and leaders to remove barriers to creativity that exist in the workplace and have been cemented in place over many years.

The key barriers to creativity are identified in Table 4.1.

Each of these creativity blocks will be explored in detail, and ideas for overcoming the blocks will be presented.

Unawareness

There are two elements of unawareness that serve to block creative thinking. The first is that we may not realize that we can be creative. Without a cognitive and proactive effort, powerful but dormant creative skills may not be recalled. Once we proactively tap into the latent skills, the creative juices of individuals will likely flow naturally unless other constraints apply. Songwriting, for example, may seem to be a talent that is limited to a gifted few. Is it reasonable that creative skills emerge through some undefined process and focus individuals to a specific area? Is it possible that songwriters are songwriters because they have a talent to write songs, or is it more plausible for an individual to try something of interest (songwriting) and discover by trying that he actually has some skills or talent in that area? How much of a songwriter's success is based on the fact that he made a proactive and cognitive effort to write songs? Clearly, anyone who has not attempted to be creative in writing a song will not succeed at writing innovative lyrics or music. Does that mean that those who do not write songs cannot write songs?

The point here is that individuals may be able to think creatively, but if they never try, they never will! This may seem like a basic and obvious

TABLE 4.1. Creativity Blockers

Awareness	Guilt
Anger	Fear
Doubt	Anxiety
Image	Habit
Judgment	Culture

conclusion, but extend the logic to problem solving in the workplace. Perhaps individuals can be more innovative and effective by using cognitive and proactive creative thinking methods—simply doing it, rather than saying they can't do it and not trying. Most workers solve problems on a daily basis, and many of those solutions may indeed be the best possible. But what if they aren't the best? This is particularly important for problems that have significant consequences. Consider the roll-out of a new product. Is it adequate for a concept merely to be perceived as a good idea? Can it be improved upon before introduction to the market? Is the roll-out program the best, or is it the first workable idea considered? The notion of creatively seeking alternatives will be developed further. For the present, simply consider the relevance of a proactive and cognitive approach to creativity, rather than leaving everything to chance. In other words, try to be creative. Employ creative techniques. You might find that your ability to generate ideas is greater than you realized!

The second aspect of the unawareness block deals with overcoming other creativity blocks. Before creativity blocks can be overcome, they must be identified, understood, and dealt with in an appropriate manner. Unawareness of these barriers, at best, limits the creative efforts and most likely prevents creative thinking. The influence of the creativity blockers must be removed before creativity can flourish.

Doubt

If we think of ourselves as lacking creative ability, we may foster a mindset that we are not creative and, therefore, cannot be creative to the full extent of our capabilities. In effect, doubting that we have what it takes to be creative becomes self-fulfilling.

If we are not sure that our creative ideas have merit and are unwilling to act on them or to bring them forward, they are of little value. If the work environment encourages creative thought and operates in a culture that recognizes value in all ideas, regardless of merit, it is easier to overcome such doubt. However, such environments are fairly rare.

Dealing with personal doubt, therefore, is an important step in the process of being creative. Fortunately, there are a number of practices that can help overcome such doubt.

As previously stated, all human beings are born with creative instincts. Over time, we are taught to conform to the norms of society, but no one tells us that it's acceptable to be childlike in our maturity, especially when developing creative ideas. The curious and explorative nature we had as children is still with us. In many respects, we have been conditioned to suppress those innovative aspects of our personality. However, we can recover those skills and erase doubt by recognizing these latent creative capabilities, dropping our inhibitions, and letting our childhood imagination return in a mature, creative context. Consider looking at issues from different perspectives, as a child may. Proactively try to be creative! Doubts about creative capabilities will soon vanish.

In addition, understand and accept that failure is an essential element of the creative process. It is perfectly normal and even desirable to generate nonworkable and suboptimized solutions when engaging in creative thought. Consider this "good failure" because it leads to optimized creative outcomes.

One must distinguish between a) the generation of creative ideas and b) the selection and implementation of such ideas. In an effective process for generating creative ideas, there are no rules. All relevant thoughts should be considered. Indeed, certain ideas are often born from others, ultimately leading to the best idea through a series of rejected thoughts. The concepts of "fail," "wrong," "can't," "won't," or "shouldn't" have no place in the idea generation phase. Doubt, therefore, should be of little concern, and recognizing the irrelevance of correctness is important in overcoming any form of doubt.

Another tool for overcoming doubt is to engage others in the thought process. Ask questions. Seek advice. Bounce ideas around. Often, such dialog helps focus the creative process and remove elements of doubt.

Eliminate doubt that arises from a perceived lack of expertise. Sometimes the most creative ideas flow from the novice. To be creative, you don't need to be an expert. In fact, expertise may be a disadvantage. Experts often become mired in history with rigid rules and paradigms. Consider, for example, a new employee's view of certain processes that are part of an organization's routine. The benefit of unfamiliarity and lack of historical paradigm allows that person to be totally objective in viewing the value of such processes and in offering creative suggestions for improvement. Even if the workplace culture tends to suppress such critical challenges to the status quo, it is important to recognize that the lack of expertise is not a disadvantage.

Understand that everyone struggles with self-doubt at times. Being creative may make some individuals particularly vulnerable to self-doubt, raising the question whether they're good enough to participate in the creative process. Keep in mind that it's okay to fail in the course of following the creative process. "Good failure" in the pursuit of creative solutions is a necessary side effect of the overall process.

In addition, consciously recognize negative thoughts that are creating doubt (thinking you're going to blow it, concern that your idea will never work, etc.) and rationalize them away by understanding the creative process. Create positive images. Imagine yourself succeeding, eliminate the doubt, and don't give up.

Functioning in an environment that encourages or even requires creative thought can sometimes be intimidating and can raise vulnerabilities that are otherwise latent. So the creative process may itself create doubt. All of the above tools apply to this situation. In addition, and most importantly, the need to remove workplace barriers plays a large role in eliminating this aspect of doubt. A nonthreatening environment clearly goes a long way in eliminating personal doubt and encouraging participation by all employees.

Image

Two forms of image can interfere with creative thinking: self-image and public image. Self-image, of course, is how we view ourselves, and public image is, for purposes of this discussion, how we perceive others to view us. In each case, it is helpful both to recognize that concern over image may interfere with the creative process and to take steps to eliminate the concern.

As we mature, we develop standards of self-image against which we try to conform our behavior. We are influenced by our environment in creating such image standards. Being creative may force us to challenge those standards and may even require that we change our benchmark for self-image. Change is often difficult, particularly when dealing with inner perceptions that have been created over the years and have become ingrained in our thinking. As with other creative blocks, it's important to bring the self-image barrier into the cognitive state. Once we are aware of the self-image creative block, we can identify the specific element of image that is holding the creative process back and rationalize it. Is it a real concern or is it baseless? Understand that self-image is something that we have built for ourselves and that it's very acceptable to change our standards, especially when engaging in creative thought.

To further help eliminate self-image concerns, consider the benefits of successful creative thought. Refuse to deny yourself those benefits. Recognize that the benefits may actually improve self-image as well as public image. Think about the image of others who have been successful through creative thinking, and recognize the value of such creativity for you. Recognize also that there is a natural comfort level associated with maintaining our image in the context of the status quo, because it's easy. Not changing requires little, if any, effort. In a competitive and changing world, however, status quo may no longer be appropriate. It may be the path to commercial extinction. Behaviors that worked in the past may not work in the present or in the future. If proactive creative thinking has not been part of past practice, it is time for a change. Accept such change and embrace it, realizing that change is often difficult because it may require acknowledgement that our current or past behavior is wrong or inappropriate for the creative mode of behavior. In reality, our behavior may have been acceptable for the past circumstances, but as the environment changes, so must we. Think of the dinosaurs.

If concern over public image interferes with the creative process, challenge that concern. Is it real or perceived? Are we concerned that others will think less of us if we offer creative ideas that don't get traction? Why be concerned? Does it really matter? Recognize how rigid our image issue is, and allow for some flexibility. Postulate what would happen to public image if the creative process were allowed to successfully run its course. Perhaps the image would improve rather than suffer. Imagine being successful in the creative process and how public image might actually be enhanced.

Judgment

Consider that there are two stages of the creative process: idea generation and decision making. Generating ideas requires imagination. To effectively develop ideas, there should be no rules. There should be no limits on the creative process. It should be free flowing, perhaps even chaotic and disruptive. Often the best ideas are found outside the boundaries of "normal thought." Judgment interferes with the free flow of ideas. Whether in a group or alone, avoid being judgmental in creative idea generation. Save judgment for the decision-making process after ideas have been generated. At the decision-making stage, all ideas can be weighed together and analyzed thoroughly with sound and critical judgment.

Idea generation is often about quantity. It may thrive on chaos, disruption, and uncertainty. Forget what has been learned about precision and control, and adopt the practice of generating ideas without rules or judgment. Consider the idea generation phase to be one of diffusion whereby concepts are expanded and quantity is more important than quality, where rules don't apply, where "different" is good and "more" is better. Check all forms of judgment at the door and let the creative process flow unimpeded. There will be time for judgment later, before final implementation decisions are made.

Guilt

Creative thinking requires breaking some rules that have been part of our behavior. It may require us to do some things differently than we have in the past. Breaking those inbred rules may give us pause and cause feelings of guilt that interfere with the creative process.

The first step in overcoming guilt is to recognize its existence and that it is impacting the effort to be creative. Uncover what the inner critic is saying. What are the "should" and "should not" types of feelings that are driving the guilt? Think about the rule that is begging to be violated. Is it really a sound rule? Can it be suspended for purposes of creativity? If not, ask why not! What is the source of the rule? Is it something that applied in the past, but is not applicable today? Consider the consequences of breaking the rule to overcome the guilt block. In all likelihood, the consequences are insignificant. Weigh the consequences of breaking the rule against the consequences of not breaking it.

Often guilt arises because of beliefs that we should not impose our opinions on others and that asserting our position may detract from the issues others raise. Such guilt suggests that we must defer rather than advance our ideas in order to avoid a self-serving appearance. In creative thinking, nothing can be further from the truth. Collective thought is a powerful force that is fueled by participation. Individual ideas stimulate the thoughts of others and allow new ideas to flow. Offering ideas is therefore totally consistent with the process and should never be the source of guilt.

Perhaps the sense of guilt is driven by the failure in the past to meet our own expectations, and we don't want to risk aggravating such feelings by being less than perfect in the creative process. Again, recognize that the guilt feeling is blocking the flow of creative thinking and that creativity is not about perfection. It's about generating ideas. Evaluate the seriousness of the behavior that gives rise to the guilt. Put the seriousness in perspective and weigh the pros and cons of harboring the guilt.

Perhaps the guilt will vanish when the act is attributed to others. Determine how you would view the seriousness of such guilt-causing actions if they were the actions of a trusted friend. Alternatively, weigh your personal responsibility for the actions. How much of the violation is your sole personal responsibility? If necessary, forgive yourself and proceed with the understanding that a lesson has been learned, which forms a foundation for future success. If necessary, talk with a trusted person about the guilt. Often the fear of how people will react is worse than the actual reaction.

Work around the issue by considering how important the guilt will be in one month, one year, or five years. Perceiving the issue to fade over time may help remove the guilt.

Fear

The fear of being wrong or the fear of asserting a position that is not accepted by others is very often a significant barrier to successful creative thinking.

In creative thinking, success and failure are not opposites. They are complementary elements of the same process. The same energy that produces creative ideas also produces errors. These are good errors born from constructive thought, not bad errors arising from wrongful or lackadaisical behavior.

Recognize that "good failure" and errors are necessary, and accept them as fundamental to the concept of creative thinking. Remember that perfection is not the goal of creative thinking. Idea generation is.

If fear remains after recognizing that the failures of the creative process are acceptable, reduce the risk of failure by doing some preparation. Research the topic to generate ideas and select ones that seem most likely to succeed. Realize, of course, that such prescreening may cause ideas that have merit to be excluded from a multiparty creative brainstorming process. An alternate to research and prescreening is to discuss issues with others for suggestions or concurrences. Such discussions may put fears to rest and may even generate new ideas. Another approach to eliminating fear by mitigating risk is to generate a number of alternatives. Remember, nonjudgmental idea generation is more about quantity than quality. Offering alternatives dilutes the risk and may lead to a more effective creative thinking process while eliminating fear.

Sometimes it helps to deal with fear by uncovering the most catastrophic fantasy and asking "What is the worst that could happen?" Carry the worst-case fantasy to the most ludicrous possible extreme. Then analyze what is really likely to happen and determine if you can live with the likely outcome. Consider short-range and long-range scenarios. This exercise helps put fear in perspective. Chances are that you will decide you can live with the most likely outcome, which is considerably less threatening than the outcome underlying the original fear.

Finally, ensure that fears aren't created by manipulation. Don't get side-tracked by the negative statements of others (e.g., "I don't see how anything will solve this problem" or "The boss will never consider changing."). Get out in front of the noncreative negative thinkers, not behind them. Understand the objective and realize that doing nothing can improve nothing.

Anxiety

Anxiety is a vague, unpleasant emotion that is experienced in anticipation of some—usually ill-defined—misfortune. It often leads to a sense of foreboding and reluctance to behave in any way that may improve the chances for the misfortune to occur. Anxiety may arise at the point when creative ideas must be delivered to others. It may arise when explaining the value of an idea to others. Or it may arise from a situation totally unrelated to the creative process. Nonetheless, it may interfere with the creative process; once recognized, it can be addressed.

There are many forms of anxiety, and some can best be resolved with professional help. For our purposes however, we will suggest some tools for eliminating simple forms of anxiety.

First, eliminate other creativity blocks using the techniques described. Those other blocks could be causing the anxiety problem; once removed, the anxiety may pass.

Consider basic relaxation strategies. Leave the premises for a leisurely lunch with a friend. Take a walk. Take a nap. Practice breathing techniques, meditation, or yoga. Sometimes it helps simply to ignore the symptoms. Often the blushing, sweaty palms, and quaking voice are not as apparent to others as they appear to you.

As you engage in creative behavior more frequently, familiarity and self-confidence will take over and the anxiety symptoms will fade away.

Habit

Engaging in the creative thinking process may be a new experience. The practices of the past must be set aside in favor of the new creative techniques.

These habits may involve a reluctance to challenge the status quo or an unwillingness to offer ideas, even when asked. They may include an absolute commitment to be logical and practical or a reluctance to break certain "breakable" rules. Fortunately, the habits we're concerned about are not addictions and are fairly easy to change. However, proactive and cognitive efforts are necessary. The desire to become more creative is the first step. By employing creative thinking techniques, the habits of the past can be identified and gradually reduced to a secondary role. Success in the creative process will play a large role in eliminating habit barriers. Generally, with success comes a new attitude.

How can the elimination of habits be accelerated? You have to work on it! Consider the following:

- Identify the habits that are getting in the way. Write them down.
- Next to each habit, write the barriers that prevent eliminating the habit.
- Write a plan to overcome each barrier and set a time frame for its elimination. This could be done by applying some creative techniques.
- List the benefits to be gained by eliminating the habits.
- Track your status against the plan.

Obviously, the more we engage in creative thinking, the sooner the habits can be overcome. Keep in mind that creative thinking is not limited to the workplace or to group sessions. Many activities of our day-to-day lives are habits. While there may be little consequence, changing those habits could heighten awareness of the creative process and help to cement our commitment to being creative. Consider, for instance, taking a different route to work, drinking a different soft drink, or reading nonfiction instead of a novel.

Proactive and cognitive efforts to be creative are the best solutions to the habit barrier, as well as for other barriers. Make a choice to be creative and commit to it.

Anger

Anger obscures our thinking. It imposes biases and channels our thought processes in a direction that may mask certain very appropriate and necessary considerations. In general, anger restricts most thinking, logical or otherwise, and it must be addressed.

Fortunately, anger is usually a short-lived mood, and for most of us, it can be checked at the door before we engage in the creative process. Nonetheless, it is important to discharge our anger before pursuing creative thinking.

Consider whether the anger is based on facts or assumptions. Examine the assumptions and attempt to determine whether they have merit to cause the anger or whether they are mere innuendo that should be forgotten. Look at the situation causing the anger from a different perspective. Attempt to be objective and understand the opposing position. If the anger persists, attempt to defer participation in the creative process until the anger subsides.

Workplace Barriers

The creative blockers previously discussed are largely individual in nature. Overcoming those individual barriers is essential for the creative process to be successful. However, in an organizational setting, creative minds and ideas have no value if they are not allowed to see the light of day. Many brilliant ideas die on the vine because they do not get a hearing. An organization of truly creative people would soon become discontented if they were inhibited from exercising their creative talents by the management team. Creative employees will keep ideas to themselves, or they may go elsewhere if the enterprise does not consider their thoughts. There is significant potential in the collective creative thinking of a group of individuals. To stay competitive, organizations must realize the potential of group creativity. The process of stimulating new ideas *must* and *can* be managed.

The workplace is an arena where creativity should play a huge role and can factor significantly in the success of the enterprise. Many businesses, however, whether intentionally or unintentionally, suppress the creative potential of the workforce or fail to fully employ the creativity of employees.

Consider the following as some of the traits of a noncreative workplace:

- Requires that communications go through the "proper" channels
- Punishes failures that occur when attempting sound innovation
- Buries mistakes and failures
- Requires conformance to turf silos
- Forbids challenging of the status quo
- Imposes too many rules that specify what can't be done, rather than what can
- Develops programs that foster conformity rather than change
- Adopts autocratic management styles with little delegation of authority.

There are many others. The personal creativity blocks previously addressed can only get worse in a noncreative workplace environment. How can the "fear" block be overcome if there are reprisals for advocating certain change? How can the "image" block be addressed if creative thought is ridiculed by the management team? How can an organization improve if it fails to capitalize on the creative thinking of its people? Peter Drucker, the renowned author and management consultant, advocated a policy of "organized abandonment," whereby the enterprise seriously challenges its portfolio of products, its processes, all internal staff activity, and other elements of its existence. How can such a cleansing be effectively undertaken without the involvement of the workforce?

It's not enough to avoid the behavior of a noncreative organization. Successful and innovative organizations must be proactive in stimulating the workforce and in establishing programs that facilitate the awesome power of collective creativity. This effort starts at the top. Leadership is the sine qua non of a creative organization. From the top, the leaders have to proactively advance the creative process. They must be personally involved, and they have to believe that the creative process is appropriate. The concept of believing in the process is important because leaders must trust and be trusted. They must be willing to accept constructive criticism of their own behavior and of their policies. The ability of employees to speak openly and challenge the status quo has to be real, and everyone must believe it's real. Leaders would have a difficult, if not impossible, time establishing the trust and commitment of a workforce that has doubts about the leadership's commitment.

Actions can be taken to create a workplace that fosters creativity. Specific suggestions for eliminating workplace blocks to creativity include the following:

- Require the most senior manager of an enterprise to personally conduct a portion of new employee orientation and define policy and expectations for the workforce. In this forum, the manager should:

  — Encourage professional outspokenness in challenging current practices, recognizing that new employees are in a unique position to view work practices objectively because they are not tainted by paradigms developed over time and are in an excellent position to ask "Why?" and "Why not?"

  — Stress the importance of risk taking. Discuss any limits or prerequisites tied to certain risks.

  — Commit to no reprisals for well-thought-out creative efforts.

  — Encourage employees to come by the office and talk (and mean it).

- Conduct creativity training and follow through with the implementation of a creativity program; drive it and stick with it.
- Recognize and reward creative activities, including those that are not successful.
- Believe in the idea of a creative organization and show it. (Perhaps everyone is not suited to lead a creative organization.)
- Truly enjoy working with creative people and show it.
- Celebrate successful ideas by giving them visibility in company news letters, or in the public press.
- Document all new ideas, big and small, and share them throughout the organization.
- Create forums and processes whereby employees can present new ideas.
- Provide funding, or at least a funding process, for implementing creative ideas. Make it easy to implement creative ideas, especially the inexpensive ones.
- Involve employees in management problem-solving sessions.
- Conduct periodic employee meetings and reinforce the principles of the creativity program.
- Conduct periodic employee surveys to test the perceptions of the creativity (and other) policies.
- Frequently discuss creativity with employees in one-on-one informal sessions.

- Conduct 360-degree evaluations whereby employees assess various managers' and supervisors' practices in support of the creativity principles. Follow up as appropriate to "adjust" supervisory behavior.
- Demonstrate a willingness to take risks, especially in dealing with internal company resistance.
- Understand change and the implications of change, and be capable of managing change.
- Explore alternatives for workplace configuration and decoration.
- Grow this list by engaging employees in the creative process.

These concepts have been used. They work!!

SUMMARY

The most important consideration in overcoming creativity blocks is to recognize them and to deal with them proactively. Practicing various creative techniques helps to cast aside the barriers.

Remember that we all have the ability to be creative. We must make proactive attempts at creative thinking. However, remember also that failure is part of the creative process. Over the years, each of us has been taught to do things right. In school, getting less than 60 percent of the questions right on a test was a failure. On the other hand, Hall of Fame baseball players got hits only 30 percent of the times they were at bat. In generating ideas in a creative process, most ideas or concepts will not be adopted, similar to major league batting stars. Even ideas that are adopted may not succeed.

The most important factor in removing workplace blocks is leadership. Some people may never have the disposition or aptitude to lead a creative organization. That needs to be recognized. Committed and communicative leaders can motivate the workforce and create the environment where creativity thrives. Once it catches on, it will feed on itself and get better. A change in leadership, however, can turn out the creative lights in a very short time, if the wrong individual is given the helm.

Picasso once said, "Every act of creation is first an act of destruction." Remember that the creative process must challenge the status quo, starting out with no preconceived notions and with no rules or restrictions. An organization composed of rigid sacred cows cannot be innovative until strong leadership with creative mindset and courage eliminates the workplace barriers and creates an enterprise that believes every policy can be challenged, except the policy on challenging policies.

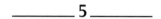

5

The Psychology of Creativity

DEAN KEITH SIMONTON

A lthough psychologists have studied creativity ever since the advent of the discipline, it has seldom been considered a mainstream research topic (Sternberg & Lubart, 1996). Nevertheless, its disciplinary status was improved when J. P. Guilford in 1950 made a plea on behalf of creativity research in his presidential address before the American Psychological Association. As a consequence, empirical and theoretical inquiries have continued to grow in number and quality. Moreover, there now exist two journals specifically devoted to creativity research—the *Journal of Creative Behavior* and the *Creativity Research Journal*—and several important handbooks have been published (e.g., Glover, Ronning, & Reynolds, 1989; Sternberg, 1999) as well as a two-volume *Encyclopedia of Creativity* (Runco & Pritzker, 1999). According to the PsycINFO electronic database, the number of publications devoted to the topic now exceeds 15,000, including over 10,000 articles in professional journals. Hence, it can no longer be considered a neglected topic in the field.

Below I provide an overview of the central findings in the psychology of creativity. I begin by defining the concept of creativity and its manifestations, and then I examine the distinct perspectives that psychologists have taken on the phenomenon.

DEFINITION AND MANIFESTATIONS

According to most psychologists who do research in this area, creativity requires the satisfaction of two independent criteria (Simonton, 2000b). To begin with, creativity demands originality, such as novelty or surprise. To be creative is to be unexpected. However, it is easy to see why this criterion is necessary but not sufficient. A schizophrenic may generate lots of original ideas that prove totally unrealistic or maladaptive. Hence arises the second criterion: an idea is not considered creative unless it is adaptive, that is, it must work or be functional. For instance, a new mousetrap, no matter how novel the design, must actually catch mice to be called creative. These two requirements of originality and adaptiveness can be usefully seen as defining creativity in terms of a multiplicative function. That is, if C stands for "creativity," O for "originality," and A for "adaptiveness," then we may define creativity according to the formula $C = O \times A$. Here it is assumed that C, O, and A are all ratio-scaled variables with zero points. Hence, if either $O = 0$ (i.e., the idea is completely commonplace) or $A = 0$ (i.e., the idea does not work at all), then $C = 0$.

This definition is extremely general, and perhaps even excessively abstract. As a result, psychologists usually investigate a particular manifestation of the phenomenon. Three manifestations are by far the most prominent (Simonton, 2000b). First, some investigators concentrate on the creative *process*, that is, they examine the cognitive mechanisms that underlie the emergence of original and adaptive ideas. These processes include intuition, insight, association, and various problem solving heuristics and algorithms (Boden, 1991; Hayes, 1989). Second, other researchers focus on the creative *person*, trying to discover how individual differences on various cognitive and dispositional variables are associated with the degree and type of creative ability (Feist & Barron, 2003). These variables include intelligence, motivation, personality, interests, and values. Third and last, some investigators narrow the examination to the creative *product*, with the goal of discerning the characteristics of the product that render it creative. For instance, this is the approach favored by those engaged in empirical aesthetics (Berlyne, 1974). Needless to say, these three manifestations of creativity—the process, the person, and the product—are closely related to each other. Presumably, the creative product is the outcome of the creative process, and the latter is the outcome of being a creative person.

PERSPECTIVES

Because creativity is a very complex phenomenon with more than one manifestation, it has become the subject of research by psychologists active in distinct subdisciplines. In particular, creativity has been investigated by cognitive psychologists, differential psychologists, developmental psychologists, and social psychologists.

Cognitive Psychology

Ever since the advent of the cognitive revolution, cognitive science has assumed an ever-increasing role in the study of creativity. Understandably, cognitive psychologists are most interested in the creative process. Although research on this topic has covered a diversity of issues, four areas have perhaps received the most signification attention: insightful problem solution, creative cognition, computer simulation, and expertise acquisition.

Insightful problem solution. The first psychologists to study problem solving were the Gestalt psychologists, whose primary interest was in the process of insight (e.g., Wertheimer, 1982/1945). Cognitive psychologists have expanded upon these early findings by introducing new methods and theories (Sternberg & Davidson, 1995). A special focus of this research is what happens during the incubation period of insightful problem solving. This is the period between the "preparation" phase, in which the individual first unsuccessfully attempts to solve a problem, and the "illumination" phase, in which the solution arrives through a flash of insight (Wallas, 1926). It is during the incubation period that unconscious information processing tends to play a major role (Bowers, Farvolden, & Mermigis, 1995; Schooler & Melcher, 1995). The mind becomes unusually open to subliminal stimuli and free association that eventually excite a fruitful route to a problem solution (Seifert, Meyer, Davidson, Patalano, & Yaniv, 1995).

Creative cognition. One of the central debates in the study of the creative process is whether creativity requires nothing more than the application of everyday cognitive mechanisms. Those psychologists who adopt the creative cognition approach believe that this is the case (Smith, Ward, & Finke, 1995; Ward, Smith, & Vaid, 1997). Their goal is to demystify creativity by showing that it entails nothing more than the coordinated use of ordinary mental processes directed at a specific problem-solving goal. To achieve this goal, researchers have conducted laboratory experiments that illustrate how visual imagery functions in the production of creative ideas (Finke, Ward, & Smith, 1992). This research also marks a special advance over the insight experiments because participants generate actual creative products rather than merely discover the solutions to problems with known solutions.

Computer simulation. Because many cognitive psychologists view creativity in terms of ordinary mental operations (Klahr & Simon, 1999), and because cognitive psychology often uses computers to model those operations, it should come as no surprise that they have also written computer programs that embody explicit models of the creative process (Boden, 1991; Johnson-Laird, 1993). For instance, Newell and Simon (1972) proposed a theory of human problem solving that later provided the basis for "discovery programs" that are designed to draw inductive conclusions from scientific data (Langley, Simon, Bradshaw, & Zythow, 1987; Shrager & Langley, 1990). Frequently these programs use the same raw data that were used by eminent scientists in making the discoveries that made them famous. In addition, other computer programs have been devised to produce creative products in art, literature, and music, at times generating works that closely emulate human creativity (Boden, 1991; Dartnall, 2002).

Expertise acquisition. So far it seems that creativity may involve nothing more than the application of general cognitive processes. Indeed, the processes are so basic that even computers can display creativity of the highest order. Yet this conclusion leads to a paradox: If creativity is so easy, then almost everybody should be creative, and perhaps even equally so. This inference appears flatly contradicted by the most straightforward observations. Certainly some creators are much more creative than others. At the extreme upper end of the distribution are figures like Albert Einstein, Jean-Paul Sartre, Igor Stravinsky, Pablo Picasso, Martha Graham, and Ingmar Bergman. What sets these world-class creators apart from those whose creativity is much less remarkable, even by more everyday standards? Many cognitive psychologists have sought an answer in the role of acquired expertise (Ericsson, 1996). Past research on domains as diverse as chess, music performance, and competitive sports has shown that normally about a decade of deliberate practice is required before an individual can attain elite competence. Moreover, some empirical studies have shown that this same "ten-year rule" applies, to a certain extent, to almost all creative domains (Hayes, 1989; Simonton, 1991, 2000a). Without this inherently arduous phase of study and practice, a person would not have the skills and knowledge necessary to make significant contributions to a domain. Hence, in this view, there is no such thing as innate talent (Howe, Davidson, & Sloboda, 1998). If Einstein and the rest stand higher than most others, it merely reflects the fact that they worked harder than most.

Differential Psychology

The implication left in the preceding section was that individual differences in creativity could be ascribed to variation in expertise. The more you know, the more creative you will be. However, empirical data show that this explanation is seriously incomplete. For instance, highly creative individuals do not necessarily have more domain-specific knowledge and skills than colleagues who are less creative (Simonton, 2000a). On the contrary, the former may actually have less expertise, not more. Einstein knew much less about physics and mathematics than his classmate and friend Marcel Grossmann, yet it was Einstein alone of the two who won a Nobel Prize. Even more significant is the fact that creators display a distinct set of personal traits that tend to set them apart from mere experts. Indeed, it is the goal of differential psychologists to identify the individual-difference variables that predict creativity independent of expertise acquisition. The traits investigated tend to fall into two broad categories: intelligence and personality.

Intelligence. Ever since the pioneering studies of Galton (1869) and Terman (1925–1959), differential psychologists have tried to link creativity with superior intellect. However, the connection is not as strong or as unambiguous as originally hypothesized. Although performance on standard IQ tests is positively correlated with creative behavior over the full range of scores, the association becomes much less pronounced in the upper end of the distribution (Barron & Harrington, 1981). As a consequence, one does not have to have a genius-level IQ to be able to originate exceptional creative products. For example, an IQ of around 120 is all that is absolutely necessary to become a high-impact scientist (Simonton, 2002). Nevertheless, many psychologists have challenged whether intelligence can be considered a unidimensional construct; rather than a single factor, it may consist of multiple factors that are fairly independent of each other (Guilford, 1967). A well-known example is Gardner's (1983) theory of multiple intelligences, a theory that incorporates abilities that are not assessed by most intelligence tests (e.g., musical, bodily-kinesthetic, interpersonal, and intrapersonal). Furthermore, these special abilities are linked with particular forms of creativity, such as painting, choreography, and psychology (Gardner, 1993).

These complications notwithstanding, it has become increasingly clear that personality traits may supercede intelligence as the primary predictors of creativity (Dellas & Gaier, 1970; Feist & Barron, 2003). So it is to personality that I must now turn.

Personality. The first systematic research on the creative personality was carried out at the Institute for Personality Assessment and Research at the University of California, Berkeley (e.g., Barron, 1969; MacKinnon, 1978). Over the years, a large literature has accumulated that provides a fairly robust personality profile of the creative individual (Feist, 1998; Martindale, 1989; Simonton, 2004b). To illustrate, such individuals are prone to have wide interests, greater openness to new experiences, and a more conspicuous behavioral and cognitive flexibility. They also tend to be more risk-taking, more independent, more nonconformist, and less conventional. At the same time, the specific details of the expected profile tend to vary according to the particular domain of creative achievement (Feist, 1998; Simonton, 2004b). For instance, artistic creators tend to display the most typical profile, whereas scientific creators are prone to have personalities somewhat closer to the population means.

Perhaps the most significant finding to emerge out of this research is the support it provides for the idea that creativity bears some linkages with psychopathology (Jamison, 1993; Ludwig, 1995; Simonton, 2005). For example, highly creative individuals are less adept at filtering out extraneous information (Ansberg & Hill, 2003; Carson, Peterson, & Higgins, 2003; Peterson & Carson, 2000), a deficiency that is apparent in psychotics as well (Eysenck, 1995). Nonetheless, these connections do not justify the conclusion that creative persons must be mentally ill. Instead, the literature indicates that (a) some creators, even high-order geniuses, have no obvious psychopathology; (b) the incidence rates depend on the domain of creativity, with some domains showing low rates; (c) creators who seem to display symptoms normally feature compensatory traits, such as intelligence and ego-strength, that allow them to channel their inclinations into adaptive activities; and (d) many attributes that seem pathological may actually prove more functional with respect to the person's lifelong well-being (see, e.g., Csikszentmihalyi, 1997; Rothenberg, 1990; Simonton, 2005). Highly creative individuals seem to have an adaptive level of madness.

Developmental Psychology

Although differential psychology has greatly enhanced our understanding of creativity beyond what was contributed by cognitive psychology, significant aspects of the phenomenon remain unaddressed. Creativity is not just a static phenomenon on which people may vary, but also a capacity that emerges and manifests itself over the course of an individual's lifespan. As a result, it is essential to examine creativity from the standpoint of developmental psychology. In general, developmental psychologists have investigated this issue from two perspectives. On the one hand, some investigators have focused on the early antecedents of creativity—the supposed factors responsible for the emergence of creative potential. On the other hand, some researchers have concentrated on how this potential is actualized over the course of adulthood—including how creativity is affected by aging.

Early antecedents. Earlier I pointed out how cognitive psychologists tend to reduce creative development to expertise acquisition; given a decade of deliberate practice and study, a person eventually acquires the knowledge and skills essential for making creative contributions to a particular domain. However, this explanation tends to ignore the important contribution of genetic endowment (Howe, 1999). After all, nurture alone cannot account for two facts: (a) there exist substantial individual differences in the time required to acquire the necessary expertise and (b) those individuals who take less time tend to be more creative than those who take more time (Simonton, 1991, 2000a). Hence, some individuals appear to have exceptional natural ability—a talent or gift—that enables them to master the requisite skills and knowledge in less time. Although the importance of biological inheritance was first argued by Galton (1869), the case really did not become fully convincing until the advent of modern behavioral genetics. Here, two findings are especially crucial. First, many if not most of the intellectual and personality traits that correlate with creativity exhibit sizable heritability coefficients (Bouchard, 1994; Eysenck, 1995; Simonton, 1999). Second, the specific form of inheritance appears to be multiplicative rather than additive, that is, creativity is an emergenic trait (Lykken, 1998; Simonton, 1999; Waller, Bouchard, Lykken, Tellegen, & Blacker, 1993). This means that creative potential depends on a configuration of genetic traits that must be inherited as a package.

Of course, we should not go overboard in the opposite direction by concluding that nature dominates over nurture. Genes seldom account for more than half of the variance in any given trait, and often explain closer to a third.

This leaves room for a large number of environmental factors that contribute to the early development of the underlying intellectual and dispositional components of creative potential. And, in fact, several decades of research have yielded a long list of environmental antecedents of creative potential (Simonton, 2004b). A significant proportion of these antecedents involve various family circumstances, such as birth order, early childhood trauma, ethnic marginality, and the availability of role models and mentors. Other developmental factors concern the person's experiences and accomplishments in primary, secondary, and higher education. Perhaps the most provocative conclusion to be drawn from both types of developmental influences is that high-level creativity does not necessarily emerge from the most supportive familial and educational experiences (e.g., Eisenstadt, 1978; Goertzel, Goertzel, & Goertzel, 1978; Simonton, 1984b; Sulloway, 1996). Instead, the acquisition of creative potential appears to demand some degree of exposure to (a) challenging experiences that reinforce an individual's ability to overcome obstacles and (b) diversifying experiences that undermine the restrictions engendered by conventional upbringing. These two influences are particularly central for the development of artistic creativity (Simonton, 2004b).

Maturity and aging. Once the person acquires the necessary creative potential in the early part of life, the next stage is to actualize that potential. This raises the question of how creativity is manifested across the lifespan. There are two major ways to address this question (Lindauer, 2003). The first applies psychometric measures of creativity to individuals of varying ages. Because cross-sectional data cannot distinguish age differences from cohort differences, the most ideal application involves testing the same persons across consecutive periods of time (Simonton, 1988). Whatever the methodological details, it is clear that performance on creativity tests, such as measures of divergent thinking, tends to decline after about age forty (e.g., McCrae, Arenberg, & Costa, 1987).

The second approach uses the product definition of creativity, counting output of products across consecutive time units across the entire adult life span (Simonton, 1988). Interestingly, this is by far the oldest method, the first study in this vein being conducted in the early nineteenth century by Quételet (1835/1968). Since then a great many empirical studies have accumulated (e.g., Dennis, 1966; Lehman, 1953; Simonton, 1997). This research leads to the following six conclusions (Simonton, 1988, 2004b). First, the longitudinal relation between age and creative output is best described as a single-peaked function characterized by a rapid pre-peak ascent and a gradual post-peak decline. Second, the output of high-impact products follows the same course as that of low-impact products, that is, quality is a function of quantity. Third, the longitudinal curve is actually a function of career age rather than chronological age. Hence, those who get a late start have their expected peaks shifted proportionately later. Fourth, the location of the peak as well as the slope of the post-peak decline varies according to the domain of creative productivity.

For instance, mathematicians and poets tend to reach their peaks at younger ages than do geologists and novelists. Fifth, there are substantial individual differences in the average output rate per unit of time, and this variation is far more conspicuous than the longitudinal fluctuations. In more concrete terms, highly prolific creators in the tail end of their careers will be more productive than less prolific creators at their career peaks. Sixth and last, under special circumstances creators can undergo a resurgence of creativity toward the end of life. Especially remarkable are the old age-style shifts of painters and the swan songs of composers (Lindauer, 1993; Simonton, 1989). This last result is provocative insofar as a parallel upsurge has never been documented using psychometric methods.

Social Psychology

Cognitive, differential, and developmental psychologists share one thing in common: They all focus on the individual creator. This shared individualistic perspective ignores the fact that creativity often occurs in a social context. As a consequence, several social psychologists have attempted to understand how creativity emerges out of this broader context (e.g., Amabile, 1996; Simonton, 2004b). Admittedly, the social psychology of creativity has not yet produced a body of research as extensive as in the preceding three instances. Even so, already social psychologists have made important contributions to our understanding of creativity. The two socio-psychological phenomena that have received the most attention are interpersonal interactions and group dynamics.

Interpersonal interactions. One of the most recurrent images of outstanding creators is that of the "lone genius." It would seem that this image is endorsed by the fact that highly creative individuals tend to be introverted rather than extroverted (Cattell & Butcher, 1968). Nevertheless, this introversion is not equivalent to the claim that such persons are social isolates. On the contrary, the empirical literature shows that creative individuals are usually embedded in social networks consisting of other persons working in the same domain of activity (Csikszentmihalyi & Sawyer, 1995). These persons may include collaborators, associates, correspondents, friends, rivals, and acquaintances of various kinds (Simonton, 1984a, 1992). In addition, the richer this disciplinary network, the more productive creators tend to be (e.g., Simonton, 1992).

The foregoing results apply to more or less equal-status relationships. Even so, interactions frequently involve individuals of unequal status. Besides the role model and mentor relations that were noted to exert an important impact on creative development, a creative person must sometimes work under supervision by some superior. An example would be the head of a research unit in industry or academe. The question then arises about the optimal supervisory strategy for maximizing the productivity of individual creators in the unit. One of the central issues addressed by research on this question is the proper use of rewards, incentives, evaluations, and direct supervision (e.g., Eisenberger & Cameron, 1996). If not applied carefully, these tools of management can stifle creativity by suppressing intrinsic motivation in favor of extrinsic motivation (Amabile, 1996).

Group dynamics. In the previous section, we saw that the creativity of individuals is contingent on the social context. There are certain social circumstances that favor individual creativity, others that may undermine individual creativity. Still, these investigations place creativity in the person, so the analysis remains individualistic. This perspective overlooks the fact that a considerable amount of important creativity entails collaborative efforts. An obvious example is cinema, a case easily demonstrated by examining the credits of any feature film (Simonton, 2004a). Another instance is "big science" research collaborations that may involve dozens of scientists (Andrews, 1979). As a result, it is essential to understand group rather than individual creativity. Social psychologists have investigated this problem three major ways (Paulus & Nijstad, 2003). First, and most commonly, investigators have examined problem solving in experimental groups. A prime instance is the extensive literature on brainstorming (e.g., Dugosh, Paulus, Roland, & Yang, 2000). Second, some investigators have taken advantage of archival data to determine the factors that enhance or hinder group creativity. An example is research on social loafing that determines whether individuals working together are less creative than the same individuals working alone (e.g., Jackson & Padgett, 1982). Third, and least common, are field studies of actual group creativity in which the investigator analyzes member interactions. For instance, researchers have scrutinized the patterns of communications that characterize laboratories that generate high-impact findings (e.g., Dunbar, 1995). Taken as a whole, these investigations suggest that group creativity is most often maximized when the membership is highly heterogeneous with respect to attitudes, experience, training, and various demographic variables (see, e.g., Nemeth, Personnaz, Personnaz, & Goncalo, 2004).

CONCLUSION

Based on the above overview, it should be evident that psychology has made substantial progress toward understanding creativity. In particular, the four subdisciplines of cognitive, differential, developmental, and social psychology have revealed the complexity of the phenomenon. Creativity is a process that is most likely to appear in persons with supportive cognitive and dispositional traits. Moreover, not only do creative individuals tend to share a specific set of developmental experiences and longitudinal changes, but their creativity also is favored or disfavored by particular social circumstances. In addition, creativity can be a group as well as an individual phenomenon.

Despite this wealth of information, psychologists still have a long ways to go before they can claim a complete comprehension of how creativity works.

Perhaps the greatest single need is for a satisfactory integration of the diverse empirical findings. Because the investigators in any one subdiscipline tend to ignore the research in the other three subdisciplines, the knowledge tends to accumulate in a disjointed rather than a unified manner (Simonton, 2003). Few have attempted to propose a theoretical model that attempts to accommodate the key results of all four subdisciplines (cf. Simonton, 2004b). Without such a theory, it is impossible to specify how all of the cognitive, differential, developmental, and social variables interact with each other to generate the creativity observed in the real world.

REFERENCES

Amabile, T. M. (1996). *Creativity in context: Update to the social psychology of creativity.* Boulder, CO: Westview.

Andrews, F. M. (Ed.). (1979). *Scientific productivity: The effectiveness of research groups in six countries.* Cambridge, England: Cambridge University Press.

Ansberg, P. I., & Hill, K. (2003). Creative and analytic thinkers differ in their use of attentional resources. *Personality and Individual Differences, 34,* 1141–1152.

Barron, F. X. (1969). *Creative person and creative process.* New York: Holt, Rinehart & Winston.

Barron, F. X., & Harrington, D. M. (1981). Creativity, intelligence, and personality. *Annual Review of Psychology, 32,* 439–476.

Berlyne, D. E. (Ed.). (1974). *Studies in the new experimental aesthetics.* Washington, DC: Hemisphere.

Boden, M. A. (1991). *The creative mind: Myths & mechanisms.* New York: Basic Books.

Bouchard, T. J., Jr. (1994). Genes, environment, and personality. *Science, 264,* 1700–1701.

Bowers, K. S., Farvolden, P., & Mermigis, L. (1995). Intuitive antecedents of insight. In S. M. Smith, T. B. Ward, & R. A. Finke (Eds.), *The creative cognition approach* (pp. 27–51). Cambridge, MA: MIT Press.

Carson, S., Peterson, J. B., & Higgins, D. M. (2003). Decreased latent inhibition is associated with increased creative achievement in high-functioning individuals. *Journal of Personality and Social Psychology, 85,* 499–506.

Cattell, R. B., & Butcher, H. J. (1968). *The prediction of achievement and creativity.* Indianapolis: Bobbs-Merrill.

Csikszentmihalyi, M., & Sawyer, K. (1995). Creative insight: The social dimension of a solitary moment. In R. J. Sternberg & J. E. Davidson (Eds.), *The nature of insight* (pp. 329–364). Cambridge, MA: MIT Press.

Csikszentmihalyi, M. (1997). *Creativity: Flow and the psychology of discovery and invention.* New York: HarperCollins.

Dartnall, T. (Ed.). (2002). *Creativity, cognition, and knowledge: An interaction.* Westport, CT: Praeger.

Dellas, M., & Gaier, E. L. (1970). Identification of creativity: The individual. *Psychological Bulletin, 73,* 55–73.

Dennis, W. (1966). Creativity productivity between the ages of 20 and 80 years. *Journal of Gerontology, 21,* 1–8.

Dugosh, K. L., Paulus, P. B., Roland, E. J., & Yang, H.-C. (2000) Cognitive stimulation in brainstorming. *Journal of Personality and Social Psychology, 79,* 722–735.

Dunbar, K. (1995). How scientists really reason: Scientific reasoning in real-world laboratories. In R. J. Sternberg & J. E. Davidson (Eds.), *The nature of insight* (pp. 365–396). Cambridge, MA: MIT Press.

Eisenstadt, J. M. (1978). Parental loss and genius. *American Psychologist, 33*, 211–223.

Eisenberger, R., & Cameron, J. (1996). Detrimental effects of reward: Reality or myth? *American Psychologist, 51*, 1153–1166.

Ericsson, K. A. (1996). The acquisition of expert performance: An introduction to some of the issues. In K. A. Ericsson (Ed.), *The road to expert performance: Empirical evidence from the arts and sciences, sports, and games* (pp. 1–50). Mahwah, NJ: Erlbaum.

Eysenck, H. J. (1995). *Genius: The natural history of creativity.* Cambridge, England: Cambridge University Press.

Feist, G. J. (1998). A meta-analysis of personality in scientific and artistic creativity. *Personality and Social Psychology Review, 2*, 290–309.

Feist, G. J., & Barron, F. X. (2003). Predicting creativity from early to late adulthood: Intellect, potential, and personality. *Journal of Research in Personality, 37*, 62–88.

Finke, R. A., Ward, T. B., & Smith, S. M. (1992). *Creative cognition: Theory, research, applications.* Cambridge, MA: MIT Press.

Galton, F. (1869). *Hereditary genius: An inquiry into its laws and consequences.* London: Macmillan.

Gardner, H. (1983). *Frames of mind: A theory of multiple intelligences.* New York: Basic Books.

Gardner, H. (1993). *Creating minds: An anatomy of creativity seen through the lives of Freud, Einstein, Picasso, Stravinsky, Eliot, Graham, and Gandhi.* New York: Basic Books.

Glover, J. A., Ronning, R. R., & Reynolds, C. R. (Eds.). (1989). *Handbook of creativity.* New York: Plenum Press.

Goertzel, M. G., Goertzel, V., & Goertzel, T. G. (1978). *300 eminent personalities: A psychosocial analysis of the famous.* San Francisco: Jossey-Bass.

Guilford, J. P. (1967). *The nature of human intelligence.* New York: McGraw-Hill.

Hayes, J. R. (1989). Cognitive processes in creativity. In J. A. Glover, R. R. Ronning, & C. R. Reynolds (Eds.), *Handbook of creativity* (pp. 135–145). New York: Plenum Press.

Howe, M. J. A. (1999). *Genius explained.* Cambridge, England: Cambridge University Press.

Howe, M. J. A., Davidson, J. W., & Sloboda, J. A. (1998). Innate talents: Reality or myth? *Behavioral and Brain Sciences, 21*, 399–442.

Jackson, J. M., & Padgett, V. R. (1982). With a little help from my friend: Social loafing and the Lennon-McCartney songs. *Personality and Social Psychology Bulletin, 8*, 672–677.

Jamison, K. R. (1993). *Touched with fire: Manic-depressive illness and the artistic temperament.* New York: Free Press.

Johnson-Laird, P. N. (1993). *Human and machine thinking.* Hillsdale, NJ: Lawrence Erlbaum.

Klahr, D., & Simon, H. A. (1999). Studies of scientific creativity: Complementary approaches and convergent findings. *Psychological Bulletin, 125*, 524–543.

Langley, P., Simon, H. A., Bradshaw, G. L., & Zythow, J. M. (1987). *Scientific discovery.* Cambridge, MA: MIT Press.

Lehman, H. C. (1953). *Age and achievement*. Princeton, NJ: Princeton University Press.

Lindauer, M. S. (1993). The old-age style and its artists. *Empirical Studies and the Arts, 11*, 135-146.

Lindauer, M. S. (2003). *Aging, creativity, and art: A positive perspective on late-life development*. New York: Kluwer Academic/Plenum Publishers.

Ludwig, A. M. (1995). *The price of greatness: Resolving the creativity and madness controversy*. New York: Guilford Press.

Lykken, D. T. (1998). The genetics of genius. In A. Steptoe (Ed.), *Genius and the mind: Studies of creativity and temperament in the historical record* (pp. 15–37). New York: Oxford University Press.

MacKinnon, D. W. (1978). *In search of human effectiveness*. Buffalo, NY: Creative Education Foundation.

Martindale, C. (1989). Personality, situation, and creativity. In J. A. Glover, R. R. Ronning, & C. R. Reynolds (Eds.), *Handbook of creativity* (pp. 211–232). New York: Plenum Press.

McCrae, R. R., Arenberg, D., & Costa, P. T. (1987). Declines in divergent thinking with age: Cross-sectional, longitudinal, and cross-sequential analyses. *Psychology and Aging, 2*, 130–136.

Nemeth, C. J., Personnaz, B., Personnaz, M., & Goncalo, J. A. (2004). The liberating role of conflict in group creativity: A study in two countries. *European Journal of Social Psychology, 34*, 365–374.

Newell, A., & Simon, H. A. (1972). *Human problem solving*. Englewood Cliffs, NJ: Prentice-Hall.

Paulus, P. B., & Nijstad, B. A. (Eds.). (2003). *Group creativity: Innovation through collaboration*. New York: Oxford University Press.

Peterson, J. B., & Carson, S. (2000). Latent inhibition and openness to experience in a high-achieving student population. *Personality and Individual Differences, 28*, 323–332.

Quételet, A. (1968). *A treatise on man and the development of his faculties*. New York: Franklin (Reprint of 1842 Edinburgh translation of 1835 French original).

Rothenberg, A. (1990). *Creativity and madness: New findings and old stereotypes*. Baltimore: Johns Hopkins University Press.

Runco, M. A., & Pritzker, S. (Eds.). (1999). *Encyclopedia of creativity* (2 vols.). San Diego: Academic Press.

Schooler, J. W., & Melcher, J. (1995). The ineffability of insight. In S. M. Smith, T. B. Ward, & R. A. Finke (Eds.), *The creative cognition approach* (pp. 97–133). Cambridge, MA: MIT Press.

Seifert, C. M., Meyer, D. E., Davidson, N., Patalano, A. L., & Yaniv, I. (1995). Demystification of cognitive insight: Opportunistic assimilation and the prepared-mind perspective. In R. J. Sternberg & J. E. Davidson (Eds.), *The nature of insight* (pp. 65–124). Cambridge, MA: MIT Press.

Shrager, J., & Langley, P. (Eds.). (1990). *Computational models of scientific discovery and theory formation*. San Mateo, CA: Kaufmann.

Simonton, D. K. (1984a). Artistic creativity and interpersonal relationships across and within generations. *Journal of Personality and Social Psychology, 46*, 1273–1286.

Simonton, D. K. (1984b). *Genius, creativity, and leadership: Historiometric inquiries*. Cambridge, MA: Harvard University Press.

Simonton, D. K. (1988). Age and outstanding achievement: What do we know after a century of research? *Psychological Bulletin, 104*, 251–267.

Simonton, D. K. (1989). The swan-song phenomenon: Last-works effects for 172 classical composers. *Psychology and Aging, 4*, 42–47.

Simonton, D. K. (1991). Emergence and realization of genius: The lives and works of 120 classical composers. *Journal of Personality and Social Psychology, 61*, 829–840.

Simonton, D. K. (1992). The social context of career success and course for 2,026 scientists and inventors. *Personality and Social Psychology Bulletin, 18*, 452–463.

Simonton, D. K. (1997). Creative productivity: A predictive and explanatory model of career trajectories and landmarks. *Psychological Review, 104*, 66–89.

Simonton, D. K. (1999). Talent and its development: An emergenic and epigenetic model. *Psychological Review, 106*, 435–457.

Simonton, D. K. (2000a). Creative development as acquired expertise: Theoretical issues and an empirical test. *Developmental Review, 20*, 283–318.

Simonton, D. K. (2000b). Creativity: Cognitive, developmental, personal, and social aspects. *American Psychologist, 55*, 151–158.

Simonton, D. K. (2002). *Great psychologists and their times: Scientific insights into psychology's history.* Washington, DC: APA Books.

Simonton, D. K. (2003). Scientific creativity as constrained stochastic behavior: The integration of product, process, and person perspectives. *Psychological Bulletin, 129*, 475–494.

Simonton, D. K. (2004a). Group artistic creativity: Creative clusters and cinematic success in 1,327 feature films. *Journal of Applied Social Psychology, 34*, 1494–1520.

Simonton, D. K. (2004b). *Creativity in science: Chance, logic, genius, and zeitgeist.* Cambridge, England: Cambridge University Press.

Simonton, D. K. (2005). Are genius and madness related? Contemporary answers to an ancient question. *Psychiatric Times, 22* (7), 21–23.

Smith, S. M., Ward, T. B., & Finke, R. A. (Eds.). (1995). *The creative cognition approach.* Cambridge, MA: MIT Press.

Sternberg, R. J. (Ed.). (1999). *Handbook of creativity.* Cambridge, United Kingdom: Cambridge University Press.

Sternberg, R. J., & Davidson, J. E. (Eds.). (1995). *The nature of insight.* Cambridge, MA: MIT Press.

Sternberg, R. J., & Lubart, T. I. (1996). Investing in creativity. *American Psychologist, 51*, 677–688.

Sulloway, F. J. (1996). *Born to rebel: Birth order, family dynamics, and creative lives.* New York: Pantheon.

Terman, L. M. (1925–1959). *Genetic studies of genius* (5 vols.). Stanford, CA: Stanford University Press.

Wallas, G. (1926). *The art of thought.* New York: Harcourt, Brace.

Waller, N. G., Bouchard, T. J., Jr., Lykken, D. T., Tellegen, A., & Blacker, D. M. (1993). Creativity, heritability, familiality: Which word does not belong? *Psychological Inquiry, 4*, 235–237.

Ward, T. B., Smith, S. M., & Vaid, J. (Eds.). (1997). *Creative thought: An investigation of conceptual structures and processes.* Washington, DC: American Psychological Association.

Wertheimer, M. (1982). *Productive thinking* (M. Wertheimer, Ed.). Chicago: University of Chicago Press (original work published 1945).

6

Creativity, Cognition, and Cyborgs: The Extended Mind Hypothesis as an Explanatory Framework for Creativity Research

TERRY DARTNALL

There is a common perception, seldom clearly articulated, that it is our ability to be creative that makes us characteristically and distinctively human and sets us apart as a species. Other species have limited problem-solving abilities, but we consistently come up with creative solutions and produce original artifacts.

I think there is some truth to this perception. But I also think that our perception of ourselves and of the nature of creativity misses the mark by a country mile. We typically think of mind and self as residing inside the skull—certainly as being inside what the philosopher and cognitive scientist Andy Clark (2003) calls the "skin and skull boundary" and "the biological skinbag." Similarly, we see cognition and creativity as taking place inside the head. We accept that pen and paper, paintbrush and palate, calculators and computers help us to be creative, but we see these things as adjuncts or add-ons: the real creativity takes place inside the skull.

Recent research in cognitive science suggests that these perceptions are radically wrong. When we solve a problem with pen and paper, or with a pocket calculator, mind and self loop out into the world, so that it is the mind-and-pen-and-paper system, or the mind-and-calculator system, that solves the problem. And even that doesn't quite capture it: it is not that mind *plus* pen and paper or mind *plus* calculator solves the problem. It is that the pen and paper, and the calculator, are *part of the mind*. Mind is our biological wetware coupled with "out there" technologies, so that cognition is an ongoing loop between our wetware and the world.

Now it just so happens that the notion of *looping* is recognized in the creativity literature as a key component of creativity. Creativity typically involves producing something (a sketch, a sentence, a proposal, an idea), evaluating it, and repeating the process until a satisfactory solution or satisfying product is produced. Evaluating the product typically gives rise to new ideas and new goals, in the light of which we modify the product—which we evaluate ... and so on, in a loop.

In this chapter, I suggest that we can gain explanatory leverage by seeing creativity loops as extended system loops. The shoe might not fit perfectly. There might be borderline, not very interesting cases of creativity that are not extended system loops, but with these uninteresting exceptions we can fruitfully see generative-evaluative loops as loops between our biological wetware and the world. There is a sense in which we would expect this to be the case. Extended Mind theory purports to give us the big picture about mind and cognition. Creativity is a complex, sophisticated form of cognition, so we would expect creativity loops to be extended system loops. Armed with this expectation, we look at accounts of the creative process in the research literature—and find the notion of a loop right at the heart of them.

Creativity research urgently needs an explanatory framework. Research into creativity is scattered and fragmentary, and no paradigm or explanatory framework is available. Treating creativity loops as extended systems loops would enable us to study creativity within the framework of the Extended Mind Hypothesis and would locate the study of creativity within the broader study of mind as a whole. Couched in a common framework, creativity research and the Extended Mind Hypothesis would complement one another. On the one hand we would have results, drawn in broad brushstrokes, about the structure of cognition and its relationship with the world, and on the other we would have more fine-grained information about creative processes, which would fill in some of the details of the bigger picture.

If creativity loops are extended system loops, it gives some credence to the claim that creativity makes us characteristically and distinctively human. But the perception is not entirely correct. What makes us distinctively human is the ability underlying our ability to be creative: namely, our ability to complement our pattern recognition abilities with manipulable technologies in the world. There is a complex package here in which we generate a product that we can reflect upon and change, and which in turn structures or "scaffolds" our cognition and serves as a focus for multiple mental modules: think of the way in which our notes for writing a paper, or a chapter on creativity, serve as a focal point where memory, thinking, reasoning, planning and language can converge—in a single, central location *out there in the world.*

In the first part of this chapter, I shall outline the recent research in cognitive science that says that mind loops into the world. Then I shall look at the role of loops in creativity, focussing on Hofstadter and FARG's[1] Letter Spirit project. In subsequent sections, I shall examine the relationship between the two kinds of loop and the relationship between the imagination, cognitive technologies, and the external world. I shall conclude by looking at some of the more traditional questions in the creativity literature.

CYBORGS AND EXTENDED MINDS: THE BIG PICTURE

One of the most vigorous developments in contemporary cognitive science is the "Extended Mind Hypothesis," also known as "Active Externalism" (Clark, 1997, 2003; Clark & Chalmers, 1998; Dennett, 1996; Donald, 1991; Hutchins, 1995). The Extended Mind Hypothesis says that mind extends, or loops out, into the world, beyond the skin-and-skull boundary. Clark and Chalmers (1998) say that cognitive *processes* extend into the world when we use pen and paper to work something out, or when we use a computer, or even when we use language, which Clark thinks was the first technology. They say that cognitive *states* extend into the world when we use physical objects, or data structures such as chips or CD-ROMs, as *external memory stores*.

The big picture is that our brains, in and of themselves, are pattern-recognition and pattern-completion engines, with limited problem-solving abilities. We have, however, learned to amplify these basic abilities with *cognitive technologies* out there in the world. A common example is arithmetic. Suppose we have to multiply 777 by 55. Few of us can do this in our heads, so we use pencil and paper. Our pattern-recognition abilities tell us that $7 \times 5 = 35$. We write this down in the first column and repeat the process, looping out into the world, until we have completed the sum. The pencil and paper complement our basic abilities and amplify our skills. Clark (2003), following Dennett (1996), thinks that language was probably the first cognitive technology. We needed to be smart in order to develop language in the first place, but once we had it, language enabled us to treat our thoughts and ideas as *objects* that we could reflect upon and change. According to Clark, it was this ability that "got the cognitive snowball rolling" (p. 83). We were then drawn upward in a virtuous circle as one technology led to another. We have upgraded our mindware from speech to writing, through increasingly flexible forms of printing, and are now entering into an intimate relationship with machines.

Clark (2003) says that we are so enmeshed with our technologies that we are what he calls "natural-born cyborgs" (the title of his 2003 book is *Natural-Born Cyborgs: Minds, Technologies and the Future of Human Intelligence*). It is our special character as human beings "to be forever driven to create, co-opt, annex, and exploit nonbiological props and scaffoldings" (p. 6). We are "*creatures whose minds are special precisely because they are tailor-made for multiple mergers and coalitions*" (p. 7, Clark's emphasis).

We are not, however, cyborgs in the standard sense of the word. The original vision of the cyborg was that the body would be altered and amplified to survive in alien or inhospitable environments (Clynes & Kline, 1960). Very little has happened on this front (with the exception of a rat that was fitted with an osmotic pump that automatically injected it with chemicals). What has happened instead is that our minds, rather than our bodies, have been modified, and this human-machine symbiosis has altered and expanded the psychological processes that make us what we are. It has provided an "array of resources to which biological brains, as they learn and grow, *dovetail* their own activities" (Clark, 2003, p. 32). This has led to the creation of "extended computational and mental organizations: reasoning and thinking systems distributed across brain, body, and world" (pp. 32–33).

Clark provides a nice example of the way in which we are dependent on our cognitive technologies. He found himself living next to the head of occupational therapy at the Washington University School of Medicine in St Louis, Missouri. She told him that Alzheimer's sufferers often lived alone in the city quite successfully when, given their condition, they should not have been able to do so. Investigation showed that they did this by leaving props and reminders everywhere: photographs of family and friends; labels and pictures on doors; "memory books" to record new events, meetings, and plans. These things were always in open view. Hospitalizing these people often had tragic consequences. They were so integrated with their home environments that removing them from those environments inflicted new damage, akin to brain damage, onto an already compromised host. This dramatically illustrates the way in which we are dependent on our technologies. Think what it would be like to lose your laptop or your diary, or (heaven forbid) your ability to use language.

CYBORGS AND EXTENDED MINDS: TWO ARGUMENTS

Two broad arguments have been advanced for the Extended Mind Hypothesis: the *parity argument* and the *complementarity argument*.[2] The parity argument (Clark & Chalmers, 1998) says that if something counts as cognitive when it is performed in the head, it should also count as cognitive when it is performed in the world. Suppose you have to rotate images of geometrical shapes on a computer screen. You can rotate them using a neural implant or you can rotate them using a "rotate" button in the world. Presumably we will say that the implant case is cognitive—so why isn't the button case cognitive as well? Clark and Chalmers say that epistemic credit is due where epistemic actions are performed, regardless of whether they are performed in the head or in the world.

This, however, only covers cognitive *processes*, and Clark and Chalmers admit that the processes might be in the world, while all of our "truly mental states—experiences, beliefs, desires, emotions, and so on" might be in the head (p. 12). They therefore take the parity argument a stage further and argue that cognitive *states* can be constituted partly by features of the environment. This brings us to the strange case of Otto's diary. Imagine some-one called "Otto" who suffers from Alzheimer's disease. Otto hears that there is an exhibition at the Museum of Modern Art. He consults his notebook, which says that the museum is on 53rd Street. He walks to 53rd Street and goes to the museum. Clark and Chalmers say that the notebook plays the same role for Otto that biological memory plays for the rest of us. It just happens that "this information lies beyond the skin" (p. 13).

Clark and Chalmers' claim is not only that Otto's belief is out there in the world. They also say that Otto believed the museum was on 53rd Street before he looked it up, courtesy of the "functional isomorphism" between the notebook entry and a corresponding entry in biological memory.

In more recent research, the parity argument has given way to the *complementarity argument* (Clark 2003). This argument has two intimately related components: the "neural opportunism argument" and what I call the "bioborg argument" (Dartnall, 2004). The bioborg argument says that we are already bioborgs (my term), with neural and biomechanical subsystems (let's call them "biobots") that we launch to do our bidding. When we go to the fridge for a beer, we do not consciously move one leg and then the other and then the other. We delegate responsibility to a subsystem (a "biobot") that takes care of the process for us. When we get to the fridge, we launch a "get that bottle" routine. And so on. We have onboard, dedicated devices that do these jobs for us. This frees up our minds for higher things and enables us to think about writing a chapter, or investing on the stock market, while we are going to the fridge for a beer. If you are not convinced, think how your fingers coordinate when you tie your shoelaces or when you sign a check. Imagine what it would be like to have to instruct your fingers what to do.

Going to the fridge for a beer, or getting our fingers to tie shoelaces or sign checks, are examples of how onboard devices do our bidding for us. Sometimes, however, the brain gets on with the job of interacting with the world without reporting to consciousness at all. This is beautifully illustrated by Aglioti's extension of the Titchener Circles Illusion (Aglioti, DeSouza, & Goodale, 1995; Gazzaniga, 1998; Milner & Goodale, 1995; Goodale & Milner, 2004). In this illusion, a big circle is surrounded by an annulus of big circles. Next to it is another big circle surrounded by an annulus of small circles. The circle surrounded by the small circles looks bigger than the circle surrounded by big ones, even though the two circles are really the same size. Aglioti replaced the two inner circles with plastic disks. At the conscious level, we now see a plastic disk as larger than it really is, but when we reach for the disk, our thumb and forefinger form the correct-sized aperture to pick it up. A plausible explanation is that we have two incoming visual pathways, the ventral and the dorsal, and only the ventral stream is fooled by the illusion. The ventral stream is routed through consciousness, reasoning, and memory, whereas the dorsal stream gets on with the job of interacting with the world and does not report back to consciousness. When we pick up the disk, we launch a "pick-it-up" routine that is guided by the information coming in through the dorsal stream—information that we do not have access to at the conscious level.

The above examples show that onboard, dedicated devices sometimes do our bidding and sometimes get on with the job of interacting with the world without reporting back to consciousness at all. This leaves us well placed for mechanical augmentation, for adding external devices to our already bioborg minds.

The neural opportunism argument has to do, not with our toolkit brains, but with the way in which we use enduring features of the world as external memory stores that we can consult as needs dictate. Cognitive scientists initially believed that we build rich inner analogs of the world—rather like inner maps. But this would be computationally expensive (and it would probably lead to infinite regress, because we would then have to understand the maps). Instead, our brains have learned to exploit the constant, enduring features of the world and to use objects and situations as external memory stores. All that we need is a high-level map of what's out there, plus the ability to zoom in and get detailed information whenever we need to—on a need-to-know basis.

When we look around a room, we continually scan and zoom, scan and zoom. The scanning is called "saccading," and the zooming is called "foveating." Experimental evidence shows that we take in very little during saccades. In a well-known experiment, the subject's saccades were monitored by a computer. Changes were made to the scene during saccades. These changes were obvious to the experimenters, who were standing behind the subject chuckling, but the subject couldn't see them at all. This is called "change blindness," and it can be demonstrated in various ways. Dan Simons and Dan Levin set up a slapstick scenario on Cornell University campus. Somebody would pretend to be lost. They would approach a passer-by and ask for instructions. At that moment, two people carrying a door would walk in between them. During this time the person who was "lost" would be replaced by somebody else—someone with different height, voice, clothes, etc. Only fifty percent of the people who were asked for instructions noticed the change!

The point is that we don't have rich inner models of the world. We have high-level maps plus the ability to zoom in and retrieve detailed information on a need-to-know basis. This is less demanding on memory than having a rich inner database. But we still have a rich database—it is *out there in the world*.

Using the world as an external memory store is a passive process, but neural opportunism has operated in consort with our bioborg brains to create *cognitive technologies* that actively complement our already-tool-kit brains. Clark thinks that the first cognitive technology was probably language. Language gives us a "cognitive short-cut" (p. 70). Research on chimpanzees shows that the use of plastic tokens enables them to reduce high-order abstract problems to lower-order problems that their brains can handle. Chimps were trained to associate a plastic token, such as a red triangle, with any pair of identical objects (such as two shoes) and to associate a differently shaped and differently colored token with any pair of different objects (such as a beer can and a banana). The chimps could then solve the more complex problem of categorizing pairs-of-pairs of objects in terms of *higher-order* sameness or difference. They could classify shoe-and-cup (different) as the same higher order relationship as beer can-and-banana (also different). They could do this because both pairs would have the same kind of token. All they had to do was to compare the tokens.

Clark thinks that words work in the same way. They label complex concepts and enable us to "freeze" our thoughts. This enables us to *think about* our thoughts and ideas. (Is it a good idea? What are my reasons for believing it?)

Language is what Clark calls a "transparent technology." We are so well integrated with it that it is almost invisible in use. We are surrounded by transparent technologies (pens, watches, telephones, etc.) and are rapidly developing new ones. Mobile phones have cheap, tiny cameras that enable us to beam information to family and friends while we are shopping ("Should I buy these avocados?"; "Do you like the color of this shirt?"). Implants in our bodies will communicate with one another—where we are and how we are. Augmented reality will overlay our experience of the world with personalized information, beamed to us by satellite. Lost on campus, we will enter "library," don an eyeglass, and see a green arrow pointing to the library.

Clark claims that we are already so well integrated with our technologies that the problem-solving system is the biological system (the brain, our ancient wetware) plus the technology. Suppose that somebody asks you if you know the time. You say that you do, and *then* you look at your watch. You say that you know the time because you know that you can easily find it out, just as we say that we know something because we know that we can retrieve it from long-term biological memory. It makes no difference where the information is stored, whether in biological memory or in external storage. What matters is ease of access. Suppose you have a chip on your shoulder that gives you easy access to information about women basketball players. There is no relevant difference between retrieving the information from the chip and retrieving it from long-term memory. You *know* the information because you have easy access to it, and what does the knowing is you-and-the-chip.

So what have we got? Our unassisted brains are pattern-recognition and pattern-completion engines with limited problem-solving abilities, but we have learned to complement and amplify them with technologies in the world—so that mind and cognition loop out into the world. We looked at a simple example of this in the case of arithmetic, where we repeatedly perform pattern-recognition tasks and record the ongoing results with pencil and paper. The problem-solving process loops out into the world and back into our heads, until we have finished the sum. Similarly, consider the way you might write a lecture, or a paper, or a chapter for a book. You probably begin with some scattered ideas, which you write down or throw at your word processor. Even at this early stage, you have externalized your ideas so that you can hold them at arm's length and think about them. You shuffle the ideas around, changing some of them, changing the sequence, removing some and adding others. You finally have an outline, but you aren't happy with it. You make yourself some coffee, still thinking about the lecture. You realize that you have left something out, but you have to go back to your office to look at the outline, which you couldn't hold in your head. Now that you have had your dose of caffeine, you realize there is a more interesting way in which you can present the material. You realize this by looking at the preliminary outline, which enables you to readjust your goals and write a lecture that is interestingly different to the one you originally had in mind.

There is nothing unusual about this process, which many of us engage in all the time. It is an example of mind looping out into the world, and the above account might have been given by any number of philosophers or cognitive scientists who subscribe to the Extended Mind Hypothesis. It is similar to accounts of the creative process that we find in the creativity literature, in which we iteratively generate and evaluate a product, so that the creative product emerges out of a generative-evaluative cycle. The difference is one of perspective and emphasis. Extended Mind theorists focus on the way in which mind loops out into the world and pay little attention to the emerging product. Creativity researchers focus on the emerging product and the tension and interaction between cognitive subsystems, which they see as a key component of the creative process.

We now turn to this account of the creative process.

THE CENTRAL FEEDBACK LOOP OF CREATIVITY

It is almost a truism to say that creativity and problem solving proceed through a process of generation and evaluation, in which we iteratively generate, evaluate, and modify the emerging product. To some extent, the Devil is in the details: What is the role and nature of the generative process? Is it largely random, or is it driven by the initial data or design? Inductivists in the philosophy of science say that theory formation is data driven, closely tied to and deeply informed by the available data, whereas Popperians, or falsificationists, say that the origin of a hypothesis is of little relevance to scientific progress or the philosophy of science. A theory might be prompted or suggested by the available data, but it might equally have been dreamt up or randomly generated. What matters, according to falsificationism, is how well the theory stands up to our attempts to falsify it. Another important detail is how flexible we can be in letting the interim product influence our goals and intentions. We can be flexible when writing a story or poem, but less flexible when working on a portrait or the plans for a house.

Talking about creativity in terms of a generative-evaluative loop can over-simplify things in another way. The kind of loop that is involved in the creative process is not the simple loop that we find in standard programming, where we repeatedly perform the same operation on an element or set of elements. The loop that we find in the creative process typically involves multiple cognitive modules generating, evaluating, modifying, and generally kicking a product around until a satisfactory solution is achieved.

We shall now look at a program called "Letter Spirit" (Hofstadter & FARG, 1995; McGraw, 1995; McGraw & Hofstadter, 2002; Rehling, 2001, 2002). Letter Spirit is the most ambitious project in a long line of research by Douglas Hofstadter and the Indiana University Fluid Analogies Research Group (FARG) into agent-based analogy engines. These programs are analogy engines because they "try to do in one framework something that has already been done in a significantly different framework" (Hofstadter & FARG, 1995, p. 450; McGraw & Hofstadter, 2002, p. 264). They are agent based because processing occurs through the collective actions of a large number of small computational agents, known as "codelets," that stochastically build up structures or break them down, without any higher-level executive process directing the overall course of events.

Letter Spirit is the most meticulous model of the creative process that I know of. What makes it especially interesting for our purposes is that it focuses on the way in which the creative process unfolds over time—in particular on the way in which cognitive modules compete and collaborate in a creative loop. Hofstadter stresses that Letter Spirit tries to capture the human creative process, rather than just producing a creative output. I shall return to this.

Letter Spirit models the way in which the lowercase letters of the Roman alphabet can be rendered in different but internally coherent styles. Letter Spirit has a general understanding about letters of the alphabet, so that it can recognize particular letters, such as *a*'s and *b*'s, when it sees them, but it has no built-in knowledge about style or *spirit*. At the beginning of a run, Letter Spirit is given one or more seed letters in a particular style and has to generate the rest of the alphabet so that all twenty-six letters have the same spirit or style. It draws these letters on a simple grid, a 3" × 7" array of points that can be connected by lines known as "quanta" to form letters (see Figure 6.1). The simplicity of the grid makes for startling stylistic and category changes: small changes to the grid can lead to dramatic changes in style or category.

As originally envisaged, Letter Spirit was to have four interacting modules. The *Imaginer* would play with the concepts behind letterforms. The *Drafter* would convert ideas for letterforms into graphical realizations. The *Examiner* would combine bottom-up and top-down processing to perceive and categorize letterforms, and the *Adjudicator* would perceive and dynamically build a

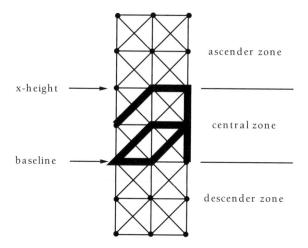

ascender zone

x-height

central zone

baseline

descender zone

FIGURE 6.1. The Letter Spirit grid, with one of the many possible sets of quanta instantiated and "a" turned on. Adapted, with permission, from "Letter Spirit: Perception and Creation of Diverse Alphabetic Styles," by Gary McGraw and Doug Hofstadter in Dartnall, Terry, *Creativity, Cognition, and Knowledge* (2002).

representation of the evolving style. These agents would engage in an iterative process of generation and evaluation that Hofstadter has called, for a long time, "the Central Feedback Loop of Creativity."

McGraw and Hofstadter (2002) provide us with an example of how these agents might work together. Letter Spirit is given a highly stylized seed letter, such as an *f* without a crossbar, and has to construct other letters in the same style. First it has to identify the letter as an *f*, which is a complex task in itself. This is done by the Examiner focusing on parts of the letter and chunking them together. The discovered structures are labeled and wake up the semantic roles *post* and *hook*, which in turn activate the letter categories *f* and *l*. *f* wins, with the attached stylistic note "crossbar suppressed." The Adjudicator files this stylistic information in a database of stylistic characteristics called the "Thematic Focus."

Letter Spirit now moves from its perceptual to its generative phase. *f* and *t* are linked as similar letters in Letter Spirit's long-term memory (known as "Conceptual Memory"), so it will probably tackle *t* next. Drawing on its knowledge of the emerging style (stored in the Thematic Focus), the Imaginer creates an abstract plan consisting of a *t* without a crossbar. It gives this to the Drafter, which draws it on the grid.[3]

Letter Spirit knows that it is supposed to have drawn a *t*, but it also knows that the stylistic changes it has made might have violated the letter category and produced something that isn't a *t* anymore. The Examiner checks this out (as part of the generative-evaluative cycle) and discovers that the new letter is not a *t* because it does not have a crossbar. This information, together with "crossbar suppressed," is sent back to the Imaginer.

The Imaginer is now in a state of creative conflict, torn between Spirit pressure ("suppress the crossbar, to make the *t* more like the *f*") and Letter pressure ("if you do that, it won't be a *t* anymore"). To resolve this conflict, the Imaginer looks at the *conceptual halo* of related concepts around "suppress" and finds the concept "underdo." It *slips* from the concept "suppress" to the concept "underdo" and draws a short crossbar on the left side of the stem (with nothing on the right side). Figure 6.2 shows the original seed letter (a barless *f*), the unsuccessful barless *t*, and the successful *t* with the "underdone" crossbar.

McGraw and Hofstadter say that replacing "suppress" with "underdo" is the "the key creative breakthrough," since it resolves the conflict between letter and spirit and allows a new structure to emerge. Creativity, they say, is an automatic outcome of the existence of sufficiently flexible, context-sensitive concepts that allow new creative forms to emerge from the resolution of conflict between inner forces. Here the conflict is between Spirit pressure, coming in from the Thematic Focus, and Letter pressure, coming in from Conceptual Memory.

We might or might not accept McGraw and Hofstadter's claim that "the key creative breakthrough" is a resolution of conflicting forces. This is certainly part of the story, but there is a good deal of collaboration as well: the Imaginer imagines something, the Drafter draws it, the Adjudicator and Examiner analyze it—and so on. What matters for our purposes is that the conflict and cooperation are possible because the modules have access to the grid. They interact with one another by accessing first the seed letter or letters, and then drafts of letters in the new, emerging style. Without access to this output, there would be no interaction or creative loop. The emerging product *holds the process together*: it is the focal point for the creative loop. I shall return to this in the next section.

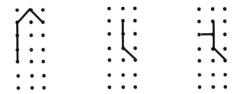

FIGURE 6.2. The *f* with no crossbar (left) gives rise in the Imaginer to a *t* with no crossbar (middle). This is rejected by the Examiner since it is too *l*-like. This leads the Imaginer to slip from "no crossbar" to "short crossbar," and a better *t* is created (right). Adapted, with permission, from "Letter Spirit: Perception and Creation of Diverse Alphabetic Styles," by Gary McGraw and Doug Hofstadter in Dartnall, Terry, *Creativity, Cognition, and Knowledge* (2002).

Hofstadter and FARG stress that they are trying to shed light on the creative process, rather than just trying to provide a program that has an interesting creative output. To illustrate this point, they contrast Letter Spirit with GridFont (Grebert, Stork, Keesing, & Mims, 1992). GridFont operates in exactly the same domain as Letter Spirit and, like Letter Spirit, "draws" its output on a simple 3" × 7" grid. Its architecture, however, is entirely different. GridFont is a connectionist system. It is trained up on letters and styles. It is then given some letters in a style that it has not seen before and has to design the remaining letters of the alphabet in the same style. It does this with only a moderate amount of success.[4]

The salient difference between GridFont and Letter Spirit is this. Letter Spirit consists of interacting modules that model the emergence of a creative product over time. Letter Spirit draws something on the grid, thinks about it, and modifies it, thus modeling the creative process as something that is spread out over time. GridFont is quite different. Once it has been trained up (which can take a *very* long time), the processing whooshes through all in one go. GridFont does not reflect upon what it is doing—nor could it, because it does not have access to its output.

So far we have looked at what McGraw and Hofstadter *thought* Letter Spirit's architecture was going to be—not what it turned out to be in fact. The original proposal was that the Imaginer would create an abstract plan for each grid letter, which would not be concerned with the actual grid. The Imaginer would hand the specifications to the Drafter, which would render them on the grid. McGraw implemented the Examiner for his 1995 doctoral dissertation (McGraw, 1995). John Rehling built upon this foundation from 1995 to 1999 and completed the system for his doctoral dissertation (Rehling, 2001). Letter Spirit had its first run as a complete system in December 1999. See Rehling (2002) for an overview of the results.

There is no Imaginer in Rehling's implementation of Letter Spirit. Instead, the Drafter carries out its work directly on the grid. Letter Spirit is given some seed letters. It then goes through two phases. In the first phase, the Examiner identifies the letters' categories, and the Adjudicator assesses their style. In the second phase, this information is passed to the Drafter, which generates different letters of the same, or similar, style. In fact, the Drafter generates many versions of the same letter, each of which is judged by the Examiner and Adjudicator, and the best one is retained. This phase of the program is a loop. The Drafter draws a letter, which is run past the Examiner and Adjudicator. If they judge it to be the best version so far for that category, the letter is retained as the current version of the category. The loop runs many more times than there are categories, so multiple attempts are made for each category. The program quits after 500 total drafting attempts. The gridfont is now complete, consisting of the best attempts for each category plus the original seeds. The loop is essential. Rehling says that the Drafter does not usually produce very good versions of letters on the first try—versions that capture both category and spirit very well. Rather, "the overall success of the program lies in the fact that many versions are drawn for each category, and the best is chosen by the top-level control" (Rehling, 2002, p. 277).

Letter Spirit's modular architecture leaves plenty of room for tinkering and improvement. In personal correspondence, Hofstadter and Rehling have suggested that the system needs a "loop within a loop": the Examiner and Adjudicator need to peer over the Drafter's shoulder as the Drafter draws on the grid and say "Fine, keep going, I recognize that" or "No, that's wrong." Under these circumstances, the Drafter would get continual feedback and direction, and the drafting process would be more fluid. The time lag between generation and feedback seems to be a critical factor. We are probably inclined to say that the lag should be as short as possible—possibly that there should be no time lag at all. This might be a mistake. We probably need a time lag so that we can put something together before we evaluate it. We need time to complete a sentence or paragraph, or to try out a series of brush strokes, or mold a pot into a particular shape, before handing these things to our internal critics. Continual, immediate feedback might freeze us up, like the centipede who is asked how he coordinates his legs and who, when he thinks about it, cannot take a single step.

In my discussion with Rehling (Rehling, 2002), he suggests another way of improving communication between modules. The Examiner and Adjudicator could say why they rated a particular grid letter poorly. A module (let's call it "The Improver") could take the grid letter and the criticism, improve the letter, and resubmit it—in a loop. Rehling says that another way to improve Letter Spirit would be for the style to evolve and develop as new letters are created. Letter Spirit's sense of style would then be based on both the seed letters and the letters it has created in the current run, so that its sense of style would be more holistic and fluid. The style it is aiming for would "drift as a run proceeds" (p. 279).

EXTENDED SYSTEM LOOPS AND CREATIVITY LOOPS

We have seen that human cognition typically loops out into the world. Extended-system loops complement and amplify our pattern-recognition and pattern-completion abilities with external objects and states of affairs, and with technologies ranging from language and pictures to computational devices. Creativity similarly involves a loop, in which we iteratively generate, evaluate, and modify an emerging product. I think we can gain explanatory leverage by treating creativity loops as extended system loops and studying creativity in an Extended Mind framework. This is not just a methodological convenience. I think that creativity loops *are* extended system loops—which is not readily apparent because the loops are seen from different perspectives. Extended-system loops are seen from the perspective of cognitive scientists and philosophers trying to understand mind and its relationship with the world, whereas creativity loops are seen from the perspective of cognitive scientists and psychologists trying to understand the creative process. From the Extended Mind perspective, the fact that mind loops out into the world:

1. enables us to treat our thoughts as objects that we can reflect upon ("Should we attack the woolly mammoth like this?") and perform operations on (think of the multiplication example)
2. structures our cognition as we build up increasingly complex structures that we could not hold in short-term memory (think about writing a lecture or a chapter for a book)

From the creativity perspective it:

1. provides a focal point for the generative-evaluative loop, which is linked up and held together by the emerging product
2. provides a focal point where modules can converge in a single, central location "out there in the world" (think of the Drafter, Examiner and Adjudicator, or, more generally, about memory, thinking, reasoning, planning and language)

I suspect that there is another perspective, from the point of view of the modularity of mind. There has been a great deal of debate and discussion about mental modules—whether they exist, and, if they do, whether they are inaccessible to other parts of the mind (variously called "informationally encapsulated" or "cognitively impenetrable") (Fodor, 1983; Karmiloff-Smith, 1992). If mental modules do exist, they might be cognitively impenetrable but still able to communicate with one another through their output, just as the informationally encapsulated components of blackboard systems communicate through a shared blackboard or workspace. I will not develop this third perspective here and will limit myself to viewing modularity from the Extended Mind and creativity perspectives.

Let us look at some of the details. We have seen that, from an Extended Mind point of view, language was probably the first cognitive technology. Language enables us to externalize our thoughts—to turn them into stable objects that we can reflect up and change ("Would it be a good idea to attack the woolly mammoth like this? What if we tried it this way instead?"). From the creativity perspective, we have a similar story. Language enables us to generate stable objects that we can iteratively evaluate and change. If we change them, we will probably adjust our goals and repeat the process, as part of a generative-evaluative loop.

Extended system loops enable us to structure or "scaffold" our thoughts. Think of the way in which the syntax of natural language makes complex cognition possible. I have just read this passage in a novel: "Here she was, the editor of the *Review of Applied Ethics*, about to go off in search of ... of a murderer is what it amounted to. And in this task she was to be assisted, although somewhat reluctantly, by a beautiful young man with whom she was half in love but who was himself in love with her niece, who in turn appeared besotted with somebody else, who was having a simultaneous affair with his sister's flatmate" (McCall Smith, 2004, pp. 61–62). The complexity of this idea is made possible because of the syntax, or structure, of the sentences in which it is expressed. And language doesn't only *structure* our thoughts. It provides us with a rich repository of shared meanings and ideas. People who are deaf from birth say that when they learned sign language their minds opened up to a rich world of shared cultural meanings and complex ideas (Sacks, 1989). In terms of the Extended Mind Hypothesis, their minds *extended out* into the world of shared meanings and ideas.

Creativity loops similarly include a product that structures our ideas. We have seen how we prepare a lecture or a chapter for a book. We begin by writing down some haphazard ideas. We work them into shape until we have an outline. To some extent, we can carry this outline in our heads, so we make ourselves a cup of coffee or pull out a few weeds in the garden while we are thinking about it, but as soon as we come up with something new, we consult the emerging outline to see where the new idea fits in. Mind continually loops out into the world, and the talk or chapter gradually takes shape.

From the creativity perspective, we can see that there is another component in the package—the way in which the emerging artifact holds our cognition together and serves as a focal point for multiple mental modules. Consider Letter Spirit's grid (strictly speaking, the contents of the grid). Letter Spirit's loop involves a complex, repetitive interaction between Drafter, Examiner, and Adjudicator. This interaction is possible because the modules have access to the contents of the grid, which serve as a focus and hold the loop together. In and of themselves, Letter Spirit's modules are black boxes that have no access to their inner workings or those of other modules. They communicate with one another through the grid. In much the same way, written notes for a new paper or chapter serve as a focal point where memory, thinking, reasoning, planning, and language can converge in a single, central location "out there in the world."

The interdependence between modularity and the emerging product is nicely illustrated by comparing Letter Spirit and GridFont in an Extended Mind explanatory framework. GridFont is a connectionist system. We can think of it as a little artificial brain, consisting of interconnected artificial neurons. GridFont learns to produce an output given a particular type of input, but without the assistance of external, cognitive technologies. We can think of it as a "naked brain" that is not complemented by external devices. This makes it difficult for it to be modular, for there are no structured objects or artifacts to hold the modularity together. And without modularity, GridFont cannot model the to-ing and fro-ing and resolution of creative tension that (according to Hofstadter and FARG) lie at the heart of the creative process. Once it has been trained up and given an input, GridFont's processing whooshes through all in one go, in an uncreative, unreflective kind of way.

Now contrast this with Letter Spirit. Letter Spirit's modules are complemented by the contents of the grid. They loop out into the grid, which enables them to access their own output and that of other modules, so that the
modules interact and communicate through their output. The planned
improvements to Letter Spirit that we saw in the previous section are possible
because of Letter Spirit's modular nature, which in turn is made possible by
the coordinating effect of the grid—by structured output "out there in the
world." Seen in this light, it seems that external objects and artifacts make
modularity, and hence creativity, possible. In turn, the modularity generates
and structures the objects that hold the creative process together.

But does the output have to be out there in the world?

IMAGINATION AND THE EXTERNAL WORLD

Suppose somebody says, "Why must the creative product be *out there in the
world*? Why can't it be in our minds, so that the creative process takes place
entirely in the imagination?" Why, for example, do we need to think of Letter
Spirit's grid as being out there in the world, rather than in Letter Spirit's
"mind"?

First, Extended Mind theory does not say that *all* cognition loops out into
the world—some, no doubt, takes place entirely in the head. Second,
Extended Mind theory says that it is *irrelevant* whether cognition loops out
into the world or whether it loops around inside the head, just as it is irrelevant whether the information about female basketball players is in biological
memory or external storage. What matters in the basketball case is availability
and access, and it is the same with cognitive loops. Clark invites us to imagine a colony of Martian artists who "by some freak of evolution" have developed a kind of biological scratchpad memory, so that they can do in their
heads what we do with our sketchpads (Clark, 2003, p. 77). Martians and
humans would then perform similar creative processes, but Martians would
perform them in their heads whereas we would use brains and sketchpads.
What it comes down to is a matter of ability and convenience—how good we
are at doing things in our heads, compared with doing them with the aid of
external devices. For humans, the external devices win every time. Think how
much more difficult mental arithmetic is than working things out with pencil
and paper (let alone with a calculator!). Think how hard it would be to prepare that lecture in your head, without being able to write anything down. In
a nightmare scenario, we might imagine losing our technologies—first our
computers, then our books, then our writing material, and finally our ability
to use language. Under these circumstances, we would not only lose our cognitive technologies. We would lose our ability to think and be creative.

Our dependence on technology is nicely illustrated by Chambers and Reisberg
(1985). Chambers and Reisberg showed subjects ambiguous pictures, such as
the duck-rabbit picture, and told them to form a mental picture so that they

could draw it later on. They then asked the subjects to rotate the image in their minds and provide the other interpretation of the picture. None of the subjects were able to do so. They were, however, able to draw the picture on paper and *then* see the alternative interpretation. One way of looking at this is to say that their imaginative abilities were extended by externalizing the images and running them through visual perception. The situation is not clear cut, however. Finke, Pinker, and Farah (1989) asked subjects to close their eyes and juxtapose or superimpose mental images, to describe the result, and then to draw the pattern in their image. A well-known example is that subjects were able to rotate a D and add it to an upright J to get an image of an umbrella. Pinker and Finke (1980) found that subjects could imagine a three-dimensional scene as viewed from a novel perspective. Finke and Slayton (1988), Anderson and Helstrup (1993), and Brandimonte, Hitch, and Bishop (1992) report similar results. Rollins (1999) provides an alternative interpretation of Chambers and Reisberg's results that combines the role of representations with attentional and other strategies.

The academic jury, then, is still out. I am going to suggest that we would *expect* something like the Chambers and Reisberg result to be correct, at least in the sense that we are a lot better at generating and evaluating things in the world than we are at generating and evaluating them in the imagination. I do not want to replace experimental evidence with intuition, but there is no harm in trying to bring about a change in perspective—so here we go. We typically think that cognition and creativity take place inside the skull. This belief is so firmly entrenched in our cognitive folklore that it affects the way in which the Extended Mind Hypothesis is stated. The hypothesis is typically seen as saying that mind "starts" in the head and then loops out into the world, so that cognition *becomes* externalized through cognitive technologies such as language and writing. I suspect that the truth is the other way around and that cognition and creativity start in our relationship with the external world and become *internalized* (Dartnall, 2005). Imagery, for example, is probably generated by redeploying mechanisms that we normally use in perception, and all but the most rudimentary kind of thought is probably internalized speech.

Let's look at the language case first. The seventeenth-century philosopher John Locke said that the meaning of a word is an idea in the speaker's head, so that we understand what a speaker means when we understand the corresponding idea in his or her head (Locke, 1964). When somebody says "My dog is a Labrador," we understand the meaning of "dog" by grasping the idea in the speaker's mind. But this account has it exactly back to front. We do not understand the meaning of a word by understanding an idea in the speaker's mind. We could not possibly do this, because the only access we have to the idea is through the public meaning of what the speaker says. Rather than understanding the meaning of what somebody says by accessing the corresponding idea in their minds, we understand the idea in their minds by understanding the public meaning of what they say (Dartnall, 1998). This strongly suggests that we have meanings in our heads courtesy of a shared, public framework of concepts and ideas. The notion of *scaffolding* that plays such a prominent role in the Extended Mind Hypothesis is derived from Lev Vygotsky's belief that public language becomes internalized and (whether vocal or internalized) structures and controls our actions (Vygotsky, 1962). It is not just a means of communicating information. Wittgenstein argued for a similar position with his Private Language Arguments (Wittgenstein, 1963).

We find a similar kind of story with imagery and perception. Stephen Kosslyn has spent many years studying imagery and perception. Much of his major (1994, 2006) study of imagery is devoted to developing a theory of perception. He then argues that imagery is generated by the same mechanisms that underlie perception: "In essence, images are formed by the same processes that allow one to anticipate what one would see if a particular object or scene were present" (1994, p. 287). "Imagery is in most respects just like vision, except that there's nothing there" (Personal communication, August 7, 2005). It is not, however, simply a case of imagery "piggybacking on perception." The relationship is stronger than that. Imagery is already present in perception. It is an "integral part of how perception operates" (1994, p. 21).

Both the cognition and imagery cases strongly suggest that we first acquired abilities to interact and problem-solve in the world and then imported these operations into our heads. If this is correct, we would expect something like the Chambers and Reisberg result to be correct—that we are better at performing cognitive operations on objects in the world than we are at performing them on things in our heads.

I will cite one more piece of evidence that supports this conclusion. Van Leeuwen, Verstijnen, and Hekkert (1999; see also Jaarsveld & van Leeuwen, 2005) provide a meticulously detailed study of why we sketch (rather than just "doing it all in our heads"). They talk about the "iterative process of imagining, sketching, and evaluating the aesthetic quality of the sketch in perception" (p.180). They say that throughout this process the artist is continually monitoring the evolution of her product, so that "the creative process draws heavily on the same resources that are involved in the aesthetic apprehension of a completed work of art" (p. 180). This aesthetic apprehension requires us to analyse the emerging product. We can do this freely and easily in the case of perception, but it is much more difficult with inner imagery: "Analytic processing occurs much less frequently in imagery than in perception. The detection of novel components by an analytic transformation is very difficult in imagery" (p. 212). This is especially true in the case of abstract art, where the artist works through multiple copies or sketches as a way of developing a structure that has layers of meaning. It seems that we can analyze the product when it is out there in front of us, but we have much more difficulty when we try to analyze it in our minds.

If the foregoing is correct, we have an interesting inversion. We typically think that creative cognition takes place in our heads and that we sometimes externalize it into the world—even the Extended Mind Hypothesis can suggest that this is the case. It now seems that the opposite may be true: we first learned to problem-solve and be creative in the world, and *then* learned to do so in our heads. This was probably a result of natural selection. Survival and natural selection would have pressured us to develop inner, portable data structures so that we could plan and problem-solve in the safety of the cave—or at least a long way from the saber-toothed tiger (Dartnall, 2005).

Armed with this reperception, let us return to Letter Spirit's grid. Does this correspond to letters on pieces of paper in the world, or does it correspond to letters "in the mind's eye"? First, it really doesn't matter. What matters is that Letter Spirit as a whole solves the problem, so that the grid and its contents are part of the problem-solving process. But I do think it is significant that, when the chips were down and Letter Spirit had to be implemented, the Imaginer was abandoned. I think this was because the rest of the system made it redundant. When it came to modeling the creative process, all that was needed was a generative-evaluative loop held together by the contents of the grid. There was no need for an abstract Imaginer. After all, what could it have done that was not already done by the combined efforts of the other modules—by Letter Spirit as a whole?

Hofstadter and FARG's original idea was that the Imaginer would come up with ideas about new letter forms and give them to the Drafter for implementation. Hofstadter and FARG provide *pictures* of the sorts of new letters that the Imaginer might come up with, but say, "Despite the picture, one has to keep in mind that the pulling-apart and reattaching operations are actually just mental, as opposed to being splicing-operations on graphic shapes" (Hofstadter & FARG, 1995, p. 445). It seems to me that these pictures are redundant, because Letter Spirit can make do perfectly well with the letters it draws on the grid. It doesn't need what Hofstadter and FARG call "Platonic letters" (p. 445) lurking in the background. Put differently, the Imaginer's letters are not "abstract" at all. They are concrete designs that just happen not to be on the grid. Even if we were to include an Imaginer in the design process, it would hand its specifications to the Drafter, which would then engage in an iterative cycle with the Examiner and Adjudicator and shut the Imaginer out of the creative loop, leaving it with no work to do. I once said to a professional photographer that he must have a good visual imagination. He said, "I don't have any imagery at all. I just look for good pictures in the world." Like Letter Spirit, he did not need abstract pictures or specifications *in addition* to the pictures he captured with his camera.

Seen in this light, the Imaginer is a ghost in the machine—a ghost that is exorcised when we implement the mechanism, because it is redundant. Gilbert Ryle (1949) talks about "Descartes' Myth" in *The Concept of Mind*. Somebody wishes to see Oxford University and is shown the colleges, libraries, playing fields, museums, scientific departments, and administrative offices. Then the visitor says, "But where is the University? I haven't seen the University yet." He has seen the University, of course. His mistake is to think that the University is something over and above the things he has already seen. In the same way, Letter Spirit's imagination is not something over and above its components working together. Letter Spirit as a whole does the imagining, which is a complex process of drafting, examining, adjudicating, and repeating the process.

I suggest that we can generalize this result. When we create something, whether a poem or a painting or a strange new font, we do not need an Imaginer in our heads. We need skill and ability and an external work space (equivalent to Letter Spirit's grid) where we can access our output and evaluate it and change it in an iterative cycle. In the 1990s, there was a lot of interest in Annette Karmiloff-Smith's notion of Representational Redescription, which says that we are endogenously driven to redescribe our implicit, procedural knowledge as explicit, declarative knowledge that we can reflect upon and change (Karmiloff-Smith, 1992). Some researchers saw this as a way of studying creativity (Dartnall, 1994; Clark, 1994), because once we have made our cognition explicit, we can access it and change it. The research program did not develop, however, mainly because of the difficulty of modeling a mechanism that would enable us to redescribe implicit, procedural representations as explicit, declarative ones. It would be interesting to revisit the problem in an Extended Mind framework—in which our implicit, procedural knowledge is redescribed as explicit, declarative knowledge that is *out there in the world*, so that modules communicate with one another through the external representations they generate, evaluate, and change.

CONCLUSION

We started this chapter with the perception that creativity makes us characteristically and distinctively human and sets us apart as a species. The Extended Mind Hypothesis suggests that the relationship is not so direct. What makes us characteristically human is our ability to complement our onboard, pattern recognition abilities with manipulable technologies in the world—and it is this ability, in turn, that enables us to be creative. It enables us to be creative in three intimately related ways. First, it enables us to hold our products at arm's length, so that we can access, manipulate, and modify them in a generative-evaluative loop. Second, the emerging product scaffolds our cognition so that we can work with increasingly complex forms of creative thought. Last but not least, the product holds the creative process together and serves as a focus for multiple mental modules.

I have not directly addressed any traditional creativity questions in this chapter, but I will mention two of them now.

Our reperception of the creative process in an Extended Mind framework strongly suggests that creativity, as Thomas Alva Edison famously said, is one percent inspiration and ninety-nine percent perspiration. We cannot, however, dismiss inspirational, "divine spark" theories of creativity out of hand. What underlie these theories are accounts of creative genius coupled with the common experience that solutions to problems magically and mysteriously pop into our heads. It seems that Mozart composed easily and effortlessly, getting it right every time, without needing to engage in generative-evaluative cycles: the original scores seem to have been written without any mistakes or corrections at all. Kekulé had a flash of insight about the structure of the benzene molecule when he was gazing into a fire. We cannot ignore these accounts of inspirational creativity, yet treating creativity as a form of revelation would be a methodological dead end. If we are to understand the creative process, we must run with the assumption that there is an underlying mechanism that can be studied and understood.

I have suggested that creativity "starts on the outside" with cognitive technologies and can become internalized (in the way in which we internalize perception to get imagery and language to get thought). To get at the mechanism underlying inspiration and revelation, we need to say that the creative loop is internalized and operates at an unconscious level, until it presents its product to consciousness in what looks like a "flash of inspiration." The mysteriousness and sense of wonder that we experience is because we see the product in a moment, without witnessing the ongoing, underlying process that gives rise to it.

In my discussion with John Rehling (2002), Rehling says that he can run Letter Spirit in either of two modes. In the first mode, all of the Drafter's letters are graphically displayed, including the ones that will be rejected by the Examiner or Adjudicator. In the other mode, only the successful letters are displayed, at the end of a run. Rehling says that in this second case, "the program *looks* a lot smarter" (pp. 280–281). When we see the output all at once, without seeing any of the intermediary stages, it surprises us and looks like divine inspiration, but we are not so surprised when we see the slow accrual of output during consecutive loops. If Letter Spirit could be run in a totally transparent mode, so that we could see the mechanisms that give rise to the letters, we would not be surprised at all. Understanding the mechanism exorcises the mystery from the imaginative machine.[5]

Studying creativity in an Extended Mind framework similarly suggests that there is no special mechanism for creativity and that creative people are just better at doing what most of us do all the time, but do not do very well. This is related to the "ninety-nine percent perspiration" view of creativity, according to which the creative process is a painstaking cycle of generating, evaluating, and modifying our output. But I do not wish to overreach myself here: the Extended Mind Hypothesis gives us a framework for studying creativity and *leads us to suspect* that there is no special mechanism, but the final answer to this question depends on the empirical results.

Finally—educationalists exercise themselves about our dependence on computers (but make no mention of our more deep-seated dependence on pens, paper, and language itself). On the other side of the fence, an entire area of creativity research is devoted to the way in which computers can enhance human creativity.[6] Isaac Asimov once said that he was not worried about having too many computers. He was worried about having too few. If there is a moral to be taken home from this chapter, it is this: "Technology enables us to be creative. Let's go for it!"

NOTES

1. FARG is the Fluid Analogies Research Group at Indiana University, Bloomington.

2. See Sutton (2006) for a study and comparison of these arguments.

3. Strictly speaking, the Drafter drafts on the Workspace, which Rehling calls a "copy of the grid" (Rehling 2001, p.255).

4. GridFont is a partially connected feed forward, back-propagation connectionist system. Its input layer has thirty-two nodes: twenty-six *letter nodes* (one for each letter) and six *style nodes*. Its output layer has fifty-six nodes, one for each line in the grid. There is a hidden layer of eighty-eight nodes, divided into two sets of forty-four each. It is trained up on all the letters in five different font styles and on fourteen letters of a sixth style, called "Hunt Four." It begins with no knowledge about letters. After about 10,000 learning cycles, it can reliably draw all of the twenty-six letters on the grid, in any of the five font styles it has learned about, as well as the fourteen Hunt Four letters it has seen. It now has to produce styles for the twelve Hunt Four letters that it hasn't seen. It does this by combining what it knows about letters in general with what it knows about Hunt Four style.

5. It is probably significant that Mozart and Kekulé were seasoned campaigners with huge amounts of thought and experience behind them. Their genius lay partly in their ability to perform complex operations in their heads that they would have originally performed in the external world and that gradually migrated inwards. I know of no accounts of flashes of insight or strokes of genius occurring in unprepared or inexperienced minds.

6. See Dartnall (1994), Part V: Human Creativity Enhancement.

REFERENCES

Aglioti, S., DeSouza, J. F., & Goodale, M A. (1995). Size-contrast illusions deceive the eye but not the hand. *Current Biology, 5,* 679–85.

Anderson, R. E., & Helstrup, T. (1993). Visual discovery in mind and on paper. *Memory and Cognition, 21,* 283–293.

Brandimonte, M. A., Hitch, G. J., & Bishop, D. V. M. (1992). Influence of short-term memory codes on visual image processing: Evidence from image transformation tasks. *Journal of Experimental Psychology: Learning, Memory, and Cognition, 18,* 157–165.

Chambers, D., & Reisberg, D. (1995). Can mental images be ambiguous? *Journal of Experimental Psychology: Human Perception and Performance, 2* (3), 317–328.

Clark, A. (1994). Connectionism and cognitive flexibility. In Dartnall, T. H., ed., *Artificial Intelligence and creativity: An interdisciplinary approach*. Dordrecht, Netherlands: Kluwer.

Clark, A. (1997). *Being there: Putting brain, body and world together again*. Cambridge, MA: MIT Bradford. Review symposium, *Metascience* (7)1, 1998, 70–104.

Clark, A. (2003), *Natural-born cyborgs: Minds, technologies and the future of human intelligence*. Oxford: Oxford University Press.

Clark, A., & Chalmers, D. (1998). The extended mind. *Analysis, 58* (1), 7–19.

Clynes, M. & Kline, N. (1960). Cyborgs and space. *Astronautics*, September 1960. Reprinted in Gray, C., ed., (1995), *The cyborg handbook*. London: Routledge.

Dartnall, T. H. (1994). Creativity, thought and representational redescription. In Dartnall, T. H. ed., *Artificial Intelligence and creativity: An interdisciplinary approach*. Dordrecht, Netherlands: Kluwer.

Dartnall, T. H. (1998). Why (a kind of) AI can't be done. In Grigoris, A., & Slaney, J. eds., *Advanced topics in Artificial Intelligence*. Berlin: Springer. pp. 1–13.

Dartnall, T. H., ed. (2002). *Creativity, cognition, and knowledge: An interaction*. Westport, CT: Praeger.

Dartnall, T. H. (2004). We have always been … cyborgs. *Metascience*, vol. 13, no. 2, July, pp. 139–148. Essay Review of Clark, A., *Natural-born cyborgs: Minds, technologies, and the future of human intelligence* (Oxford: Oxford University Press, 2003).

Dartnall, T. H. (2005). Does the world leak into the mind? Active externalism, "internalism" and epistemology. *Cognitive Science*, vol. 29, no. 1, January/February, pp. 135–143.

Dennett, D. (1996). *Kinds of minds*. New York, NY: Basic Books.

Donald, M. (1991). *Origins of the modern mind*. Cambridge, MA: Harvard University Press.

Finke, R. A., & Slayton, K. (1988). Explorations of creative visual synthesis in mental imagery. *Memory and Cognition, 16*, 252–257.

Finke, R. A, Pinker, S., & Farah, M. (1989). Reinterpreting visual patterns in mental imagery. *Cognitive Science, 13*, 51–78.

Fodor, J. A. (1983). *The modularity of mind: An essay on faculty psychology*. Cambridge, MA: MIT/Bradford.

Gazzaniga, M. (1998). *The mind's past*. Berkeley: University of California Press.

Goodale, M.A., & Milner, A. D. (2004). *Sight unseen: An exploration of conscious and unconscious vision*. Oxford: Oxford University Press.

Grebert, I., Stork, D, Keesing, R, & Mims, S. (1992). Connectionist generalization for production: An example from GridFont. *Neural Networks*, vol. 5, pp. 699–710.

Hofstadter, D., & FARG (Fluid Analogies Research Group). (1995). *Fluid concepts and creative analogies: Computer models of the fundamental mechanisms of thought*. New York: Basic Books.

Hutchins, E. (1995). *Cognition in the wild*. Cambridge, MA: MIT Press.

Jaarsveld, S. & van Leeuwen, C. (2005). Sketches from a design process: Creative cognition inferred from intermediate products. *Cognitive Science, 29*, 79–101.

Karmiloff-Smith, A. (1992). *Beyond modularity: A developmental perspective on cognitive science*. Cambridge, MA: MIT Bradford.

Kosslyn, S. M. (1994). *Image and brain: the resolution of the imagery debate*. Cambridge, MA: MIT Press.

Kosslyn, S. M., Thompson, W. L., & Ganis, G. (2006). *The case for mental imagery.* Oxford: Oxford University Press.

Locke, J. (1964). *An essay concerning human understanding.* London: Collins. First published in 1690.

McCall Smith, A. (2004). *The Sunday Philosophy Club.* London: Little, Brown.

McGraw, G. (1995). *Letter Spirit (Part One): Emergent high-level perception of letters using fluid concepts.* Doctoral thesis. Dept of Computer Science and the Cognitive Science Program, Indiana University, Bloomington.

McGraw, G., & Hofstadter, D. (2002). Letter Spirit: Perception and creation of diverse alphabetical styles. In Dartnall, T. H., ed., *Creativity, cognition and knowledge: An interaction.* Westport, CT: Praeger

Milner, A. D., & Goodale, M. A. (1995). *The visual brain in action.* Oxford: Oxford University Press.

Pinker, S., & Finke, R. A. (1980). Emergent two-dimensional patterns in images rotated in depth. *Journal of Experimental Psychology: Human Perception and Performance, 6,* 244–264.

Rehling, J. (2001). *Letter Spirit (Part Two): Modeling creativity in a visual domain.* Doctoral thesis. Department of Computer Science and the Cognitive Science Program, Indiana University, Bloomington.

Rehling, J. (2002). Results in the Letter Spirit project. In Dartnall, T. H. ed., *Creativity, cognition and knowledge: An interaction.* Westport, CT: Praeger.

Rollins, M. (1999). Pictorial representation: When cognitive science meets aesthetics. *Philosophical Psychology, 12* (4), 387–413.

Ryle, G. (1949). *The concept of mind.* London: Hutchinson.

Sacks, O. (1989). *Seeing voices: A journey into the world of the deaf.* Berkeley: University of California Press.

Sutton, J. (2006). Exograms and interdisciplinarity: History, the extended mind, and the civilising process. In Menary, R. (ed.), *The extended mind.* Aldershot, England: Ashgate.

Van Leeuwen, C., Verstijnen, I., & Hekkert, P. (1999). Common unconscious dynamics underlie common conscious effects: A case study in the interactive nature of perception and creation. In Jordan, J. S., ed., *Modeling consciousness across the disciplines.* Lanhan, MD.: University Press of America. 179–218.

Vygotsky, L. S. (1986). *Thought and language* (translation of 1962 edition). Cambridge, MA: MIT Press.

Wittgenstein, L. (1963). *Philosophical investigations.* Oxford, England: Blackwell.

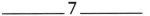

The Role of Effective Organizational Culture in Fostering Innovation and Entrepreneurship

ERIC G. FLAMHOLTZ and RANGAPRIYA KANNAN-NARASIMHAN

This chapter examines the role of organizational culture and climate in nurturing innovation and corporate entrepreneurship. We have two related objectives: first, to review the literature dealing with organizational culture and climate with respect to innovation and entrepreneurship, and second, to present a conceptual framework that is based upon the literature and is intended to help tie the insights of previous research together into a useful "lens" or tool for dealing with research and practical aspects of innovation and entrepreneurship in organizations.

The field of organization studies holds increasing evidence that organizational culture and climate are indispensable for nurturing innovation and entrepreneurship within existing organizations.[1]

We begin the chapter with a critical examination of the current state of the art of literature on organizational culture and climate with respect to innovation and entrepreneurship. Based on the literature review, we will develop an effective culture model for innovation and corporate entrepreneurship.

The next section of the chapter will identify critical organizational culture characteristics and discuss how organizations can encourage entrepreneurial behaviors among the workforce. We will also describe some innovative practices, "experiments," and success stories from real-world organizations regarding the role of corporate culture in promoting innovation and entrepreneurship. Examples from a variety of organizations (including 3M, Starbucks, Hewlett-Packard, GE, and Dow Corning) will be presented.

Finally, we will conclude the chapter by suggesting implications of this study for organizations and suggest directions for future research and new theory development.

REVIEW OF LITERATURE ON ORGANIZATIONAL CULTURE AND CLIMATE, INNOVATION, AND ENTREPRENEURSHIP

The field of organizational studies and corporate entrepreneurship contains numerous definitions for the four key concepts that will be used frequently in this chapter: organizational culture, climate, entrepreneurship, and innovation. However, the definitions used for each of these terms vary considerably between researchers. Moreover, these terms might also mean different things in varying contexts. In order to avoid ambiguity in the use of these concepts in this chapter, we will first define and clarify these terms.

Since the focus of this chapter is on studying entrepreneurship and innovation within existing organizations, these key concepts will be defined in the context of an existing organization (and not in the context of new ventures or start-ups).

Key Concepts: Definitions and Explanations

The first two constructs that will be defined and distinguished from one another are "culture" and "climate."

Organizational culture and climate. All organizations have cultures or sets of values that influence the way members behave in a variety of areas, including innovation.[2] Culture, whether the context is organizational or national, refers to patterns of fundamental assumptions rooted in values, and contextual artifacts that are shared by a group of people.[3] Culture is reflected in shared patterns of beliefs, values, and expectations that produce norms that powerfully shape behaviors exhibited, thought processes, and feelings held by groups or individuals.[4]

In contrast, climate is typically discussed in the context of organizations or groups. It is based on employees' perceptions of aspects of the work environment.[5] Climate is also defined as how employees in an organization understand and execute in their everyday work behaviors the guiding principles encapsulated in the organization's culture.[6] According to Schneider, climate reflects practices, policies, procedures, and rewards of various aspects of organizational life (e.g., climate for safety or climate for service).[7] Correspondingly, climate for innovation or entrepreneurship refers to the general feelings one has, at a given moment in time, about how the group or organization with which one is associated is supporting (through procedures, practices, policies, and rewards) entrepreneurial behaviors.

When focusing on the organizational context, in particular, it is often useful to think about the difference between climate and culture in terms of *what* happens in an organization (i.e., organizational climate) and *why* the "what" happens in an organization (i.e., organizational culture).[8] This distinction is very helpful when the organizational climate and culture are in alignment with one another. For example if risk takers in an organization are rewarded ("what" happens in an organization") and the organization believes in risk taking as a core cultural value ("why" risk takers get rewarded), then the organizational climate is in alignment with the organization's culture. However, in the real world, there may be a lack of alignment between the culture values that an organization believes in (organizational culture) and the cultural values that are encouraged by the organization, as perceived by the employees (organizational climate).

Daley and Vasu demonstrate this dichotomy by making a distinction between "professed culture" versus "effective culture" within organizations.[9] For example, an organization might profess that risk taking is a core culture value, but in reality the organization might be averse to risk taking. This is evident when risk takers in the organization are penalized while conservative risk-averse employees are rewarded by the organization. When this occurs, the internal allocation of rewards and punishments is in strong contrast with the organization's professed culture values; as a result, there is a disconnect between the organization's professed versus effective or actual culture. The employees of this type of organization will perceive the organization to be risk averse (organizational climate), whereas the stated organizational culture value is that of risk taking.

It is extremely important for organizations to create and maintain an effective organizational culture, or a culture where the organization's cultural values are in alignment with its climate. This is because effective cultures not only enable organizations to achieve their stated objectives but also influence organizational performance. For example, a previous study found that divisions of the company whose culture was perceived to be closer to the desired culture of the company by the employees had better performance (as measured by financial performance) than those divisions whose employees perceived a dichotomy between their division's climate and the organization's culture values.[10] Accordingly, effective organizational culture or effecting an organization's climate that is reflective of an organization's culture is one of the most critical tasks faced by top management.[11] Yet very few real-world organizations succeed in achieving this critical alignment between culture values and organizational climate.

Innovation and Corporate Entrepreneurship

The next two constructs that are important are "innovation" and "corporate entrepreneurship." We will first define each term and then discuss their relationship to one another.

Corporate entrepreneurship. There are a variety of different definitions of "entrepreneurship" and "corporate entrepreneurship," as examined below.

Entrepreneurship in the context of an existing organization or corporate entrepreneurship has been defined as the aborning of new businesses within existing business and the transformation of organizations through a renewal of
new ideas.[12] Corporate entrepreneurship is an organizational process for
transforming individual ideas into collective actions by managing uncertainties
in the process, and refers to innovation that is initiated and implemented by
employees within an organization.[13] Jones and Butler refer to internal corporate entrepreneurship as entrepreneurial behavior occurring within the context
of one firm.[14] Internal entrepreneurship has been defined as entrepreneurial
activities carried out in an organization in a "formalized" manner, or where
explicit organizational support and resources have been committed for
encouraging innovative corporate endeavors, such as new product developments or improvements or new processes and procedures.[15]

The commonality of all of these notions is that corporate entrepreneurship
refers to entrepreneurial activities that are carried out by the employees *within
a given organization*. These activities have the organization's explicit support—
top management commitment and the organization's resources are mobilized
to support these entrepreneurial activities.

Innovation within an organization or entrepreneurial innovation at the
organizational level refers to "willingness to introduce newness and novelty
through experimentation and creative processes aimed at developing new
products and services, including new processes."[16]

Existing research indicates that innovation has been constantly viewed as a
fundamental endeavor of an entrepreneurial organization and that innovation
is *the* common theme of corporate entrepreneurship.[17] Zahra reiterates this
view by stating that the hallmark of an entrepreneurial organization is its
capability to create and introduce new products in the market, especially
ahead of its competitors.[18]

It is important to note that innovation has traditionally been defined as
involving products and processes. However, in recent times there has been a
change in the way in which organizations are defining innovation. One of the
primary areas in which organizations are focusing their innovation efforts is
in the area of customer experience. For example, although the primary product for Starbucks Corporation is coffee beverages, innovations from this organization are not restricted to developing various versions of coffee beverages.
In fact, Starbucks' primary focus is on the way in which customers perceive
the coffee-based experience at their stores or cafés, not just the coffee itself.

Recent innovations by Starbucks such as providing wireless Internet access
to customers and Starbucks music bars to download music when customers
are in the coffee shop are all primarily targeted at providing this customer experience. This is not to say that Starbucks does not focus on product or process innovations; rather, the concept of innovation is simply broader. This
broader notion of innovation has not been adequately addressed by the existing literature on innovation.

Relationship between innovation and entrepreneurship. The relationship between innovation and entrepreneurship has been discussed thoroughly in entrepreneurship literature for many years.[19] The first scholar to introduce the concept of innovation with reference to entrepreneurship was Schumpeter, in 1934.[20] Schumpeter stated that the fundamental endeavor of an entrepreneurial organization was the creation of new products and process. Since then, numerous researchers have repeatedly stated that innovation is central to the concept of entrepreneurship.[21]

Although some scholars argue that there might be an overlap between innovation and enterpreneurship (e.g., Schumpeter), and some state that they might be synonymous (e.g., Carrier), both these concepts are mostly viewed in the literature as two distinct but complementary constructs.[22] For example, Russell and Russell found a strong correlation between an organizational culture that supports innovation and successful entrepreneurial strategies.[23] Covin and Slevin argued that an organization's entrepreneurial orientation was the summation of top management's proclivity to take business-related risks, in order to bring about change and innovation resulting in a competitive advantage for their firm to compete aggressively with other firms.[24] Zhao found that entrepreneurship and innovation are positively related to each other and are complementary in nature.[25]

Entrepreneurship needs innovation as its primarily tool, while innovation requires entrepreneurship in order to achieve commercial success.[26] In brief, innovation seems to be the key to corporate entrepreneurship, and the existence of corporate entrepreneurship or the entrepreneurial spirit within an organization is required for bringing innovative ideas to fruition. More specifically, it appears that innovation is a *critical* component of entrepreneurship, but not a synonym for it.

THE ROLE OF ORGANIZATIONAL CULTURE IN FOSTERING INNOVATION AND ENTREPRENEURSHIP

Organizational culture plays a critical role in fostering innovation and entrepreneurship in organizations. In this section, we examine some studies that have addressed the relationship between organizational culture, innovation, and corporate entrepreneurship.

Organizational Culture and Innovation

Lemon and Sahota note that organizational culture is a primary determinant of innovation.[27] An organizational culture of innovation provides an organization the necessary ingredients to innovate.[28] It is therefore necessary to understand the relationship between innovation and organizational culture in order to nurture innovation. Lemon and Sahota do not make a distinction between innovation and a culture of innovation, and state that innovation by itself is inseparable from a culture of innovation.[29]

A culture of innovation is, however, not limited to a culture that proliferates new products or processes or services. In an organizational context, an innovation culture or innovation subculture is receptive to and encourages new ideas, change, and risk, and promotes autonomy among employees.[30] Highly innovation-supportive cultures are linked to new product development, which is an objective index of an organization's innovative capability by encouraging teamwork, risk taking, and creativity that are important for new product development.[31] Brannen, in a case study of Japanese organization, found that organizational culture as a very critical factor for fostering innovations within organizations.[32] In brief, the research literature provides substantial support for the notion that building an innovative culture is a critical step for nurturing innovation in organizations. In contrast, the organizational culture factors that serve as "killers" of innovation within an organization include reinforcers such as short-term thinking, risk aversion, and top-down decision making.[33]

Additionally, it is important to note that organizational culture is important not to just foster innovation for its own sake, but also for the organizations to take advantage of the competitive advantage that results for organizations due to their innovative capability. For example, the "Resource Based View" (RBV) of culture views organizational culture as a source of strategic advantage because it promotes learning, risk taking, and innovation, and these competencies can in turn be used by organizations to maintain sustainable competitive advantage.[34]

Organizational culture and corporate entrepreneurship. Organizational culture is also a key driver of corporate entrepreneurial growth. An organizational culture that promotes growth and encourages employees to exploit new market opportunities is seen as a key factor for driving entrepreneurial growth within an organization.[35] As Hope and Hendry, in their article "Corporate cultural change" state, the injection of entrepreneurial behavior in organizations requires the organizational redesign where personal influence, negotiation, and culture replace traditional hierarchy.[36]

Herbig, Golden, and Dunphy found that organizational culture is a primary determinant of both entrepreneurship and innovation in organizations.[37] Zhao found that organizational culture in addition to management style is a critical factor in developing innovative and entrepreneurial behavior in organizations.[38]

This section has examined the relationship between organizational culture, innovation, and corporate entrepreneurship. Later in the chapter, we will identify specific elements of an organization's culture and climate, which are conducive to innovation and entrepreneurship.

Effective Organizational Cultures and Reinforcers

When commenting on organizations that are effective in fostering innovation state, Roberts and Hirsch state that "[t]he most effective organizations at fostering creativity and innovation deeply implant what their company stands for, where it is going, and how it does business in the hearts and minds of its employees. These are organizations with remarkably strong cultures and belief systems that keep people from going too far astray" (p.175).[39] This statement clearly elucidates the distinction between organizational culture and climate in the context of innovation and entrepreneurship. It also comments on the alignment between organizational culture and climate or the effective organizational culture. Specifically, the "deeply implants what their company stands for" refers to the organizational culture for creativity and innovation "in the hearts and minds of its employees" and indicates how the organization's employees perceive the culture of the organization or the organizational climate.

The next question that arises is: how is this alignment achieved? The concept of organizational reinforcers is useful in answering this question, because organizational reinforcers help to create an effective organizational culture, as explained below.

Organizational reinforcers. Organizational reinforcers are defined as elements of an organization that are instrumental in aligning the culture of an organization with the climate of the organization.* These reinforcers help in aligning an organization's culture to its climate, thereby creating an effective organizational culture as well as maintaining it.

The concept and usefulness of organizational reinforcers can be further explained in the context of the cultural value of risk taking. Risk taking is an important culture value for nurturing innovation and corporate entrepreneurship.[40] For the organization to have an effective culture of risk taking, the employees must perceive that the organization encourages them to take risks. If the employees at large do not perceive a climate for risk taking, then the organization does not have an effective culture for risk taking.

One of the ways in which an organization can promote an effective culture for risk taking is by "recognizing" (reinforcing) employees when they take risks, irrespective of the outcome of such risk-taking behaviors. For example, at Johnson & Johnson back in the 1960s, the CEO failed with the first major product that was launched for the company. However, instead of being condemned for failure, the CEO received a congratulatory note from the company chairman for taking that risk.[41] This example demonstrates how the culture value of risk taking is "reinforced" through the use of organizational reinforcers (in this case the congratulatory note), irrespective of the final outcome. These reinforcers, as well as subsequent "organizational culture stories" on how the organization responded in this particular instance, enables employees to perceive that the organization believes in risk taking.

The model of effective culture presented in the next section will explain the relationships between organizational culture, climate elements, and reinforcers.

---

*From a managerial standpoint, a "reinforcer" might be thought of as a practical tool to reinforce one or more cultural values.

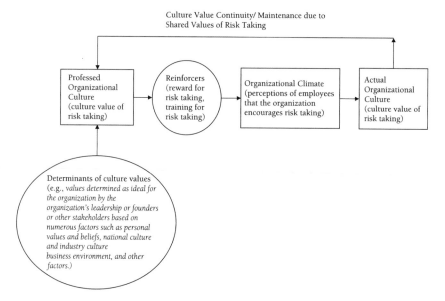

FIGURE 7.1   A Model for Effective Organizational Culture

We propose that for organizations to be effective in nurturing innovation and entrepreneurship, both the organizational culture and the climate for innovation and entrepreneurship should be in alignment. This means that the effective culture of organizations should contain elements that nurture innovation and corporate entrepreneurship.

A MODEL FOR ORGANIZATIONAL CULTURE, CLIMATE, AND REINFORCERS

Based upon the previous discussion, this section presents a model for organizational culture, climate, and reinforcers.* This model is shown schematically in Figures 7.1–7.3 and explained below. The schematics in Figures 7.1–7.3 show the hypothesized relationship among these variables, as well as a model of effective and ineffective organizational cultures.

Organizational Culture, Climate, Reinforcers and Effective Cultures

Figure 7.1 shows the differences between organizational culture, climate, organizational reinforcers, and effective culture illustrated by the example (discussed above) of an organization that wishes to nurture an effective culture for

---

*The above model is based partly on the social learning theory by Bandura,[42] which states that learning occurs within a social context and that the environment influences behavior modeling. This model is, however, not all-inclusive and merits an entire paper to its discussion. The purpose of providing the above model in this chapter is to help readers conceptualize the differences between these concepts.

risk taking. Possible organizational reinforcers for achieving an effective culture for risk taking might be training programs that encourage, educate, and train employees on the benefits of risk taking and effective risk-taking techniques (e.g., how to gauge risks versus benefits). Another reinforcer is organizational reward systems (organizational reinforcers) that reward risk takers.

The expected result of this process is that the employees will realize the value of risk taking (reinforcing risk taking as a shared value), and perceive that risk takers are being rewarded (organizational climate). This in turn is expected to help employees internalize the value of risk taking, take risks, and, in turn, convert risk taking into a shared value in the organization, and not a directive from the top management.

Organizational Culture, Climate, Reinforcers, and Ineffective Cultures

On the contrary, if an organization has a value for risk taking but reinforces risk-averse behaviors by rewarding employees who do not take risks, then the organizational climate for risk taking will cease to exist and shared values on risk taking will not be achieved.[43] The expected net result of this process is an irreconcilable dichotomy where the professed culture for the organization will be risk taking and the effective organizational culture is for risk aversion.

Figure 7.2 shows a model wherein the actual culture for risk aversion is further perpetuated by organizational reinforcers that encourage risk aversion. Specifically, the professed culture will be for risk-taking behavior, and the

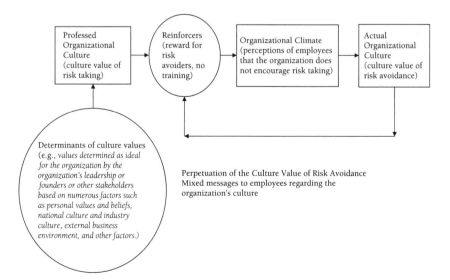

FIGURE 7.2   A Model of Ineffective Organizational Culture

actual culture will be for risk-averse behavior. The organization's professed culture and actual culture will be different, thereby creating confusion among the workforce regarding the organizational values.

Effective and Ineffective Organizational Cultures

Figure 7.3 shows effective and ineffective organizational cultures as a continuum. The left-hand side shows perfect alignment between professed and actual cultures, that is, effective organizational cultures. The right-hand side of the continuum shows ineffective cultures where there is a complete dichotomy between professed and actual cultures. In the real world, most organizations fall in the middle, where the organizational cultures are moderately effective.

The ultimate aim for most organizations is to be on the extreme left-hand side, wherein there are no differences between the actual and professed cultures of organizations. Organizational reinforcers assist organizations in moving toward the left-hand side of the continuum

Limitations of organizational reinforcers. Although reinforcers serve as a powerful means for communicating the organizational values to the employees, having effective reinforcers alone does not guarantee that an organization will have an effective culture for entrepreneurship. Certain other factors in the organization's environment, such as organizational politics, might negate the impact of reinforcers even if the latter are in alignment with the organization's culture. For example, if organizational rewards are given a few employees who might be perceived as management's "favorite employees," then the effectiveness of the rewards as a reinforcer for a given culture value will be attenuated. Similarly, other factors such as supervisor-subordinate relationships, leadership styles, the effectiveness of the organizational communication

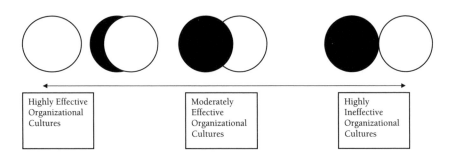

White Circle Denotes Actual Culture, Black Circle Denotes Professed Culture.

FIGURE 7.3 Effective and Ineffective Organizational Cultures

mechanisms, etc., might also influence the effectiveness of these reinforcers. The above model does not account for the influence of all these variables on effective organizational culture. However, it is outside the scope of this chapter to discuss these relationships in detail.

Effective Culture Elements in Organizations for Innovation and Entrepreneurship

In the previous section, we presented a model of organizational culture, climate, and reinforcers. In this section, we will identify the specific organizational culture values to identify recurring organizational culture elements that are known to foster innovation and entrepreneurship within organizations.

Numerours researchers in the field have identified various organizational factors that are conducive to innovation and entrepreneurship. Some of the recurring organizational culture values for creating innovation and corporate entrepreneurship include:

- autonomy with special emphasis on employee empowerment[44]
- risk taking, including a high tolerance for failure[45]
- proactiveness[46]
- competitive aggressiveness[47]
- cultural emphasis on achievement[48]
- an open learning culture that encourages constructive dissent[49]
- creativity (with reduced emphasis or lack of emphasis on consensus)[50]
- emphasis on teamwork values[51]

The reinforcers that enable the conveying of these cultural values to employees include:

- Managerial support for and top management involvement in entrepreneurship and innovation activities[52]
- Reward systems, with explicit goal setting, feedback, and rewards based on results[53]
- Explicit resource commitment (e.g., time, monetary resources) for innovation and entrepreneurship[54]
- Decentralized decision making structures with minimal formalization and bureaucracy[55]
- Participative leadership styles that offer maximum autonomy to employees, which in turn leads to employee empowerment[56]
- Challenging work assignments and team structures for task assignments whenever possible[57]

Table 7.1 summarizes the detail results of the literature review.

In Figure 7.4, a model of an Effective Culture for Innovation and Entrepreneurship is presented. Figure 7.4 shows the relationships between culture values

TABLE 7.1. Fostering an Effective Culture for Innovation and Entrepreneurship

Authors	For fostering......	Effective Organizational Culture Factors	Organizational Reinforcers	Other Organizational Factors
Ahmed, P. K.[58]	Innovation	▪ Autonomy ▪ Equal emphasis on technical abilities and team sharing and cooperation	▪ Balanced autonomy ▪ Personalized recognition ▪ Integrated socio-technical system	Existence of slack resources over a period of time.
Chandler, Keller, and Lyon[59]	Innovation		▪ Supervisory support ▪ Reward systems ▪ Less formalization	Fewer resources
Claver, Llopis, Garcia, & Molina[60]	Innovation	Worker empowerment		
Damanpour[61]	Innovation		▪ Managerial support ▪ Decentralized ▪ Decision making	
De Brentani and Kleinschmidt[62]	Innovation (measured by new product development)		▪ Resource commitment ▪ Top management involvement	
Dimitratos & Plakoyiannki[63]	International corporate entrepreneurship	(International) ▪ Learning orientation ▪ Innovation propensity		

- Risk taking
- Networking orientation
- International motivation

Gibbs[64]

Entrepreneurship (Entrepreneurial-learning organization)

- Creating or reinforcing strong individual ownership of activities
- Reinforcing freedom/control to make things happen
- Maximizing control for wide individual task structure responsibility
- Creating responsibility to see things over time
- Appraising individual/organizational excellence through stakeholder eye
- Maximizing potential for staff to develop own networks
- Linking rewards to meeting stakeholder needs (particularly customers)

(continued)

TABLE 7.1 (*CONTINUED*)

Authors	For fostering......	Effective Organizational Culture Factors	Organizational Reinforcers	Other Organizational Factors
			■ Tolerating ambiguity, managerial overlap, and mistake making	
			■ Encouraging individual strategic thinking without formal plan constraints	
			■ Emphasize the importance of formal networks through know-who and strategic networking	
			■ Building ways of learning by doing into the job and learning particularly from stakeholders	
			■ Maximizing potential for holistic management	
			■ Worker empowerment in decision making	
Gudmundsen, Tower, & Hartman[65]	Innovation	■ Worker Empowerment		
Hall, Melin, & Nordqvist[66]	Entrepreneurship	■ High Order Learning—explicit and open culture		

Author	Topic		
Hornsby, Montagno, & Kuratko[67]	Corporate entrepreneurship		▪ Management support ▪ Autonomy/work discretion ▪ Rewards/reinforcement ▪ Time availability ▪ Organizational boundaries.
Hornsby, Naffziger, Kuratko, & Montagno[68]	Corporate entrepreneurship	▪ Risk taking and tolerance for failure.	▪ Reward systems (based on goals, feedback, emphasis on individual responsibility, and rewards based on results) ▪ Management support ▪ Resources for entrepreneurship
Jaskyte & Dressler[69]	Organizational innovativeness	▪ Culture of dissent ▪ Aggressiveness ▪ Low stability	
Kanter[70]	Innovation	▪ Creativity	▪ Provide broad, non-routine challenging assignments to employees

(continued)

TABLE 7.1 (*CONTINUED*)

Authors	For fostering……	Effective Organizational Culture Factors	Organizational Reinforcers	Other Organizational Factors
Kozlowski & Hultz[71]	Innovation	■ Achievement ■ Innovative change ■ Achievement orientation	■ Recognition of individual excellence ■ Management policy wherein job assignments provide challenge, stretch skills, and utilize state-of-the-art technical knowledge	
Kuratko, Hornsby, Naffziger, & Montagno[72]	Entrepreneurship		■ Explicit goals ■ Feedback ■ Positive reinforcement ■ Emphasis on individual responsibility ■ Rewards based on results	
Lumpkin & Dess[73]	Entrepreneurship	Entrepreneurial orientation consisting of ■ Autonomy ■ Innovativeness ■ Risk taking ■ Proactiveness ■ Competitive aggressiveness		

Author	Theme			
Ogbonna & Harris[74]	Innovation		■ Participative leadership ■ Less bureaucracy	
Saleh & Wang[75]	Innovation and entrepreneurship	■ Calculated risk taking ■ Group and collective orientation	■ Management commitment to entrepreneurial activities and innovation ■ Integration and intermingling of talents in teams and task forces ■ Reward systems	
Stopford & Baden-Fuller[76]	Corporate Entrepreneurship	■ Team orientation ■ Aspiration beyond current resources ■ Proactiveness		Learning capability Capability to resolve dilemmas.
Wilson, Ramamurthy, & Nystorm[77]	Innovation	■ Encourages risk taking		
Zahra, Hayton, & Salvato[78]	Entrepreneurship	None defined	■ High strategic control ■ Low financial control	Individualism (nation's culture values) External orientation of firms

Culture Value Continuity/ Maintenance due to
Shared Values for Innovation and Entrepreneurship

| Professed Organizational Culture Values for Innovation & Entrepreneurship for *autonomy (with special emphasis on employee empowerment), risk taking (including high tolerance for failure), proactiveness, competitive aggressiveness, cultural emphasis on achievement, an open learning culture that encourages constructive dissent and creativity, and an emphasis on teamwork values.* | Reinforcers *(managerial support for and top management involvement in entrepreneurship and innovation activities, reward s that encourage entrepreneurial and innovative behaviors, explicit resource commitment time, monetary resources) for innovation and entrepreneurship, decentralized decision-making structures with minimal formalization and bureaucracy and participative leadership styles that offer maximum autonomy to employees (which in turn leads to employee empowerment), challenging work assignments and team structures* | Organizational Climate for *autonomy (with special emphasis on employee empowerment), risk taking (including tolerance for failure), proactiveness, competitive aggressiveness, cultural emphasis on achievement, an open learning culture that encourages constructive dissent and creativity, and an emphasis on teamwork values.* | Actual Organizational Culture for Innovation & Entrepreneurship for *autonomy (with special emphasis on employee empowerment), risk taking (including tolerance for failure), proactiveness, competitive aggressiveness, cultural emphasis on achievement, an open learning culture that encourages constructive dissent and creativity (and does not emphasize consensus), and an emphasis on teamwork values.* |

FIGURE 7.4 A Model for Effective Organizational Culture for Innovation and Entrepreneurship

and reinforcers and how these elements relate to one another in the proposed model.

Although the culture values and reinforcers identified through this literature review is exhaustive, it is not all-inclusive. Only the most important and recurring elements from various research studies have been included in Table 7.1 and in Figure 7.4.

Creating and maintaining an effective culture for corporate entrepreneurship and innovation is an organizational change process. As with any other organizational change process, this is also an extremely challenging task. However, one of the steps to ensure the successful implementation of the cultural change is to enact all the reinforcers simultaneously in order to communicate the underlying cultural values. This means that all the reinforcers that are necessary for fostering innovation and entrepreneurship should be enacted together, and not in a phased manner. Enacting all reinforcers at once will ensure that the culture values underlying innovation and corporate entrepreneurship are clearly communicated by the reinforcers. Enacting some reinforcers and not others might lead to confusion in the minds of the employees and undermine the process.

The proposed model is intended to help managers of organizations in visualizing how to create and maintain a culture for innovation and entrepreneurship.

Effective organizational culture at different stages of organizational growth and growing pains. Once a culture for innovation and entrepreneurship has been established, the next challenge is to nurture this culture through the various organizational growth stages. This is because as organizations grow they are expected to experience a variety of "growing pains."[79] The growing pains are symptoms of organizational distress. They are hypothesized to result from the lack of fit between the organization's infrastructure and its stage of growth.[80] The nature of growing pains is such that as a result, organizations experiencing them might not be in a position to maintain the organizational environment for entrepreneurship or nurturing the corporate entrepreneurial spirit. Growing pains are known to inhibit corporate entrepreneurship.[81] Managers of organizations have to constantly work on establishing and maintaining an effective culture for innovation and entrepreneurship.

Effective organizational culture and entrepreneurial behaviors. An effective culture of innovation and entrepreneurship wherein the employees perceive an organizational climate for entrepreneurship and innovation is expected to bring about the following entrepreneurial behaviors that are commonly associated with entrepreneurship among employees.[82]

- Opportunity seeking and grasping
- Taking initiative to make things happen
- Solving problems creatively
- Managing autonomously
- Taking responsibility and ownership of things
- Seeing things through
- Networking effectively to manage interdependence
- Putting things together creatively
- Using judgment to take calculated risks

Role of human resources in nurturing an effective organizational culture for innovation and entrepreneurship. For encouraging such behaviors among the workforce, managers of organizations might find it useful to hire employees with entrepreneurial skills and attitudes such as project management skills, high locus of control, etc.[83] Some of the other traits that are usually associated with innovators are that they are creative, have broad interests, are highly motivated, are resourceful, and, most importantly, solve problems.

Human resource managers for organizations must find people with the right kind of skills and train them on the essential competencies required for being entrepreneurial. As Gibbs notes, the essential competencies can be "pulled" by the environment.[84] Therefore, culture can nurture entrepreneurial tendencies of employees as well as drive the organization to recruit individuals who "fit" into the organization's entrepreneurial culture, thereby leading to maintenance of the shared values of the organization for innovation and entrepreneurship. Moreover, because one of the core values of entrepreneurial organizations is a learning orientation, the values of the organization might change over a period of time due to the learning process. Accordingly, entrepreneurial organizations must select employees who not only match with the current culture but who also are capable of adapting themselves to the future organizational culture.[85] In brief, we expect that hiring the employees with entrepreneurial attitudes and skills, and creating and sustaining an effective culture of innovation, will lead to an organization's success in creating and nurturing innovation and entrepreneurship among its ranks.

CASE EXAMPLES

The next section of this chapter examines a few case studies of actual organizations that have successfully fostered innovation and entrepreneurship through their organizational culture. We will discuss some organizations that are widely known to be successful in fostering an effective culture for innovation and entrepreneurship, including 3M, Hewlett-Packard, Starbucks, General Electric, and the Dow Corning Company.

Minnesota Mining and Manufacturing

Minnesota Mining & Manufacturing Co. (3M) is known for its successful history of innovation. The company has over 50,000 products, ranging from Scotch tapes and Post-it notes to machines that assist in heart surgeries.[86] The organization's Web site boldly states "The Spirit of Innovation: That is 3M." This organization, also referred to as the "hotbed" of innovation, has one aphorism that sums up the innovation and entrepreneurial culture of the company: "it is better to seek forgiveness than to ask for permission." That is, it is better to take risks and learn from failures than to be afraid to failure and not try at all.[87]

3M promotes a culture of innovation by providing employees the freedom to pursue their innovative ideas and encouraging employees to take the initiative to start programs in their laboratories in a collegial, informal environment. It reinforces these culture values through the 15 percent rule. Employees at 3M are provided the freedom to spend 15 percent of their time exploring new ideas and projects, and most products from 3M are a product of the 15 percent of time given to the employees. Moreover, although this organization has an R&D focus, innovation is not the responsibility of just R&D but is spread across other functions (such as marketing, sales, and manufacturing) in order to take advantage of the skill sets from these departments.[88] The other reinforcers that create a climate for innovation are setting stretch goals for innovators, rewarding and recognizing them publicly, and providing seed capital to innovators for developing innovative ideas further.[89]

The text box summarizes the reinforcers for innovation at 3M that are instrumental in fostering a climate for innovation and entrepreneurship, and for bringing about an effective corporate culture for innovation and entrepreneurship.

REINFORCERS FOR CREATING A CORPORATE CULTURE OF INNOVATION AND ENTREPRENEURSHIP[90]

Reinforcers of Innovation for Corporate Entrepreneurship

The 15 Percent Rule: Employees of 3M can spend 15 percent of their workweek working on projects of their choice that are beneficial to the organization. They are often not expected to inform their manager or justify the project.

Seed Capital: Employees who wish to develop their innovative ideas can request their business units for seed capital to develop their ideas further. In case their ideas are not accepted by their own business units, they can approach other business units for help. If those efforts also fail, employees can request a Corporate Genesis Grant for independent R&D awards.

Dual Career Path: Employees are given the opportunity for a career in management or technology with equal advancement opportunities so that they do not lose out by being on one of the tracks as opposed to the other.

Rewards and Recognition: Employees at 3M are rewarded through twelve global-based and four U.S.-based programs when they make significant contributions to the company. These include:

Carlton Society Awards—to honor employees for outstanding scientific achievements, contributions to new products or technologies and for high standards of achievement, dedication and integrity.

Circle of Technical Excellence and Innovation Awards—to recognize employees who have made exceptional contributions to 3M's technical capabilities.

Pyramid of Excellence Awards—to recognize administrative employees for their exceptional achievements.

Quality Achievement Awards—to reward employees for individual and team outstanding quality efforts.

Thus, the organizational culture of 3M encourages risk taking, initiative, and proactiveness as its core values for innovation. These values are reinforced through the 15 percent rule, the rewards, recognition, and performance management systems, and resource availability (seed capital) for innovators.

Hewlett-Packard

Hewlett-Packard is another company known for its success in innovation. Hewlett Packard, or HP, is one of the heroic stories of innovation that have set the tone for entrepreneurship in the entire Silicon Valley.[91] Even today, the focus of HP's culture is to encourage creativity and entrepreneurship.[92]

HP began its roots in a one-car garage in 1938 and has grown to more than $80 billion in revenues (as of 2004). It is an enterprise with business units in over 170 countries.

Cultural values espoused by this organization include innovation, risk taking, proactivenesss, care for customers, openness in culture allowing sharing of ideas at every level, and a culture of trust, loyalty, and respect. This is achieved through employee empowerment, personal ownership, and responsibility among employees for customer issues. The ultimate aim for HP is to "deliver meaningful invention to meet global needs."

HP reinforces these values by using reinforcers such as performance management systems based on management by objectives principles, using decentralization in decision making and divisionalization, practices such as "management by walking around," and teamwork. The text box elaborates on these reinforcers in detail.

BEST PRACTICES AT HEWLETT-PACKARD[93]

Best Practices

— **Establish performance measures, set high goals, and hold people accountable.**

✓ Management by objectives, where managers are rated and ranked annually for their contributions and participate in detailed annual and group business reviews.

✓ New products must have the promise of at least six times the engineering investment.

— **Break complex business into logical strategic business units that people can understand and manage. Push decision making down as far as possible.**

✓ Use decentralization and divisionalization for different product lines.

✓ Improve processes to reduce mistakes, balancing the need for written practices and personal involvement and initiative at each step.

✓ Providing feedback by communicating how individual divisions, groups and departments perform relative to objectives.

— **Share best practices and knowledge.**

✓ Understand customer needs and respond proactively.

✓ Learn and adopt best practices from other companies such as General Electric and General Radio.

— **Change before you need to change.**

✓ Using product innovation and continuously seeking new ideas that make a "contribution" force continuous change.

✓ Promoting innovation heritage by adopting the "invention" tagline to encourage more innovation.

Although these practices widely acclaimed as the "HP Way" have been instrumental in fostering growth, the "HP Way" has been called into question in recent years. The core issue is whether HP's cultural values are at odds with the industry values. For example, the emphasis at HP regarding consensus in decision making serves as an obstacle to the core computer industry value of speed.[94] HP is now adapting to these challenges by developing the "HP Way 2.0." This notion of the "HP Way 2.0," which borrows the notion of different "editions" or "releases" from software practice, is a symbolic message to reflect the need for change in the company's culture in response to the increased competitiveness of today's computing industry, while simultaneously giving recognition to the "old HP Way." For example, such hallowed HP practices as profit sharing and rewards for past performance remain a part of the culture.[95] The new HP emphasizes an "agile organization," with "think imaginatively, act decisively, and deliver quickly" as its core cultural values. The critical drivers that reinforce these values are keeping a track of time-to-market, time-to-customer, time-to-revenue, and time-to-profit. Thus, HP's culture values for innovation and entrepreneurship are reinforced by its best practices and the HP way in order to make innovation and entrepreneurship not just its nominal culture but also its effective culture.

Starbucks Coffee Company

Another organization that encourages innovation and corporate entrepreneurship is Starbucks, a corporation that went from a small start to a world-class brand and an icon of American culture. Starbucks redefined coffee and its role in society. As a result, Starbucks as well as its major competitors in the beverage industry now offer variety in coffee that was not available previously.[96]

Starting as a "local coffee roaster" in Seattle, Starbucks now has over 20,000 permutations and combinations of beverages, 8,000-plus stores, and 90,000 employees. Influenced by the romance of the coffee bars in Italy, the conception of Starbucks as a "third place experience," or a place beyond work and home, is an innovative concept in itself. This helped the company define who it was and who its customers were.

The leadership of this organization encourages and acknowledges creative ideas from all levels of the organization and turns them into feasible innovations that contribute to this organization's bottom line. For example, the Frappuccino product, which is a multi-hundred-million-dollar business for Starbucks, was invented by a store manager, who was duly recognized for this innovation through the president's award.[97] Similarly, the food group of this organization was responsible for the invention of the Chantico—a version of drinking chocolate. These ideas for innovation were not from the top but from the employees from all levels who were duly recognized for their contributions to the company.

Starbucks' efforts at innovation are not restricted to its products alone but also extend to its processes. For example, the introduction of debit cards to allow people to pay in advance for their coffee was an innovation in the food industry.[98] Other process innovations include the gift card, providing wireless Internet access to its customers, and its experimentation with the Starbucks Express—a system where customers can order online and pick up without waiting in long lines.

The emphasis from the company is on the constant reinvention of the reorganization through its partners (including employees, who are considered internal partners). Starbucks also believes that its external innovations—that is, product—and its process innovations stem from its internal innovations or its innovative human resource policies. For example, Starbucks was the first organization in the United States to give comprehensive health benefits and stock options to every employee, including part-timers. The organization has the lowest attrition level among national retailers. The top management of the organization believes that these internal innovations are threaded into the organization's external innovations.

The organization has had it share of failures due to its constant tryst with experimentation and risk taking. Two of its most notable failures are "Joe" (the magazine) and an Internet lifestyle portal in which the organization invested during the dotcom boom. Starbucks also experienced failure in its first joint venture with PepsiCo, when the two companies introduced a coffee-flavored soft drink named "Mazagran." This was later followed by the successful venture with PepsiCo involving the introduction of bottled Frappuccino.

The organization's culture of acknowledging failure and learning from past mistakes enables it to recover from its failures and move forward. For example, the CEO of Starbucks takes complete responsibility for the failure of the magazine and has kept a rack of issues in the office as a memento. This rack acts as a reinforcer and is intended to convey the message that one must have the courage to fail and to keep pushing by not embracing the status quo.[99]

Another experiment by Starbucks is the Hear Music media bars, where customers can download music from the Starbucks music library. This has been questioned by a few critics regarding its potential for success.[100] Starbucks, however, maintains that the organization's passion and commitment to this new venture will enable it to be an innovator in the industry.[101]

As seen above, there is evidence that Starbucks believes in the core cultural values of innovation, encourages risk taking, embraces failures, takes care of its internal partners, who in turn take care of the organization, and constantly looks for ways to reinvent itself to provide customers with the best possible coffee experience.

General Electric (GE)

GE is another example of a business that emphasizes innovation and the creation of the corporate entrepreneur. General Electric's focus has shifted from its past paradigm of creating and maintaining a culture and mantra of "six sigma"—where the emphasis was on quality, productivity, and bottom line results—to a new culture of innovation and creativity.[102] The result that GE wants to achieve is "imagination at work."

Although this is a radical transformation for this leviathan organization, the message from the top leadership of the organization is clear: it is acceptable to take risks.[103] The leadership of this organization believes that GE's former emphasis on the bottom line (under the leadership of the legendary Jack Welsh), where the bottom 10 percent of the performers were weeded out, made it difficult to take risks. In the new culture, it is a badge of honor to risk failure.

The new cultural values are reinforced through various initiatives. For example, GE plans to invest about $5 billion in eighty "Imagination Breakthrough" projects. "Imagination Breakthrough" projects are expected to extend the current boundaries of GE and include projects that range from creating microjet engines to overhauling the brand image of 3,000 consumer-finance locations.[104] The compensation structure has been revised to link bonuses to new ideas, customer satisfaction, and sales growth, compared to the previous emphasis on bottom line results. In stark contrast to the previous culture values of promoting from within, outsiders are brought in at all levels, including senior levels, in order to create industry experts as opposed to the traditional notion of professional managers.[105]

Dow Corning

Another example of how organizations nurture innovation and entrepreneurship is the Dow Corning Company. The company believes that empowering a select group of employees by placing them in leadership roles, encouraging them to take risks, and supporting them with the necessary resources helped bring a cultural transformation of innovation within the company.[106] Employees at all levels are encouraged to innovate and take risks. This organization also believes that having employees interact in teams with different groups provides a fresh lens for innovative ideas. Ideas that might have been turned down by the organization as "unworkable" previously are sometime revised and made feasible. Finally, the organization believes that culture cannot be changed by setting out to change it; rather, Dow believes that changing the working environment and rewarding people for giving their best is the best way to bring about a culture of transformation.[107]

Other Examples

Corporate America abounds with examples of multitude of organizations with varying profiles from different industries, such as Sony, Toyota, IBM, and eBay, which have been extremely successful with their efforts in innovation and nurturing corporate entrepreneurship. The common theme that runs through all their success stories is that all of them nurture a *culture of innovation and corporate entrepreneurship.*

All these organizations have been successful in establishing and maintaining an effective culture of innovation and risk-taking. These organizations believe in the core cultural values of risk taking, autonomy, proactiveness, competitive aggressiveness, emphasizing achievement, promoting an open learning culture that encourages constructive dissent and creativity, and emphasizing teamwork values. These core values are encouraged through organizational reinforcers such as dedicated support from management, including through times of adversity and failures, top management involvement in entrepreneurship and innovation activities, reward systems, explicit resource commitment for innovation and entrepreneurship, decentralized decision-making structures with minimal formalization and bureaucracy, and participative leadership styles that offer maximum autonomy to employees, challenging work assignments, and team structures.

CONCLUSION

This chapter has examined the role of organizational culture and climate in nurturing innovation and corporate entrepreneurship. We had two related objectives: first, to review the literature dealing with organizational culture and climate with respect to innovation and entrepreneurship, and second, to present a conceptual framework, based upon the literature and intended to help tie the insights of previous research together into a useful "lens" or tool for dealing with research and practical aspects of innovation and entrepreneurship in organizations.

We believe that our review of the literature (both research and practical examples) clearly shows that organizational culture plays a very critical role in ensuring the success of innovation and corporate entrepreneurship efforts in the organization.

Next Steps for Future Research

The next question is: where do we go from here? Case examples from industry indicate convergence between theory and practice. Specifically, organizational culture elements that have been identified by theory as critical for fostering innovation and corporate entrepreneurship are perceived as critical elements by organizations as well. If most organizations are aware of the critical role of organizational culture in nurturing innovation and corporate entrepreneurship, then why have some organizations been more successful than others in creating and maintaining an effective culture?

The answer to this question may be found in the concept of organizational reinforcers. Simply stated, organizations that have effective cultures also have strong reinforcers. This means that organizations that have succeeded in creating and maintaining an effective culture have strong reinforcers that convey the underlying cultural values of innovation and entrepreneurship. Therefore, the task facing managers of organizations is not only to espouse the core cultural values of innovation and corporate entrepreneurship but also to convey them effectively to employees. In many organizations, this might mean the crucial difference between succeeding and failing in their efforts to nurture an environment for successful innovation and corporate entrepreneurship efforts.

In terms of future theory development, although innovation and corporate entrepreneurship in organizations have been studied extensively, one area in which research is lacking is the relationship between organizational growth and corporate entrepreneurship.

Previous research in the area of innovation management and entrepreneurship has identified elements in an organization's culture that contribute to an organization's successful innovation and entrepreneurial outcomes. However, most studies have focused on two types of organizations, new ventures and large established organizations. In reality, organizations typically go through seven different growth stages before they reach organizational maturity. One framework for defining stages of growth was developed by Flamholtz and Randle.[108] Under this view, there are seven stages, including new venture stage, expansion stage, professionalization stage, consolidation stage, diversification stage, integration stage, and decline-revitalization stage. In each of these seven stages, the organization's focus, its critical development areas, structure, and size are different. Accordingly, organizational culture factors that are effective in fostering innovation and entrepreneurship in one stage of an organization's growth may not be appropriate for another stage. Future research should identify the elements in an organization's culture that encourage innovation and entrepreneurship during each of these different growth stages. It is important for researchers to determine how cultural values and reinforcers might differ in each of these growth stages and the resulting implications for management.

In conclusion, creating and maintaining an organizational culture for innovation an entrepreneurship is an art. Like music, the framework we have provided serves only as the basic notes or blueprint for nurturing an effective culture of innovation. But blueprints and notes can go only so far. Just as the rhapsody of the music results from the way the musician plays the notes, the creation of an effective culture depends on the effectiveness with which organizational managers implement the blueprint. What we have tried to do here is to ensure that they have the right "notes" to begin the development of the song.

NOTES

1. Donald Kuratko et al., "Implement Entrepreneurial Thinking in Organizations," *Advanced Management Journal* 58, no. 1 (1993): 28–39. Other researchers who have emphasized the importance of organizational culture and climate in nurturing

entrepreneurship include Rule & Irwin, 1988; Sathe, 1988; 2003; and Sykes & Block, 1989. See also Eric Rule and Donald Irwin, "Fostering Intrapreneurship: The New Competitive Edge" *The Journal of Business Strategy* 9, no. 3 (1988): 44–47; Vijay Sathe, "From Surface to Deep Corporate Entrepreneurship," *Human Resource Management* 27, no. 4 (1988): 389–411.

2. Eric Flamholtz, "Corporate Culture and the Bottom Line," *European Management Journal* 19, no. 3 (1993): 268–275.

3. Edgar Schein, "Organizational Culture," *American Psychologist* 45 (1990): 109–119.

4. Geert Hofstede, *Culture's Consequences: Comparing Values, Behaviors, Institutions, and Organizations across Nations* (Thousand Oaks, CA: Sage, 2001). Also see Howard Schwartz and Stanley Davis, "Matching Corporate Culture to Business Strategy," *Organizational Dynamics* 10, no. 1 (1981): 30–48.

5. Charles Glisson and Lawrence James, "The Cross-Level Effects of Culture and Climate in Human Service Teams," *Journal of Organizational Behavior* 23, no. 6 (2002): 1–28.

6. Dennis Daley and Michael Vasu, "Fostering Organizational Trust in North Carolina," *Administration & Society* 30, 1 (1998): 62–84.

7. Benjamin Schneider, "Organizational Climates: An Essay," *Personnel Psychology* 28, no. 4 (1975): 447–479.

8. Benjamin Schneider, Sarah Gunnarson, and Kathryn Niles-Jolly. "Creating the Climate and Culture of Success," *Organizational Dynamics* Vol. 23, no. 1 (1994): 17–29.

9. Daley and Vasu, op. cit.

10. Eric Flamholtz, "Corporate Culture and the Bottom Line," *European Management Journal* 19, no. 3 (2001): 268–275.

11. Daley and Vasu, op. cit.

12. William Guth and Ari Ginsberg. "Guest Editors' Introduction: Corporate Entrepreneurship," *Strategic Management Journal* 11 (1990): 5–15.

13. Hong Chung and Patrick Gibbons, "Corporate Entrepreneurship: The Roles of Ideology and Social Capital," *Group and Organization Management* 22, (1997): 10–30. Also see Camille Carrier, "Intrapreneurship in Small Businesses: An Exploratory Study," *Entrepreneurship Theory and Practice* 21 (1996): 5–20.

14. Gareth Jones and John Butler, "Managing Internal Corporate Entrepreneurship: An Agency Theory Perspective," *Journal of Management* 18, no. 4 (1992): 733–749.

15. Hans Schollhammer, "Internal Corporate Entrepreneurship" in *Encyclopedia of Entrepreneurship*, eds. C. A. Kent, D. L. Sexton, and K. H. Vesper, 209–229 (Englewood Cliffs, NJ: Prentice Hall).

16. Gregory Dess and G. T. Lumpkin, "The Role of Entrepreneurial Orientation in Stimulating Effective Corporate Entrepreneurship," *Academy of Management Executive* 19, no. 1 (2005): 147–156.

17. Danny Miller and Peter Friesen," Innovation in Conservative and Entrepreneurial Firms: Two Models of Strategic Momentum," *Strategic Management Journal* 3, no. 1 (1982): 1–25. Also see Joseph H. Schumpeter, *The Theory of Economic Development* (Cambridge, MA: Harvard University Press, 1934) and Jeffrey Covin and Morgan Miles, "Corporate Entrepreneurship and the Pursuit of Competitive Advantage," *Entrepreneurship Theory and Practice* 23, no. 3 (1999): 47–63.

18. Shaker Zahra, "New Product Innovation in Established Companies: Associations with Industry and Strategy Variables," *Entrepreneurship Theory and Practice* 18, no. 2 (1993): 47–69.

19. Fang Zhao, "Exploring the Synergy between Entrepreneurship and Innovation," *Entrepreneurship and Innovation* 11, no. 5 (2005): 25–41.

20. Schumpeter, op. cit.

21. See Foard Jones and Michael Morris, "HR Practices That Promote Entrepreneurship," *HR Magazine* 40, no. 5 (1995): 86–94. Also see Patrick Kreiser et al., "Assessing the Psychometric Properties of the Entrepreneurial Orientation Scale: A Multi-Country Analysis," *Entrepreneurship Theory and Practice* 26, no. 4 (2002): 71–94; Michael Morris et al., "Individualism and the Modern Corporation: Implications for Innovation and Entrepreneurship," *Journal of Management* 19, no. 3 (1993): 595–612; Michael Morris et al., "Fostering Corporate Entrepreneurship: Cross-cultural Comparisons of the Importance of Individualism versus Collectivism," *Journal of International Business Studies* 25, no. 1 (1994): 65–89.

22. See Schumpeter, op. cit. and Carrier, op. cit.

23. Robert Russell and Craig Russell, "An Examination of the Effects of Organizational Norms, Organizational Structure and Environmental Uncertainty on Entrepreneurial Strategy," *Journal of Management* 18, no. 4 (1992): 639–656.

24. Jeffrey Covin and Dennis Slevin, "A Conceptual Model of Entrepreneurship as Firm Behavior," *Entrepreneurship Theory and Practice* 16, no. 1 (1991): 7–25.

25. Zhao, op. cit.

26. Ibid.

27. Lemon and Sahota, "Organizational Culture as a Knowledge Repository for Increased Innovative Capacity," *Technovation* vol. 24, no. 6 (2004): 483–498.

28. Pervaiz Ahmed, "Culture and Climate for Innovation," *European Journal of Innovation Management* 1, no. 1 (1998): 30–43.

29. Lemon and Sahota, op. cit.

30. Charles O'Reilly, "Corporations, Culture and Commitment: Motivation and Social Control in Organizations," *California Management Review* 31, no. 4 (1989): 9–25.

31. Avan Jassawalla and Hemant Sashittal, "Cultures That Support Product-Innovation Process," *Academy of Management Executive* 16, 3 (2002): 42–54.

32. Mary Yoko Brannen, "Culture as the Critical Factor in Implementing Innovation," *Business Horizons* 34, no. 6 (1991): 59–67.

33. John Bessant, Julian Birkinshaw, and Rick Delbridge, "Innovation as Unusual," *Business Strategy Review* 15, no. 3 (2004): 32–35.

34. Shaker Zahra, James Hayton, and Carlo Salvato, "Entrepreneurship in Family versus Non-Family Firms: A Resource-Based Analysis of the Effect of Organizational Culture," *Entrepreneurship: Theory & Practice* 28, no. 4 (2004): 363–381.

35. John Eggers, "Developing Entrepreneurial Growth," *Ivey Business Journal* 63, no. 4 (1999): 76–81.

36. Hope and Hendry, "Corporate Cultural Change—Is It Relevant for the Organizations of the 1990s?" *Human Resource Management Journal* 5, no. 4 (1995): 61–73.

37. Paul Herbig, James Golden, and Steven Dunphy, "The Relationship of Structure to Entrepreneurial and Innovation Success," *Marketing Intelligence and Planning* 12, no. 9 (1994): 37–49.

38. Zhao, op. cit.

39. Russ Roberts and Paul Hirsch, "Evolution and Revolution in the Twenty-First Century: Rules for Organizations and Managing Human Resources," *Human Resource Management* 44, no. 2 (2005): 171–176.

40. See Kreiser, Maurino, and Weaver, op. cit. and Morris, Avila, and Allen op. cit.

41. James Higgins, "Innovate or Evaporate," *Futurist* 29, no. 5 (1995): 42–48.

42. Albert Bandura, *Social Learning Theory* (New York: General Learning Press, 1977).

43. Steven Kerr, "On the Folly of Rewarding A, While Hoping for B," *Academy of Management Journal* 18, no. 4 (1975), 769–783.

44. Ahmed, op. cit. Also see G. T. Lumpkin and Gregory Dess, "Clarifying the Entrepreneurial Orientation Construct and Linking it to Performance," *Academy of Management Journal* 21, no. 1 (1996): 135–172.

45. See Pavlov Dimitratos and E. Plakoyiannaki, "Theoretical Foundations of an International Entrepreneurial Culture," *Journal of International Entrepreneurship* 1, 2 (2003): 187–215. Also see Jeffrey Hornsby et al., "An Interactive Model of the Corporate Entrepreneurship Process," *Entrepreneurship Theory and Practice* 17, (1992): 29–37.

46. Lumpkin and Dess, op. cit. Also see John Stopfod and Charles Baden-Fuller, "Creating Corporate Entrepreneurship," *Strategic Management Journal* 15, no. 7 (1994): 521–536.

47. Kristina Jaskyte and William Dressier, "Organizational Culture and Innovation in Nonprofit Human Service Organizations," *Administration in Social Work* 29, no. 2 (2005): 23–42. Also see Lumpkin and Dess, op. cit.

48. Steve Kozlowski and Brian Hultz, "An Exploration of Climates for Technical Updating and Performance," *Personnel Psychology* 40 (1987): 539–563.

49. Annika Hall, Leif Melin, and Mattias Nordqvist, "Entrepreneurship as Radical Change in the Family Business: Exploring the Role of Cultural Patterns," *Family Business Review* 14, no. 3 (2001): 193–208. Also see Dimitratos and Plakoyiannki, op. cit.

50. Rosabeth Kanter, *The Change Masters* (New York: Simon and Schuster, 1983).

51. See Ahmed, op. cit. and John Stopford and Charles Baden-Fuller, "Creating Corporate Entrepreneurship," *Strategic Management Journal* 15, no. 7 (1994): 521–536.

52. See Gaylon Chandler, Chalon Keller, and Douglas Lyon, "Unraveling the Determinants and Consequences of an Innovation-Supportive Organizational Culture," *Entrepreneurship Theory and Practice* 25 (2000): 59–76. Also see Ulrike de Brentani and Elko Kleinschmidt, "Corporate Culture and Commitment: Impact on Performance of International New Product Development Programs," *Journal of Product Innovation Management* 21, (2004): 309–333.

53. See Jeffrey Hornsby, Donald Kuratko, and Ray Montagno "Perception of Internal Factors for Corporate Entrepreneurship: A Comparison of Canadian and U.S. Managers," *Entrepreneurship, Theory & Practice* 24 (1999): 9–24. Also see Kuratko et al., op. cit.

54. Hornsby et al., op.cit., De Brentani and Kleinschmidt, op. cit.

55. Fariborz Damanpour, "Organizational Innovations: A Meta-Analysis of Effect of Determinants and Moderators," *Academy of Management Journal* 34, no. 3 (1991): 555–590.

56. Emmanuel Ogbonna and Lloyd Harris, "Leadership Style, Organizational Culture and Performance: Empirical Evidence from UK Companies," *International Journal of Human Resource Management* 11, no. 4 (2000): 766–788.

57. See Kanter, op. cit., Kozlowski and Hultz, op. cit.

58. Ahmed, op. cit.

59. Chandler, Keller, and Lyon, op. cit.

60. Enrique Claver et al., "Organizational Culture for Innovation and New Techno-logical Behavior," *Journal of High Technology Management Research* 9, no. 1 (1998): 55–68.

61. Damanpour, op. cit.

62. Brentani and Kleinschmidt, op. cit.

63. Dimitratos and Plakoyiannaki, op. cit.

64. Alan Gibbs, "Corporate Restructuring and Entrepreneurship: What Can Large Organizations Learn from Small?" *Enterprise & Innovation Management Studies* 1, no. 1 (2000): 19–35.

65. Donald Gudmundsen, Burk Tower, and Alan Hartman, "Innovation in Small Businesses: Culture and Ownership Structure do Matter," *Journal of Developmental Entrepreneurship* 8, no. 1 (2003): 1–17.

66. Hall, Melin, and Nordqvist, op. cit.

67. Jefferey Hornsby, Ray Montagno and Donald Kuratko, "A Study of the Factors in Corporate Entrepreneurship," *Proceedings of the United States Association for Small Business and Entrepreneurship* (1990): 239–243.

68. Hornsby et al., op. cit.

69. Jaskyte and Dressier, op. cit.

70. Kanter, op. cit.

71. Kozlowski and Hultz, op. cit.

72. Kuratko et al., op. cit.

73. Lumpkin and Dess, op. cit.

74. Ogbonna and Harris, op. cit.

75. Shoukry Saleh and Clement Wang, "The Management of Innovation: Strategy, Structure, and Organizational Climate," *IEEE Transactions on Engineering Management* 40, no. 1 (1993): 14–21.

76. Stopford and Baden-Fuller, op. cit.

77. Alla Wilson, K. Ramamurthy, and Paul Nystorm, "A Multi-Attribute Measure for Innovation Adoption: The Context of Imaging Technology," *IEEE Transcactions on Engineering Management* 46, no. 3 (1999): 311–321.

78. Zahra, Hayton, and Salvato, op. cit.

79. Eric Flamholtz and Yvonne Randle, *Growing Pains: Transitioning from an Entre-preneurship to a Professionally Managed Firm* (San Francisco: Jossey-Bass, 2000). Also see Eric Flamholtz and Wei Hua, "Strategic Organizational Development, Growing Pains and Corporate Financial Performance: An Empirical Test," *European Management Journal* 20, no. 1 (2002): 527–536.

80. Eric Flamholtz, "Managing Organizational Transitions, Implications for Corpo-rate and Human Resource Management," *European Management Journal* 13, no. 1 (1995): 39–51. Also see Flamholtz and Randle, op. cit.

81. Kannan-Narasimhan and Flamholtz, *Growing Pains: A Barrier to Successful Cor-porate Entrepreneurship* (2005), unpublished manuscript.

82. Gibbs 2000, op. cit. Also see Kelly Shaver and Linda Scott, "Person, Process, Choice: The Psychology of New Venture Creation," *Entrepreneurship: Theory & Practice* 16, no. 2 (1991): 23–45.

83. Gibbs, op. cit.

84. Ibid.

85. Robert Heneman, Judith Tansky, and Michael Camp, "Human Resource Management Practices in Small and Medium-Sized Enterprises: Unanswered Questions and Future Research Perspectives," *Entrepreneurship: Theory & Practice* 25, no. 1 (2000): 11–26.

86. Geofferey Nicholson, "Keeping Innovation Alive," *Research Technology Management* 41, no. 3 (1998): 34–40.

87. Ibid.

88. Tim Stevens, "3M reinvents its innovation process," *Research Technology Management* 47, no. 2 (2004): 3–5.

89. Nicholson, op. cit.

90. Tim Studt, "3M—Where Innovation Rules," *R&D Magazine*, 45, no. 4 (2003): 20–24.

91. David Plotnikoff and Michelle Quinn, "Breakup Raises Questions on H-P's Culture," *Denver Post,* March 1999.

92. Murray Hiebert, "Treasure Island," *Far Eastern Economic Review,* December 1997, 60–61.

93. Anonymous, "Best Practices at Hewlett-Packard," *Dealerscope*, March 2000.

94. Plotnikoff and Quinn, op. cit.

95. Ibid.

96. Vijay Vishwanath and David Harding, "The Starbucks Effect," *Harvard Business Review* 78, no. 2 (2000): 17–18.

97. Howard Schultz and Dori Jones Yang, *Pour Your Heart into It: How Starbucks Built a Company One Cup at a Time* (New York: Hyperion, 1997).

98. David Kirkpatrick and Gary Hamel, "Innovation Do's and Don'ts," *Fortune,* September 2004, 239–240.

99. Abrahm Lustgarten, "A Hot, Steaming Cup of Customer Awareness," *Fortune,* November 2004, 192.

100. Stanley Holmes, "Strong Lattes, Sour Notes," *Business Week,* June 2005, 58–60.

101. Howard Schultz, Letter to the editor, "Starbucks' Founder on Innovation in the Music Biz," *Business Week*, July 2005, 16.

102. Diane Brady, "Bringing Innovation to the Home of Six Sigma," *Business Week*, August 2005, 68.

103. Ibid.

104. Diane Brady, "The Immelt Revolution," *Business Week*, March 2005, 64–73.

105. Ibid.

106. Interviews with Scott Fuson (chief marketing officer, Dow Corning Corp.) and Scott Antony, "Instilling a Culture of Innovation," *Chemical Week*, September 2004, 16.

107. Ibid.

108. Flamholtz and Randle, op. cit.

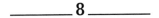

8

The Social Context of Innovation

DEAN KEITH SIMONTON

P sychologists study individuals. As a result, they tend to see creativity and innovation as individual-level phenomena. In particular, psychologists examine creativity in terms of individual thought processes, personality characteristics, and developmental conditions. Yet other social scientists—especially sociologists and cultural anthropologists—have advanced a rather contrary view. Rather than psychological reductionism, they have argued for a sociological reductionism: the position that innovations constitute exclusively societal-level phenomena. It is the sociocultural system that creates, the individual innovators serving as mere agents, or perhaps even as mere epiphenomena. Interestingly, this conflict between individualistic and sociocultural conceptions of creativity has become intimately intertwined with other debates in the behavioral sciences, such as the comparative influence of nature and nurture on individual development or the relative impact of ethnocentrism and cultural relativism in cross-cultural comparisons. Accordingly, to understand fully the social context of innovation requires that I first provide a brief history of the controversy.

HISTORY

In his classic *Hereditary Genius*, Francis Galton (1869) attempted to show that exceptional creativity was born, not made. That is, creative genius depended on the biological inheritance of a very high level of "natural ability." To make

155

his case, he presented extensive family pedigrees of eminent creators in a diversity of domains—science, literature, music, and the arts. Because most great innovators tended to come from familial lineages with other major innovators, creative genius had to be genetically inherited. In fact, those who had the highest levels of natural ability would attain distinction no matter what their environmental circumstances. Galton's position was not only highly individualistic, but also based his psychological reductionism on an extreme biological determinism.

This twofold extremism was immediately attacked. Ironically, the first criticism came from Alphonse de Candolle, the distinguished French botanist who came from a lineage of famed scientists included in Galton's (1869) treatise. Candolle thought that Galton ignored the critical part played by the environment in the emergence of major innovators. To make his case, Candolle (1873) compiled an impressive quantity of information that demonstrated the impact of several environmental factors on scientific creativity. Galton picked up the challenge at once (Hilts, 1975). He sent out questionnaires to the top scientists in the United Kingdom, requesting that they indicate the familial and educational circumstances that might have supported their creative development. The resulting survey responses were published just one year after Candolle's work, in *English Men of Science: Their Nature and Nurture* (Galton, 1874). As the book's subtitle reveals, Galton conceded that exceptional creativity was not merely the manifestation of superior genetic endowment (nature). The environment (nurture) also had a major role.

Even so, it is now evident that Galton (1874) actually overlooked Candolle's (1873) principal argument. Galton still viewed the environment in highly individualistic terms: family background and educational experiences distinguish individual lives. In contrast, Candolle focused on external influences of a higher order of magnitude, namely those that operate at the level of entire nations or civilizations. Part of the reason for Galton's oversight might be ascribed to his methods: because he surveyed only British scientists, his respondents came from more or less the same sociocultural context. Yet perhaps a more crucial reason was that Galton had a strong theoretical bias. Although he was willing to allow biographical circumstances some explanatory power with respect to individual differences in creativity within a given society, Galton maintained quite emphatically that contrasts between cultures must be the consequence of biological differences. Societies that feature the most innovation are those that are peopled by the superior races (Galton, 1869). Indeed, an entire chapter in *Hereditary Genius* treats "The Comparative Worth of Different Races," and this is followed by another chapter that relates these supposed racial differences to the comparative "natural ability" of whole nations. Although Galton recognized that civilizations could rise and decline, he attributed these fluctuations to eugenic and dysgenic practices that either improved or undermined the genetic basis of genius. For example, the creativity of Greek civilization was undermined when the Greeks intermarried with "barbarians" after the conquests of Alexander the Great. The days of the Athenian Golden Age could never return once Greece had become infused with "inferior" genes.

In this chapter, I will show that the coming and going of innovators in various times and places can be better ascribed to fluctuations in the social context of creativity. Certain cultural, political, and economic circumstances establish a milieu that affects either the development of creative potential or the adulthood manifestation of that acquired potential. To make this case, I review the research that has emerged since Candolle's (1873) pioneering effort. This research tends to adopt two rather distinct yet mutually reinforcing methodologies. Both methods focus on aggregates of creators rather than on individual creators, but examine those aggregates in contrasting ways. On the one hand, cross-sectional research concentrates on variation in the level of innovative behavior in whole groups, such as cultures, societies, nations, or civilizations. This approach aspires to detect the Ortgeist, or "Spirit of the Place," that best supports the development and manifestation of creativity. On the other hand, time-series investigations look at the level of creativity exhibited by a single social entity as it fluctuates over history. The unit of analysis in this case is a period of some specified length, such as a year, decade, generation, or century. The aim of this analysis is to discern the Zeitgeist, or "Spirit of the Times," that is most conductive to creativity at the aggregate level.

THE ORTGEIST: CROSS-SECTIONAL RESEARCH

Investigators have often tried to assess how creativity varies across culturally distinct groups (e.g., Lehman, 1947; Murray, 2003). However, such comparisons often suffer from a severe methodological bias. This bias is ethnocentrism. Galton's (1869) own work provides a prime example. Because he started by assuming that extreme natural ability must necessarily take the form of outright genius, Galton felt free to draw inferences about superior versus inferior races according to the distribution of eminent innovators among diverse populations. Those nations who claimed the most geniuses were the ones with the greatest natural ability. Galton utterly ignored how his conclusions were vulnerable to ethnocentric biases in the reference books from which he drew his data. The fact that he identified more Europeans than Africans or Asians reveals more about the ethnocentrism of nineteenth-century British biographical dictionaries and encyclopedias than about the differential creativity of the various societies that have populated this globe.

To avoid this problem, below I concentrate on those investigations that have implemented special measures to control ethnocentrism. These studies are of two kinds, depending on the nature of the unit of analysis. On the one hand are cross-cultural comparisons, and on the other are cross-national comparisons.

Innovative Cultures

Perhaps the question that features the most instances of the pernicious operation of ethnocentrism is the matter of whether cultures can be ranked along an evolutionary scale. Is it possible to distinguish "savage" or "primitive" societies from those that are "civilized" or "advanced"? Almost invariably, when a given investigator engages in such evaluations, his or her own cultures somehow manage to emerge at the top of the hierarchy. The key reason for this self-flattering outcome is that the investigators' judgments are largely based on values and priorities that are characteristics of their own culture. Fortunately, means are available that are far more objective. These means rely on criteria that are more culture free. Carneiro's (1970) research on evolutionary scales provides an excellent example. Carneiro began with the assumption that cultural evolution entails a transformation from simplicity to complexity. As societies evolved from simple to complex, changes would take place that could be objectively and quantitatively assessed. These changes would entail the accumulation of specific political, military, economic, social, legal, technological, religious, and artistic traits. That is, rather than emerge randomly, some traits would appear earlier in cultural evolution, whereas other traits would appear later, the former traits defining the prerequisites for the appearance of the latter traits. Carneiro then assessed 100 world cultures on 354 traits regarding subsistence, settlements, architecture, economics, social organization and stratification, political organization, law and judicial process, warfare, religion, ceramics and art, tools, utensils, and textiles, metalworking, watercraft and navigation, and special knowledge and practices. A standard statistical analysis indicated that an evolutionary scale could be devised based on 90 percent of these traits. Because the traits were objectively assessed and because a computer program did the rankings, the opportunity for the intrusion of ethnocentric bias was substantially reduced. This reduction is revealed in the results. The societies in the top ten in complexity came from every continent except Antarctica and represented every major racial group.

Although it was not his main goal, Carneiro's (1970) evolutionary scaling has implications for the social context of innovation. These implications arise from the fact that many of the scaled traits are clearly related to creativity. For instance, the following traits form a temporal sequence within the evolutionary scale: craft specialization, craft production for exchange, full-time craft specialists, monumental stone architecture, full-time painters or sculptors, and full-time architects or engineers. This ordering clearly reflects the transformation of artisans to professional artists. Furthermore, the traits associated with creativity display a connection with other cultural traits. This means that a society must reach a specific degree of economic and political complexity before the appearance of full-time painters, sculptors, architects, or engineers. This cultural complexity can be said to embody the minimal conditions for the emergence of a highly innovative society.

Probably the single most critical condition associated with this emergence is population growth (Simonton, 1999b). As a population grows in size, its members can differentiate into more specialized occupations (Carneiro, 1970; see also Peregrine, Ember, & Ember, 2004). Part-time artisans can thereby evolve into full-time artists. Indeed, some forms of creativity do not even emerge until the appearance of urban centers with substantial population concentrations. An obvious example is monumental architecture, such as the pyramids of Egypt and the temples of Mexico.

Innovative Nations

The first scientific inquiry into cross-national differences in creativity was conducted by Candolle (1873) as part of his attack on Galton's (1869) biological reductionism. Candolle focused on scientific innovation. His goal was twofold. First, he wanted to measure the per-capita output of creative scientists for various nations. Second, he hoped to identify variables that correlated with these cross-national contrasts. By concentrating on science, Candolle was able to lessen the intrusion of ethnocentric bias. After all, innovations in science are evaluated by less culture-bound standards than innovations in other areas, such as literature. In more modern times, the comparative universality of science is witnessed in the fact that the Nobel prizes awarded in physics, chemistry, and physiology or medicine tend to be much less controversial than those awarded in literature. Yet Candolle went a step farther toward reducing ethnocentrism in his cross-national assessments. He would only count a scientist as sufficiently eminent to be included in the per-capita counts if he or she had achieved an international reputation. The latter was discerned by the scientist earning honors in a nation different from his or her own. Thus, a British scientist who was only a Fellow of the Royal Society could not be credited in the measure of the scientific creativity of Great Britain. By this criterion, Galton did not count, but his cousin Charles Darwin did. By implementing this method, Switzerland was the clear winner among the nations of the world. And as testimony to Candolle's success in removing ethnocentric bias, his own nation, France, came out somewhat worse: the per-capita representation of scientific innovators in Switzerland surpassed than in France by a ratio of about five to one.

Having thus scored nations on scientific productivity, Candolle's (1873) next task was to identify the national characteristics that were associated with output. These characteristics would define the Ortgeist most favorable to creative science. These attributes can be enumerated as follows:

1. The nation has a substantial class of individuals who do not have to devote most of their effort to earning a livelihood through manual labor. This class provides a pool of persons who have the leisure and the desire to engage in intellectual and cultural enterprises.

2. The nation has a strong cultural tradition that channels this available pool toward scientific inquiry. In particular, the society places a high value on knowledge about the real world rather than placing the emphasis on the otherworld (see also Sorokin, 1937–1941). These pro-science values, moreover, should take the form of institutions that are supportive of scientific research. These institutions include libraries, observatories, laboratories, and special collections.

3. The nation should encourage or at least tolerate basic freedoms, such as free speech, freedom of association, and freedom to travel freely within and outside the nation's borders. Such freedoms should enable scientific debate and exchange without fear of persecution or punishment. Closely related to these conditions is a nation's openness to the influx of foreigners who have a high degree of educational and intellectual resources, regardless of their religion or ethnicity.

4. The nation's system of education is free of political and religious control, or at least nearly so. If there is any political or religious influence, it is benign and supportive so that the institutions can encourage open intellectual inquiry in both teachers and students.

5. The nation tends to be a comparatively small independent state, or else a country that involves the integration of several autonomous states. In other words, the nation is not subordinate to an overbearing empire state. At the same time, the nation is usually situated very near other highly civilized nations, rather than being isolated. In addition, the nation is most likely to be located where the climate is moderate rather than extremely hot or cold.

6. Certain languages tend to be most conductive to scientific innovation, namely French, German, and English. Because these three languages can serve as the lingua franca of scientific exchange, those nations will have a decided advantage if (a) they have one of these three as their native tongue or (b) they encourage their citizens to acquire one of these three as a second language. Curiously, Candolle (1873) concluded from an analysis of worldwide demographic trends that eventually English would become the dominant language of science. This conclusion provides additional support for ability to avoid ethnocentric biases.

Unfortunately, despite all of his efforts, Candolle's (1873) work suffers from one fundamental limitation: it does not contain the statistical analyses that would place his conclusions on firmer ground. Ironically, the correlation coefficient needed for such analyses was developed about two decades later by Francis Galton and his student Karl Pearson. Nevertheless, most of his inferences have been replicated in more rigorous investigations (Szabo, 1985). Furthermore, several of the variables that Candolle linked with scientific activity have been shown to correlate with creative activity in general, no matter what the specific domain. This extension became evident in the research using time-series analysis.

THE ZEITGEIST: TIME-SERIES RESEARCH

During World War II, Galton's (1869) individualistic genetic determinism was again challenged, this time by Alfred Kroeber (1944), the distinguished cultural anthropologist. Kroeber argued that creativity was not the product of innate genius but rather the manifestation of the sociocultural system. He made his case in the classic book *Configurations of Culture Growth*. Here, Kroeber used a methodological approach that bore a superficial resemblance to Galton's (1869). In particular, Kroeber collected extensive lists of major innovators in diverse domains of creativity, including science, philosophy, literature, art, and music. Unlike Galton, however, Kroeber took great pains to ensure that his compilations were truly cross-cultural in scope. His lists included the great creators of Islamic, Hindu, Chinese, and Japanese civilizations, as well as those of European civilization. In addition, unlike Galton, who listed his names in alphabetical order to emphasize family pedigrees, Kroeber arranged his names in chronological order to stress historical placement. As a result, he was able to show that eminent innovators tend to cluster into cultural configurations (see also Sorokin & Merton, 1935; Spiller, 1929). In some periods, a civilization is blessed with a Golden Age of creativity, other periods witness a Silver Age, and still others are characterized as a Dark Age in which creative activity comes to a halt. Significantly, the rate by which these creative clusters rise and decline is far too fast to be explained by changes to the gene pool. The Periclean Age of Athens or the Elizabethan Age of England lasted but a few generations, yet it would require hundreds of years of massive eugenic interventions to have any comparable effect.

Kroeber's (1944) work is complementary to Candolle's (1873). Where the latter showed that creators were not equally distributed across space, the former showed that they were not equally distributed across time. Nonetheless, Kroeber did not collect any data about the sociocultural conditions that were responsible for the Golden and Silver ages. Even so, several investigators have attempted to identify the factors underlying these events (e.g., Gray, 1958, 1961, 1966; cf. Kroeber, 1958). In addressing this question, these researchers have introduced a diversity of methods. Some use years or decades as the temporal unit of analysis (Simonton, 1980a), whereas others favor large time-series units such as generations or centuries (Naroll et al., 1971). Some investigators tabulate the number of creative products, such as patents or discoveries (Simonton, 1975b), whereas others count the number of eminent creators per unit of time (Simonton, 1988). Lastly, where some researchers examine the ups and downs in creativity in whole civilizations (Simonton, 1975c), others scrutinize the fluctuations in single nations (Simonton, 1976a). Taken together, the resulting studies have accumulated a substantial inventory of sociocultural factors that support or hinder creativity across historical time. These influences are of two general types: short term and long term.

Short-Term Influences

Creators during the course of their adulthood careers are often subject to the impact of various sociocultural events. These influences can be grouped into two categories: quantitative and qualitative.

Quantitative effects. International war provides a prime case of a short-term quantitative influence. For instance, the frequency and intensity of balance-of-power wars among European nations between 1500 and 1903 are negatively associated with the year-to-year fluctuations in the number of notable inventions and discoveries over the same period (Simonton, 1980a). Interestingly, although some argue that wartime conditions can stimulate medical and technical innovations (Norling, 1970), the overall impact of war remains negative even for medicine and technology (Simonton, 1976d, 1980a). This implies that resources tend to be channeled into that subset of innovations most obviously and directly connected with the war effort (e.g., the atomic bomb), a shift that occurs at the cost of other potential developments (e.g., television). The repercussions are much worse for forms of creativity with even less wartime utility. For example, military events can have an adverse effect on literary creativity (Simonton, 1983a).

Qualitative effects. Creative products generated under wartime conditions differ in content, form, and style from those generated under peacetime circumstances (Simonton, 1977b, 1983a, 1986a). For example, the thematic content of the plays attributed to Shakespeare tends to reflect contemporary military events (Simonton, 1986b, 2004b). Although this connection is fairly obvious, other qualitative effects are less so. For instance, territorial conquests are positively associated with the popularity of the Don Juan theme in European literature, an association based on the power motivation linked with both variables (Winter, 1973). The consequences of war for classical music are even more subtle: composers change the form of their melodies and harmonies in those works that are conceived under wartime circumstances (Cerulo, 1984; Simonton, 1986a, 1987b). The melodies, for example, become less predictable and more chaotic, just like the external conditions in which the melodies are created.

Such qualitative effects are not confined to war. The classic research on the authoritarian personality indicates that authoritarianism tends to increase when individuals feel threatened by uncontrollable external forces (Adorno, Frenkel-Brunswik, Levinson, & Sanford, 1950). The same principle operates at the collective level: when a nation feels itself similarly threatened, it will exhibit many authoritarian symptoms, including increased superstition, anti-intraception, and conventionality. As an example, one inquiry found that if the economy goes bad, as evidenced by increased unemployment, then highly authoritarian churches tend to increase membership relative to more liberal churches (Sales, 1973). More important for our purposes here, the positive relation between authoritarianism and economic stress has consequences for the types of creativity that are most likely to be popular at a given time (Doty, Person, & Winter, 1991). For instance, books concerning superstitious beliefs, such as astrology, display better sales figures (Padgett & Jorgenson, 1982). In contrast, books that discuss "intraceptive" topics, such as psychoanalysis, are prone to become less popular by the same criterion (Sales, 1973). A final illustration concerns the place of parapsychological studies—such as "ESP"—in psychological research: such studies tend to become more prominent in threatening times (McCann & Stewin, 1984).

Long-Term Influences

So far we have examined external effects that are more or less temporary. Military and economic events fluctuate rapidly over time. For instance, a nation is seldom at war for more than a few years at a time. The following influences are not nearly so transient. Instead, long-term effects assume two major forms, namely inertial and developmental.

Inertial effects. Nations and civilizations are large systems that do not change rapidly across time. Insofar as the milieu displays appreciable inertia, then their consequences require long time periods to develop (e.g., Blaha, 2002; Gray, 1958, 1961, 1966). Hence, whereas economic circumstances may rise and fall over short time intervals, the economic systems that generate those conditions may maintain themselves over much longer periods.

An illustration of such inertial consequences may be found in Pitirim Sorokin's (1937–1941) *Social and Cultural Dynamics*. Sorokin claimed that a particular "mentality" dominates a civilization during any given point in history. This mentality consists of a system of beliefs and values that define a culture's worldview. Three such culture mentalities are especially conspicuous. First, the Sensate mentality emphasizes such ideas as empiricism, materialism, determinism, individualism, and hedonism. Second, the Ideational mentality stresses such ideas as rationalism, idealism, collectivism, and principled ethics. Third, the Idealistic mentality aims at a balanced integration of these divergent ideas. Furthermore, according to Sorokin, civilizations experience slow cyclical shifts in the prevalent mentality. Ideational civilizations often transform into Idealistic civilizations, which in their turn transform into Sensate civilizations. These transformations occur at a glacial pace because several generations must pass before the advantages and disadvantages of a particular mentality become completely realized. What makes this gradual evolutionary process relevant to the present discussion is that the dominant mentality very strongly influences the types of creativity that are most favored. For instance, the Sensate mentality tends to favor scientific creativity, whereas the Ideational mentality tends to favor religious innovation. Even within a given domain of creativity, each mentality will have its distinctive impact. Sensate times are conducive to highly realistic art, whereas Ideational times are supportive of highly spiritual art. Thus, both the quantity and quality of creativity should gradually change according to the slow transformations of the culture mentality.

Unfortunately, although Sorokin (1937–1941) gathered massive amounts of data in support of his theory, his statistical analyses were rather deficient (Simonton, 2003). Even so, more recent research has provided some endorsement to some of his most general conclusions (Ford, Richard, & Talbutt, 1996). As a case in point, the philosophical components of the three mentalities are best described in terms of massive cycles instead of momentary fluctuations (Klingemann, Mohler, & Weber, 1982; Simonton, 1976b). A civilization cannot alter its ontological, epistemological, and ethical commitments in just a few generations. Moreover, research indicates that creative activity is associated with several features of the culture mentality. For instance, the Sensate mentality does indeed support both technological invention and scientific discovery (Simonton, 1976b).

The above investigations all involved secondary analyses of Sorokin's data. Nevertheless, other investigations based on new data lead to similar conclusions. Gradual transformations in the sociocultural system can leave an impression on both the quantity and quality of creativity and innovation displayed at a particular time in history (e.g., Dressler & Robbins, 1975; Hasenfus, Martindale, & Birnbaum, 1983; Naroll et al., 1971; Simonton, 1975c).

Developmental effects. Sometimes a long-term effect results because a specific condition may function via an extended time lag. The principal causal root for this lagged influence is that a particular Zeitgeist may have its impact on creative development rather than creative output. The acquisition of creative potential begins early in life, and in all likelihood continues into early adulthood. Although part of this development may be under genetic control (Simonton, 1999c), it is apparent that environmental factors also have a role. Yet as observed earlier, psychologists, like Galton (1874), have tended to concentrate on family and educational experiences (Simonton, 1987a). The assumption is clearly that home and school exert a massive influence on creative development. Nonetheless, it is evident that beyond this most immediate environment exists a powerful and pervasive world consisting of military, political, economic, social, and cultural conditions. One can run away from home or drop out of school, but one cannot escape civil wars or economic depressions. Furthermore, a large body of evidence has indicated that diverse aspects of the larger sociocultural milieu do indeed shape the acquisition of creative potential (Simonton, 1984b). Most of this evidence is based on generational time-series analyses (Simonton, 1984b). This technique allows the researcher to investigate how the frequency and intensity of specific events in generation g affect the number of creators and innovators who emerge in generation g + 1 (where the duration of the generation is usually taken as twenty years). Using this approach, investigators have identified the following five sets of conditions (cf. Simonton, 1999a, 1999b):

1. Those periods that feature a large number of independent states provide a positive setting for the appearance of ideological diversity (Simonton, 1976c). That is, political fragmentation is most likely to nurture the emergence of thinkers who advocate a wide array of different philosophical positions. Furthermore, because general creative activity is positively correlated

with ideological diversity (Simonton, 1976c), this relation indicates that political fragmentation also has a lagged effect on creativity.

2. The opposite of political fragmentation is political integration—the circumstance when a civilization is under the hegemony of a large empire. Thus, it is not surprising that whenever such large imperial states display instability in the form of nationalistic uprisings, popular revolts, and other violent mass movements, then innovative activity resuscitates after a delay of one generation (Simonton, 1975c, 2004a). Riots, revolts, rebellions, and other civil disturbances—whether or not they occur within empire states—also have a qualitative impact on philosophical thought. Specifically, after a one-generation delay, such events excite a polarization of intellectual debate, with philosophers tending to take extreme positions on key intellectual issues (Simonton, 1976f).

3. Sometimes it is the "power elite" that displays instability rather than the civilization or nation as a whole. This instability takes the form of coups d'etat, political assassination, conspiracies, military revolts, and other manifestations of anarchy. These events have a devastating impact on the creative development (Simonton, 1975c). In particular, the aftermath is a decline in innovations in science, philosophy, literature, and music.

4. Civilizations vary across time in the extent to which they are open to the influx of ideas from outside. Sometimes a culture or society will totally shut itself off from such influences, whereas other times the sociocultural system will be open to immigration, foreign travel, and foreign masters. This openness has a positive consequence for creativity (Simonton, 1997). Curiously, the lag for this effect is not one generation, but two. Evidently, the society must assimilate the alien ideas into the native culture before it can leave an imprint on the innovativeness of the civilization.

5. Creativity in one field can often affect creative development in a closely related field (Simonton, 1975a). For example, a high level of activity in chemistry, medicine, and geology in one generation tends to have a positive impact on major advances in biology in the subsequent generation (Simonton, 1976d). These cross-generational influences can be qualitative as well as quantitative. For instance, the beliefs that make up the philosophical Zeitgeist in one generation leave an impression on related beliefs in the next generation (Simonton, 1978).

The above list makes a strong case that to a very large extent, the creativity displayed by a generation of creators may reflect the conditions and events to which they were exposed in childhood and adolescence.

CREATIVITY IN CONTEXT

I began this chapter with the debate between Galton (1869) and Candolle (1873), a debate that Galton (1874) framed in terms of the nature-nurture issue. Since that time, the debate has broadened far beyond that question. Especially crucial is the recognition that environmental influences, which Galton (1874) viewed as involving home and school, also included the political, economic, social, and cultural milieu, just as Candolle (1873) had originally argued. This milieu defines the Ortgeist and Zeitgeist that shape not just the amount of creativity, but also the type of creativity. Sometimes these effects are transient, and other times the effects are more durable, even stretching out across generations. But whatever the details of a specific process, it should now be evident that innovation ensues out of a specific social context.

It is essential to recognize that the fact that creativity is contingent on context is not equivalent to saying that the individual is irrelevant. It would be most unwise to engage in a complete sociological reductionism. There are five major reasons why individual psychology still has a major place in any explanatory account of innovation:

1. Although the number of innovators in a particular generation may be a function of sociocultural factors, not all innovators within a single generation can be considered equally creative. On the contrary, tremendous individual differences characterize the creative output of persons even though they emerged under the same Ortgeist and Zeitgeist (Simonton, 1991, 1997). In fact, the larger the number of creators active in a given cohort, the larger the variation in creativity exhibited by those creators (Simonton, 1999b).

2. The most conspicuous innovators in any given time and place tend to conform less to the sociocultural milieu than do their less prominent colleagues (Simonton, 1976e, 1980b; cf. Simonton, 1992b). Coupled with this intellectual independence is a strong inclination to espouse extreme positions and to advocate systems of beliefs that integrate ideas in rather uncommon packages (Simonton, 1976e, 2000).

3. Factors that determine creativity at the sociocultural level can sometimes have different causal repercussions at the level of the individual creator (Simonton, 1976e, 1977a, 1996). That is, the variables that distinguish Golden from Dark ages are not identical to those that distinguish creative geniuses from the practitioners of more everyday forms of creativity. In fact, occasionally the correlation can change directly when we switch from the group to the individual.

4. The causal connection between the sociocultural context and the individual creator may sometimes be mediated by psychological processes (Simonton, 1984a, 1992a, 1992c; see also Simonton, 1983b). A potential case concerns how creative activity in a civilization is enhanced by the influx of foreign ideas and persons (Simonton, 1997). This causal relationship may be partly mediated by a developmental phenomenon, such as the positive association between bilingualism and creative development (Simonton, in press).

5. Often psychological processes, such as cognitive and motivational variables, underlie sociocultural circumstances. For example, the probability that a nation becomes entangled in war is partly the consequence of how its political leaders score on integrative complexity (Suedfeld & Bluck, 1988; Suedfeld & Tetlock, 1977) and the power and affiliation motives (Winter, 1973, 1993). In a sense, the amount of creativity displayed at a particular time is partly contingent on the psychological makeup of heads of state.

In light of the forgoing considerations, the social context of innovation makes the phenomenon more complex without making it any less psychological.

REFERENCES

Adorno, T. W., Frenkel-Brunswik, E., Levinson, D. J., & Sanford, R. N. (Eds.). (1950). *The authoritarian personality.* New York: Harper.

Blaha, S. (2002). *The life cycle of civilizations.* Auburn, NH: Pingree-Hill.

Candolle, A. de (1873). *Histoire des sciences et des savants depuis deux siècles.* Geneve: Georg.

Carneiro, R. L. (1970). Scale analysis, evolutionary sequences, and the rating of cultures. In R. Naroll & R. Cohn (Eds.), *A handbook of method in cultural anthropology* (pp. 834–871). New York: Natural History Press.

Cerulo, K. A. (1984). Social disruption and its effects on music: An empirical analysis. *Social Forces, 62,* 885–904.

Doty, R. M., Peterson, B. E., & Winter, D. G. (1991). Threat and authoritarianism in the United States, 1978–1987. *Journal of Personality and Social Psychology, 61,* 629–640.

Dressler, W. W., & Robbins, M. C. (1975). Art styles, social stratification, and cognition: An analysis of Greek vase painting. *American Ethnologist, 2,* 427–434.

Ford, J. B., Richard, M. P., & Talbutt, P. C. (Eds.). (1996). *Sorokin and civilization: A centennial assessment.* New Brunswick, NJ: Transaction.

Galton, F. (1869). *Hereditary genius: An inquiry into its laws and consequences.* London: Macmillan. (Original work published 1892)

Galton, F. (1874). *English men of science: Their nature and nurture.* London: Macmillan.

Gray, C. E. (1958). An analysis of Graeco-Roman development: The epicyclical evolution of Graeco-Roman civilization. *American Anthropologist, 60,* 13–31.

Gray, C. E. (1961). An epicyclical model for Western civilization. *American Anthropologist, 63,* 1014–1037.

Gray, C. E. (1966). A measurement of creativity in Western civilization. *American Anthropologist, 68,* 1384–1417.

Hasenfus, N., Martindale, C., & Birnbaum, D. (1983). Psychological reality of cross-media artistic styles. *Journal of Experimental Psychology: Human Perception and Performance, 9,* 841–863.

Hilts, V. L. (1975). *A guide to Francis Galton's English men of science.* Philadelphia: American Philosophical Society.

Klingemann, H.-D., Mohler, P. P., & Weber, R. P. (1982). Cultural indicators based on content analysis: A secondary analysis of Sorokin's data on fluctuations of systems of truth. *Quality and Quantity, 16,* 1–18.

Kroeber, A. L. (1944). *Configurations of culture growth.* Berkeley: University of California Press.

Kroeber, A. L. (1958). Gray's epicyclical evolution. *American Anthropologist, 60,* 31–38.

Lehman, H. C. (1947). National differences in creativity. *American Journal of Sociology, 52,* 475–488.

McCann, S. J. H., & Stewin, L. L. (1984). Environmental threat and parapsychological contributions to the psychological literature. *Journal of Social Psychology, 122,* 227–235.

Murray, C. (2003). *Human accomplishment: The pursuit of excellence in the arts and sciences, 800 B.C. to 1950*. New York: HarperCollins.

Naroll, R., Benjamin, E. C., Fohl, F. K., Fried, M. J., Hildreth, R. E., & Schaefer, J. M. (1971). Creativity: A cross-historical pilot survey. *Journal of Cross-Cultural Psychology, 2*, 181–188.

Norling, B. (1970). *Timeless problems in history*. Notre Dame, IN: Notre Dame Press.

Padgett, V., & Jorgenson, D. O. (1982). Superstition and economic threat: Germany 1918–1940. *Personality and Social Psychology Bulletin, 8*, 736–741.

Peregrine, P. N., Ember, C. R., & Ember, M. (2004). Universal patterns in cultural evolution: An empirical analysis using Guttman scaling. *American Anthropologist, 106*, 145–149.

Sales, S. M. (1973). Threat as a factor in authoritarianism: An analysis of archival data. *Journal of Personality and Social Psychology, 28*, 44–57.

Simonton, D. K. (1975a). Interdisciplinary creativity over historical time: A correlational analysis of generational fluctuations. *Social Behavior and Personality, 3*, 181–188.

Simonton, D. K. (1975b). Invention and discovery among the sciences: A p-technique factor analysis. *Journal of Vocational Behavior, 7*, 275–281.

Simonton, D. K. (1975c). Sociocultural context of individual creativity: A transhistorical time-series analysis. *Journal of Personality and Social Psychology, 32*, 1119–1133.

Simonton, D. K. (1976a). The causal relation between war and scientific discovery: An exploratory cross-national analysis. *Journal of Cross-Cultural Psychology, 7*, 133–144.

Simonton, D. K. (1976b). Do Sorokin's data support his theory? A study of generational fluctuations in philosophical beliefs. *Journal for the Scientific Study of Religion, 15*, 187–198.

Simonton, D. K. (1976c). Ideological diversity and creativity: A re-evaluation of a hypothesis. *Social Behavior and Personality, 4*, 203–207.

Simonton, D. K. (1976d). Interdisciplinary and military determinants of scientific productivity: A cross-lagged correlation analysis. *Journal of Vocational Behavior, 9*, 53–62.

Simonton, D. K. (1976e). Philosophical eminence, beliefs, and zeitgeist: An individual-generational analysis. *Journal of Personality and Social Psychology, 34*, 630–640.

Simonton, D. K. (1976f). The sociopolitical context of philosophical beliefs: A transhistorical causal analysis. *Social Forces, 54*, 513–523.

Simonton, D. K. (1977a). Eminence, creativity, and geographic marginality: A recursive structural equation model. *Journal of Personality and Social Psychology, 35*, 805–816.

Simonton, D. K. (1977b). Women's fashions and war: A quantitative comment. *Social Behavior and Personality, 5*, 285–288.

Simonton, D. K. (1978). Intergenerational stimulation, reaction, and polarization: A causal analysis of intellectual history. *Social Behavior and Personality, 6*, 247–251.

Simonton, D. K. (1980a). Techno-scientific activity and war: A yearly time-series analysis, 1500–1903 A.D. *Scientometrics, 2*, 251–255.

Simonton, D. K. (1980b). Thematic fame, melodic originality, and musical zeitgeist: A biographical and transhistorical content analysis. *Journal of Personality and Social Psychology, 38*, 972–983.

Simonton, D. K. (1983a). Dramatic greatness and content: A quantitative study of eighty-one Athenian and Shakespearean plays. *Empirical Studies of the Arts, 1*, 109–123.

Simonton, D. K. (1983b). Intergenerational transfer of individual differences in hereditary monarchs: Genes, role-modeling, cohort, or sociocultural effects? *Journal of Personality and Social Psychology, 44*, 354–364.

Simonton, D. K. (1984a). Artistic creativity and interpersonal relationships across and within generations. *Journal of Personality and Social Psychology, 46*, 1273–1286.

Simonton, D. K. (1984b). Generational time-series analysis: A paradigm for studying sociocultural influences. In K. Gergen & M. Gergen (Eds.), *Historical social psychology* (pp. 141–155). Hillsdale, NJ: Lawrence Erlbaum.

Simonton, D. K. (1986a). Aesthetic success in classical music: A computer analysis of 1935 compositions. *Empirical Studies of the Arts, 4*, 1–17.

Simonton, D. K. (1986b). Popularity, content, and context in 37 Shakespeare plays. *Poetics, 15*, 493–510.

Simonton, D. K. (1987a). Developmental antecedents of achieved eminence. *Annals of Child Development, 5*, 131–169.

Simonton, D. K. (1987b). Musical aesthetics and creativity in Beethoven: A computer analysis of 105 compositions. *Empirical Studies of the Arts, 5*, 87–104.

Simonton, D. K. (1988). Galtonian genius, Kroeberian configurations, and emulation: A generational time-series analysis of Chinese civilization. *Journal of Personality and Social Psychology, 55*, 230–238.

Simonton, D. K. (1992a). Gender and genius in Japan: Feminine eminence in masculine culture. *Sex Roles, 27*, 101–119.

Simonton, D. K. (1992b). Leaders of American psychology, 1879–1967: Career development, creative output, and professional achievement. *Journal of Personality and Social Psychology, 62*, 5–17.

Simonton, D. K. (1992c). The social context of career success and course for 2,026 scientists and inventors. *Personality and Social Psychology Bulletin, 18*, 452–463.

Simonton, D. K. (1996). Individual genius and cultural configurations: The case of Japanese civilization. *Journal of Cross-Cultural Psychology, 27*, 354–375.

Simonton, D. K. (1997). Foreign influence and national achievement: The impact of open milieus on Japanese civilization. *Journal of Personality and Social Psychology, 72*, 86–94.

Simonton, D. K. (1999a). The creative society: Genius vis-á-vis zeitgeist. In A. Montuori & R. Purser (Eds.), *Social creativity* (Vol. 1, pp. 265–286). Cresskill, NJ: Hampton Press.

Simonton, D. K. (1999b). *Origins of genius: Darwinian perspectives on creativity.* New York: Oxford University Press.

Simonton, D. K. (1999c). Talent and its development: An emergenic and epigenetic model. *Psychological Review, 106*, 435–457.

Simonton, D. K. (2000). Methodological and theoretical orientation and the long-term disciplinary impact of 54 eminent psychologists. *Review of General Psychology, 4*, 1–13.

Simonton, D. K. (2003). Kroeber's cultural configurations, Sorokin's culture mentalities, and generational time-series analysis: A quantitative paradigm for the comparative study of civilizations. *Comparative Civilizations Review, 49*, 96–108.

Simonton, D. K. (2004a). Creative clusters, political fragmentation, and cultural hetero-geneity: An investigative journey though civilizations East and West. In P. Bernholz & R. Vaubel (Eds.), *Political competition, innovation and growth in the history of Asian civilizations* (pp. 39–56). Cheltenham, United Kingdom: Edward Elgar.

Simonton, D. K. (2004b). Thematic content and political context in Shakespeare's dra-matic output, with implications for authorship and chronology controversies. *Empirical Studies of the Arts, 22,* 201–213.

Simonton, D. K. (in press). Bilingualism and creativity. In J. Altarriba & R. R. Heredia (Eds.). *An introduction to bilingualism: Principles and practices.* Mahwah, NJ: Erlbaum.

Sorokin, P. A. (1937–1941). *Social and cultural dynamics* (Vols. 1–4). New York: Ameri-can Book.

Sorokin, P. A., & Merton, R. K. (1935). The course of Arabian intellectual develop-ment, 700–1300 A.D. *Isis, 22,* 516–524.

Spiller, G. (1929). The dynamics of greatness. *Sociological Review, 21,* 218–232.

Suedfeld, P., & Bluck, S. (1988). Changes in integrative complexity prior to surprise attacks. *Journal of Conflict Resolution, 32,* 626–635.

Suedfeld, P., & Tetlock, P. (1977). Integrative complexity of communications in inter-national crises. *Journal of Conflict Resolution, 21,* 169–184.

Szabo, A. T. (1985). Alphonse de Candolle's early scientometrics (1883, 1885) with refer-ences to recent trends in the field (1978–1983). *Scientometrics, 8,* 13–33. *Who said what when: A chronological dictionary of quotations.* (1991). New York: Hippocrene Books.

Winter, D. G. (1973). *The power motive.* New York: Free Press.

Winter, D. G. (1993). Power, affiliation, and war: Three tests of a motivational model. *Journal of Personality and Social Psychology, 65,* 532–545.

9

Creative Cognition in the Workplace: An Applied Perspective

SAMUEL T. HUNTER, TAMARA L. FRIEDRICH,
KATRINA E. BEDELL-AVERS, and MICHAEL D. MUMFORD

Innovation, the implementation of new, original, useful ideas, is viewed by many as the key to sustaining a competitive advantage.[1,2,3] By introducing new products and processes first—ahead of competitors—organizations are able to carve a substantial marketplace niche, oftentimes solidifying their role in a current business environment best characterized as turbulent, dynamic, and rapidly changing. Moreover, organizational innovation provides companies with the tools to exist at the cusp of environmental shifts, allowing them to both stay ahead of, and simultaneously shape, the direction of business itself.[4]

The implementation of new ideas, however, is one step removed from a particularly critical aspect of the innovation process. Specifically, before original ideas can be implemented at an organizational level, they must first be generated at the individual level. Put more precisely, substantial organizational resources as well as a willingness to use such resources are of minimal utility if an organization lacks ownership of creative ideas. This is not to say that the organization-wide implementation of original, new ideas is unimportant, or even less important than the cognitive generation of new ideas. Rather, the cognitive generation and exploration of novel ideas is a necessary, albeit not wholly sufficient, condition for organizational innovation.

At its core, the generation and exploration of creative ideas is a cognitive or mental activity.[5] Going one step further, this mental process, or series of mental processes, may thusly be viewed as a starting point for organizational innovation. Not surprisingly, then, the generation and exploration of new ideas has been the topic of a number of scientific investigations. Researchers have conducted numerous field investigations, examining which aspects of the creative process were most relevant in an organizational setting.[6,7] Other researchers have explored creative processes in the laboratory—examining, with notable detail and control, the components of creativity that are essential to creative performance.[8,9] The results of such efforts have been particularly fruitful in identifying the processes involved in the generation and exploration of original ideas. The goal of the present effort, then, is to explore these processes and their impact on the generation of new, creative products. Throughout the discussion of these processes, a series of propositions will be provided. Such propositions are put forth as tools for those attempting to increase and enhance organizational innovation. Again, it is only through the generation and exploration of creative ideas that innovation can occur, and as such, these processes appear elemental to organizational success.

EARLY PROCESS MODELS

Early views of creativity, much to the lament of modern creativity researchers, portrayed the generation of new ideas as a "mystical" activity.[10] Such conceptualizations have hampered, in many ways, the study of creativity and innovation. Researchers have noted: "Many people seem to believe, as they do about love, that creativity is something that just doesn't lend itself to scientific study, because it is a spiritual process."[10] Thus, the more recent and empirically supported view of creativity as a series of interconnected stages is largely welcomed by most scientists and practitioners. Put another way, by viewing creativity as a relatively knowable, understandable, and therefore predictable phenomenon, we can in turn examine the factors that either hamper, or enhance, idea generation and, ultimately, organizational innovation.

One of the earliest process models appears to have been developed by Wallas,[11] who proposed that there are four processes involved in creativity: (a) preparation, (b) incubation, (c) illumination, and (d) verification. This approach has been used by a number of researchers who have expanded, somewhat, on Wallas's original ideas. For example, in her model for organizational innovation, Amabile[12] also proposed four processes: (a) problem identification, (b) preparation, (c) response generation, and (d) response validation. Empirically, the four-stage model has received some notable success and has, at a very minimum, helped guide a better understanding of creativity. As such, it seems reasonable to contend that:

> **Proposition 1:** *Creativity is best understood as a process—or series of interconnected stages—rather than a singular mystical or spiritual activity.*

The four-stage model, however, is not without its subtle critics. Some have contended that to fully understand creativity we need to further examine the subprocesses involved. More precisely, it appears necessary to examine the four-process model in finer detail.[13] In response, several researchers have explored multiple, more elaborate creative process models. One of the most notable is that put forth by Finke, Ward, and Smith,[14] who proposed a two-stage model containing multiple subprocesses. Termed the genoplore model, the approach includes, broadly, a generation stage as well as an exploration stage—with each comprised of multiple elaborate subprocesses. What is particularly noteworthy about the model is that the researchers contend that individuals may cycle back and forth between stages, suggesting that although the creative process may follow a basic pattern, the process is dynamic and shifting rather than a rote path along specified operations. Given the success of the genoplore model, it seems reasonable to contend that:

Proposition 2: *Creativity appears to involve a dynamic process pattern, whereby individuals may shift between generating and exploring ideas at multiple points in time.*

EIGHT-PROCESS MODEL OF CREATIVE THINKING

Relatively recently, Mumford and colleagues[15,16] proposed an eight-stage process model of creativity. Building off the work of Wallas[11] and Dewey,[17] as well as more recent conceptualizations such as the genoplore model,[14] the researchers proposed that there are eight core processes involved in creative thought: (a) problem construction, (b) information gathering, (c) concept selection, (d) conceptual combination, (e) idea generation, (f) idea evaluation, (g) implementation planning, and (h) monitoring. There is compelling evidence to support the model, and it is regarded by many as the most comprehensive and clearest conceptualization of the creative process.[18,16,19]

Problem Construction

Before a new idea can be generated to solve a given problem or situation, the situation must first be clearly understood. What is critical to understanding creativity, however, is that the situations requiring the generation of creative solutions differ substantially from more straightforward, typical problem-solving scenarios. Specifically, situations requiring creative ideas tend to be complex and ill defined.[20,21] As such, providing some structure—a framework for interpreting the problem—is critical to creative thought. Because problem construction is essentially the initial stage of cognitive idea generation, it plays a particularly important role via its impact on later stages. The notion that problem construction is a critical component of creative problem solving has been supported by a number of studies, all demonstrating that the degree to which individuals can identify and understand the nature of a problem is significantly related to creative performance. The results, moreover,

suggest that problem construction is important, even when one's creative ability (e.g., divergent thinking ability) is taken into account.[22,20,23] Thus, it
seems reasonable to contend:

> **Proposition 3:** *Identifying and understanding the nature of the problem at hand is
> critical to creative performance.*

Information Gathering

Once a problem is understood, the tendency may be to begin generating
new ideas. Such an approach, however, would be premature. Instead, upon
gaining an understanding of the nature of the problem, it appears best to then
begin gathering and considering information—particularly information that is
relevant to the situation at hand. In fact, research has shown that individuals
who are able to attend to relevant information, while ignoring irrelevant information, are more likely to produce creative ideas.[24] As such:

> **Proposition 4:** *Searching for and gathering information relevant to the situation at
> hand is critical to creative performance.*

Concept Selection

Following an intensive search for information relevant to solving a problem, one is oftentimes left with a fairly large and wide range of data to sort
through. Consequently, the next step in the creative process is to select for
further exploration the concepts—or bits of knowledge—most relevant to the
situation at hand.[25] These knowledge structures have been the center of attention in numerous studies,[9] with the exact nature of such concepts and their
antecedent components still being explored. What seems clear, however, is
that individuals who can clearly organize ideas into relevant concepts and
then select those concepts most pertinent to the current situation are best able
to generate creative ideas. Thus:

> **Proposition 5:** *The selection of the most relevant concepts in a given situation is criti-
> cal to the generation of new, original ideas.*

Conceptual Combination

Of the processes discussed thus far, it appears that the act of combining
new concepts, or conceptual combination, may be the most critical to creative
performance. As may be suspected, conceptual combination involves taking
the relevant notions from the concept selection stage and combining them in
new, unique ways. What is less clear, however, is how such ideas are ultimately combined. Mumford and colleagues[26,21] suggest that when a situation
requires the combination of ideas that are characterized by similar features,
one may simply apply the combination rules used in previous attempts. When
the situation is notably different, however, an individual may use something

akin to a metaphor—or abstract guiding concept—to direct the combination of relevant concepts. As such, two propositions appear relevant:

> **Proposition 6:** *When a situation requires the combination of concepts that are similar to what was done in previous experiences, such experience and similarity will guide the combination process.*

> **Proposition 7:** *When a situation requires the combination of concepts that share little in common with previously combined concepts and each other, abstract frameworks such as metaphors may aid in conceptual combination.*

Idea Generation

Once ideas have been reorganized and combined in new ways, the next step is to formally generate ideas deriving from the new reorganization. As may be surmised, combining concepts and formally generating new ideas are closely related cognitive processes. Where the two processes differ, however, is in their degree of abstractness. During the conceptual combination stage, individuals are attempting, globally, to combine previously unrelated concepts—to get a feel for what broad ideas may be placed together. During the idea generation stage, individuals are attempting to formally take those conceptual combinations and create new, workable ideas. Thus:

> **Proposition 8:** *Once concepts have been combined conceptually, it is necessary to formally generate workable, concrete ideas.*

Idea Evaluation

When considering the creative processes described by Mumford et al.,[15] it appears that idea evaluation has received relatively less attention than the other processes. Such a lack of investigation might at first glance suggest that this process is of lesser importance. Recent research, however, indicates that idea evaluation may be a particularly important aspect of creativity.[27,28,29,30] Idea evaluation involves the consideration of ideas in light of potential outcomes deriving from, and resources needed for, its implementation.[31] Idea evaluation appears most critical to the generation of new ideas by focusing resources on ideas that are most likely to be of utility for the situation at hand. Conversely, ideas that have little usefulness are often discarded at this stage. This is particularly important upon consideration of creative problems—problems or situations often characterized by few, or limited, resources. Thus, in light of recent research, the following proposition appears warranted:

> **Proposition 9:** *The evaluation of ideas, or consideration of potential outcomes and resources necessary to produce such outcomes, is a critical aspect of creative performance.*

Implementation Planning

Once ideas have been properly "fleshed out" and taken from abstract to relatively concrete, their implementation must ultimately be considered. Recent research suggests that planning, specifically, is an important determinant of organizational innovation.[32] More precisely, planning appears critical for three main reasons: (a) plans help properly guide and maximize limited resource scenarios characterizing creative efforts, (b) without plans, it is particularly difficult to align broader business strategies with creative efforts, and (c) for organizations to sustain innovation, they must have plans, preferably multiple plans, to implement projects and ideas over time[32] Thus:

> **Proposition 10:** *Planning for idea implementation is a process critical to creative achievement.*

Monitoring

No idea, however well conceived, is guaranteed success. As such, monitoring ideas and their implementation is an important element of the creative process. Specifically, monitoring activity is vital due to the feedback, good or bad, that may be gleaned from an idea's implementation. Such feedback helps guide and facilitate additions, deletions, adjustments, or alterations that may be made to creative ideas or processes. It is important to note that monitoring information may be used to make changes at nearly any stage in the creative process—reiterating, again, the dynamic, oscillating nature of creative idea generation. Put another way, monitoring is critical to the *continual* improvement of creative ideas. As such, the following proposition appears warranted:

> **Proposition 11:** *The monitoring of the implementation of creative ideas is an important part of the creative process—largely due to feedback and subsequent adjustment mechanisms.*

Summary

Because organizational innovation inherently requires the generation of new ideas, the cognitive processes involved in generating and implementing ideas appear notably relevant to understanding how to improve innovation in the workplace. Research suggests that by viewing creativity as a series of processes, we are better able to understand, and in turn enhance, creative performance. Early process models have had notable success, with calls being made for their enhancement and expansion rather than full reconsideration. Not surprisingly, then, recent expansion efforts have been especially fruitful in gaining and providing insight into means and methods of improving creativity. Specifically, the eight-stage process model put forth by Mumford and colleagues appears particularly noteworthy.

APPLICATIONS OF THE EIGHT-STAGE MODEL

Having considered each stage of the model broadly, we turn now to more specific applications and considerations of the eight-stage model. More precisely, we will now examine the eight-stage process model in relation to: (a) ability and creative personality, (b) knowledge and creative thinking, (c) errors in idea evaluation, (d) causal analysis and its influence on idea generation, (e) multilevel influences, and (f) enhancing creative processes through training. Finally, we conclude with a discussion and brief commentary on the role of creative thinking in the workplace.

The Role of Ability and Creative Personality in Problem Construction

As noted earlier, the first stage in the generation of a creative solution involves identifying and considering the exact nature of the problem or situation. Upon examination of research conducted examining this creative process, it is clear that this stage is particularly important to innovation. Until relatively recently, however, the question remained as to what factors, specifically, influenced success or failure at this stage. Fortunately, recent work by Reiter-Palmon and colleagues[33,34] has shed some light onto these factors. The authors investigated problem construction ability as well as personality in relation to creative performance. Reiter-Palmon et al.[33] provided participants with six different problems across three domains: leadership, school, and social. Prior to engaging in these problems, researchers measured problem construction ability—or the capacity to frame problems in multiple creative ways. The results of the study revealed that problem construction ability was positively related to the originality and usefulness of solutions generated across all three domain types. Similar positive correlations were also found in a later study,[34] where ability and personality fit were conjointly examined. The unique contribution of the second study, however, was the additional investigation of personality fit. According to the authors, fit between one's personality—operationalized as the goals, problems, or life tasks the individual chooses to engage in—and the situation at hand will result in increased creativity. The results of the study supported this contention, with fit between personality and situation accounting for additional variance above and beyond that were accounted for by ability and requisite covariates. In light of these results, the following two propositions appear warranted:

> **Proposition 12:** *Having the capacity, or ability, to frame problems in several alternative, creative ways is related to creative performance.*

> **Proposition 13:** *Fit between one's personality and creative problem solving situation will result in enhanced creative output.*

Knowledge Structures and Creative Thinking

There is an old adage that one cannot create something from nothing. Accordingly, during the conceptual combination and idea generation stages, individuals are cognitively combining something—be they termed concepts, notions, or ideas. Such concepts, notions, or ideas may more accurately be labeled knowledge. Knowledge, then, stands as the ultimate building block of the combination process. Broadly defined, knowledge may come in several forms: schematic, associational, or case-based.[9] Schematic knowledge refers to generalized concepts derived from experience. Obtaining schematic knowledge takes substantial effort—it involves abstracting relevant and exemplary attributes of ideas and boiling them down to only the key relevant concepts. Associational knowledge, on the other hand, requires little effort and in many cases is unconscious. Associational knowledge is derived from repeated pairings and/or exposure of ideas. Finally, case-based knowledge is based on past experience and, in this way, is somewhat similar to schematic knowledge. Case-based knowledge, however, is organized by such factors as goals attained, causes of performance, and resources needed for solution rather than exemplar information.

Following work by Mumford et al.[3] and Hunter, Bedell, and Mumford[9] set out to examine how these different types of knowledge structures impacted the conceptual combination and idea generation processes. Specifically, the researchers manipulated the number and type of knowledge structures salient to participants. For example, in one condition, only a single knowledge structure was made salient (e.g., associational knowledge). In other conditions, two knowledge structures were elicited (e.g., schematic and case-based knowledge), and in a third condition all three knowledge structures were made salient. The results of the study revealed that the elicitation of either schematic or associational knowledge alone resulted in a greater number of ideas generated. Use of multiple knowledge structures, however, resulted in higher quality and more original ideas—particularly when schematic or associational structures were paired with case-based knowledge. It seems that previous experience (i.e., case-based knowledge) is relevant to creative performance—but only if individuals also have additional knowledge to enhance knowledge based on past experience.

> *Proposition 14: Past experiences are important to conceptual combination and idea generation—but only if they are supplemented with additional knowledge structures such as schematic or associational.*

Idea Evaluation and Errors

As noted earlier, the evaluation of ideas is a critical creative process and one that has, overall, been underinvestigated by the majority of creativity researchers. Fortunately, work by Mumford and colleagues has shed notable light onto this critical creative process. A model put forth by Lonergan, Scott, and Mumford[30] proposes that idea evaluation is an aspect of idea implementation, where ideas are "forecasted" into future situations. Potential ideas, then, are appraised in relation to a variety of standards, including popularity, potential impact, workability, risk, and cost. What is particularly noteworthy about Lonergan et al.'s model is the generativity involved in the evaluation process. Ideas may be reshaped and reformed during this stage, depending on the evaluative outcome. Thus, evaluation is not only a judging or decision tool whereby ideas are either kept or tossed aside—it is also a dynamic generative process, where ideas are potentially reformed and adjusted. The generative nature of the stage underscores the importance of this stage, meaning that ideas with potential problems or issues may be kept in the system, rather than removed completely—provided, of course, an adequate adjustment may be found allowing for their continuation.

As is implied by the model, the quality and originality of adjusted ideas is only as good as the standards applied in the evaluation process. Unfortunately, errors are inherent in the evaluation process—particularly for the evaluation of *creative* ideas. We simply make mistakes in our assessment of whether an idea is worth pursuing.[35] The question brought to fore, then, is: What factors influence the likelihood of these errors? A series of recent studies[35,36,30] have attempted, rather successfully, to shed some light onto this question.

By definition, creative ideas are novel. Taken a step further, novel ideas are inherently *different* from ideas or processes currently in use. This break from the status quo has led to a variety of errors occurring when highly original ideas are evaluated. Specifically, three reasons may account for the evaluation errors associated with very *novel* ideas. First, evaluation standards are generally based on the current goals of the organization. Because a creative idea is novel, it may not fit with current organizational goals but rather with new (potentially better), differing goals. Second, evaluations often occur in relation to past performance. The rarity and relative infrequency of creative ideas makes it difficult to compare them to previous instances of achievement. Finally, the novelty of creative ideas makes it difficult to recognize the key and critical attributes that could potentially contribute to greater organizational performance. In other words, it is difficult to see, at first, how an idea may benefit an organization. All three of these factors have led individuals to discount the potential contribution of highly novel ideas. In fact, a study by Licuanan et al.[35] found that there was a greater frequency of errors associated with very novel ideas than with less novel ideas. Similar results were also found in a study by Blair and Mumford[36]; participants preferred unoriginal ideas when asked which ideas should be used for further exploration. In light of these findings, it seems reasonable to suggest:

Proposition 15: *When evaluating very new or novel ideas, it is critical to carefully consider such ideas with regard to potentially new, and unforeseen, positive outcomes.*

Unfortunately, idea novelty is only one factor that has led to errors in creative idea evaluation. Building on the notion that individuals use standards to evaluate the utility of an idea, Blair and Mumford[36] hypothe-sized that participants would apply social consequence standards to idea evaluation—or consider ideas in light of potential social outcomes. Specifi-cally, Blair and Mumford theorized that risky ideas would be less preferred because (a) they have the potential to produce negative outcomes, (b) their pursuit may be viewed as irresponsible by others, and (c) the pursuit of such ideas may be associated with self-indulgence and self-centeredness. The results of their study supported their hypothesis, with risky ideas being pre-ferred less by participants. As such, the following proposition appears rea-sonable:

Proposition 16: *When evaluating creative ideas, be aware that potentially beneficial ideas are often dismissed due to an overweighing of perceived risk.*

One final process impacting errors during the idea evaluation phase is tied to forecasting. Again, during the idea evaluation stage, ideas are mentally placed, or forecasted, into future scenarios. Similar to standard comparison,[36] this process of future prediction and consideration is also open to potential biases and errors. Elements such as underprediction of requisite resources and overconfidence in potential success may lead individuals to be somewhat optimistic in their assessment of an idea during this forecasting stage. In fact, in a study examining forecasting errors, Dailey and Mumford[37] provided par-ticipants with several case studies and asked them to evaluate the ideas with regard to resource requirements and potential consequences. The responses were then compared against actual case results, providing a strong, realistic estimate of idea evaluation accuracy. The results of the study revealed that when participants had some familiarity with the issue in the case study, they overestimated potential outcomes and underestimated resource requirements. In this sense, it may appear that expertise (i.e., familiarity with a given topic) is a detriment to creative performance. Closer examination of the results revealed that this is not, in actuality, the case. In fact, expertise was associated with greater accuracy of future predictions—particularly with regard to organ-izational impact and difficulties involved in implementation and novelty. The results, then, reveal somewhat of a paradox: to reduce errors in idea evalua-tion, expertise is both desired and not desired. To solve this paradox, it would seem best to involve expertise in the evaluation process, but also have indi-viduals with less familiarity paired with experts during the idea evaluation process. Put another way, expertise will reduce errors in idea evaluation, but that expertise must be tempered with the opinions of others who have less expertise. In light of these results, the following proposition appears war-ranted:

Proposition 17: *When evaluating new, original ideas, experts are largely beneficial—but should be paired with individuals with less expertise to reduce forecasting errors.*

The Role of Causal Analysis in Idea Generation for Social Innovation

Thus far, innovation has referred to the generation and implementation of new ideas and processes. However, exactly where innovation occurs—or the domains in which innovations are born—can vary substantially. Recently, the research emphasis has been placed on innovation occurring in areas where creativity is thought to commonly occur, such as the visual arts, writing, engineering, and the sciences.[38,39,40,41,42] A domain receiving less emphasis, though of seemingly equal or potentially greater importance, has been social innovation. Marcy and Mumford[8] defined social innovation as "the generation and implementation of new ideas about people and their interactions within social systems" (p. 3). Witness the work of Henry Ford, who implemented the assembly line in the automotive industry, thus revolutionizing how cars were manufactured. Such innovation not only required the consideration of shop floor plans, requisite tools, and expense forecasts—it also involved the employees and their interactions as social beings. Based on the final outcome of Henry Ford's work, it is evident that social innovations have potentially far-reaching and substantial workplace implications.

From the above example, one thing is readily apparent: social innovations are complex phenomena.[8] In fact, there appear to be four reasons why social innovation is more complex than most other types of innovation. First, a multitude of individuals are involved in social systems, all having personal agendas and, potentially, competing goals. Second, there are multiple simultaneous activities occurring in a social system, resulting in, at times, a system best described as chaotic. Third, the success of one individual or group is dependent on the success of other individuals and groups—all of which are additionally impacted by the environment itself. Finally, the actions and reactions among multiple contingencies occur in a context best characterized as dynamic, and oftentimes highly ambiguous. Given the complex nature and high potential for impact of social innovations, an important question is brought to fore: what factors may be identified that influence idea generation occurring in the social domain?

Efforts by Mumford and colleagues[8,43,44] provide some insight into the elements influencing social innovation. In a study examining concept selection, idea generation and implementation planning, Marcy and Mumford[8] gave participants six social innovation problems occurring in business and educational domains. Prior to solving these problems, researchers provided participants with training in causal analysis. Similar to the concept selection process, causal analysis refers to the consideration of factors that influence, or cause, certain outcomes. Because social innovations are so complex, having the ability to determine the importance of relevant causes is particularly critical to creative success in the social domain.[45] Once solutions to problems were generated by participants, Marcy and Mumford[8] also manipulated implementation planning by asking participants to forecast their ideas into future scenarios. This forecasting manipulation was further augmented by requiring half of the participants to forecast ideas into future scenarios where their friends or family were involved, while the remaining half forecasted scenarios where their friends and family where removed from the situation. The results of the study suggest that training in causal analysis resulted in more original ideas. More-over, by having participants forecast future scenarios that contained family members and friends, solution quality and originality were also increased. Thus, it seems that by creating personal involvement and providing individuals with the tools to better understand problems through training, creative idea generation is enhanced. As such, the following propositions appear warranted:

> *Proposition 18:* Training in causal analysis—or providing individuals with the cognitive tools for understanding what factors impact or cause desired outcomes—is beneficial to idea generation.

> *Proposition 19:* Personal involvement in a problem tends to increase the quality and originality of idea generation.

Cognitive Processes—A Multilevel Perspective

The generation of original ideas appears to be an inherently individual-level phenomenon and, in many ways, this is indeed the case. However, denying the multilevel impacts (i.e., team, organization, and environmental factors) influencing creative idea generation at the individual level may result in a substantially narrowed—and potentially misleading—view of creativity. For example, idea generation often occurs in a team-based setting where each individual level cognitive process occurs in the presence of other team members. Undeniably, these teammates will have varying levels of expertise, knowledge, personality, and creative ability. The comments and viewpoints of team members, then, can have a substantial impact on individual-level processes such as problem construction and idea generation. Moreover, an organization with few resources and high demand for output (organizational-level factors) may leave employees with little "extra" time for deliberation and consideration of new ideas, in turn impacting the creativity of ideas put forth by individuals. Though many more examples exist,[3] the above suffice to make our basic point: creativity is an inherently multilevel phenomenon and must be considered as such before a full realization of creative potential may be made. Further, failure to take into consideration multilevel conflicts may result in notable decreases in organizational innovation.[3] Thus:

> *Proposition 20:* Creative processes, despite their individual level origins, must be considered in light of other multilevel influences.

Individual- and team-level processes. Recent efforts by Palmon, Herman, and Yammarino[18] have resulted in a relatively comprehensive multilevel review of the eight-process model. More precisely, the authors reviewed each process, considering both individual and team level influences—exploring how such processes may be maximized to enhance innovation. The reader is invited to examine the chapter for greater detail and discussion of this topic, but a summary of the work reveals at least three notable points. First, in a team setting, individuals may arrive at various creative process stages at different times. This varied creative stage arrival may be due to differing degrees of importance held by individuals (i.e., one team member may have a preference for concept selection), or the back-and-forth nature of the creative processes themselves. Second, because individuals may be at differing stages of consideration and cognition, the team-based approach to innovation may require more time than individual-level exploration. This extra time is necessary for each team member to arrive on the "same page" as the other team members. Finally, team creativity may be best facilitated by comprising teams of varying levels of creative personality and ability. Though there may be some conflict due to differences of opinion, the ideas generated will benefit from these varied inputs. In sum, the work by Palmon et al.[18] suggests three propositions:

Proposition 21: The use of teams for creative idea generation will likely result in team members arriving at differing creative process stages at different times.

Proposition 22: The team-based approach to innovation is likely to result in a longer time frame than individual-level idea generation.

Proposition 23: Team composition may play an important role in creative idea generation—with greater creativity occurring in expertise-diverse teams.

Planning from a multilevel perspective. The multilevel investigative efforts by Reiter-Palmon et al.[18] represent a fairly comprehensive review of the eight-process model. In slight contrast, however, other researchers have chosen to focus on one multilevel aspect of creative thought. Specifically, recent efforts by Mumford, Bedell, and Hunter[32] explored implementation planning from a multilevel perspective. Again, planning plays a critical role in creative efforts by helping focus resources onto those ideas that are most feasible, are of greatest utility, and are consistent with goals determined in earlier creative processes (e.g., problem construction). What is noteworthy about the work by Mumford et al.,[32] however, is the exploration of planning from a multilevel perspective. More precisely, Mumford et al. presented a multilevel model of innovation planning where individual-level factors (e.g., mission planning), impact group factors (e.g., relationships), organizational factors (e.g., climate), and environmental factors (e.g., environmental trends) either directly, or indirectly vis-à-vis other factors. Moreover, each factor may then have an impact on other factors, resulting in a recursive, dynamic relationship. The point, broadly made, is that although planning is an individual-level cognitive phenomenon, it is impacted by a host of other inputs in dynamic, interrelated fashion. Thus:

Proposition 24: Planning, despite being an individual level phenomenon, both impacts and is impacted by a host of team-, organization-, and environmental-level factors.

From a multilevel perspective, planning is a complex, resource-intensive task. Fortunately, a few suggestions have been provided to aid in this seemingly daunting task.[32] First, organizations are advised to make use of project portfolios. Such portfolios should be comprised of multiple projects guided by a basic theme consistent with the organization's overall strategy. This approach allows for project failures, an inevitable by-product of creative endeavors, yet allows an organization to have a fairly consistent pipeline of innovations that are, again, congruent with a general organizational strategy. Planning is then possible because the projects are guided by a common theme and therefore share similar constraints, resource requirements, and goals. Second, as decision makers in organizations begin the planning process, it is suggested that they consider potential team, organization, and environmental impacts. Clearly, no planning effort will be able to take into account every possible input—yet those that consider such multilevel factors have an advantage over those who do not. Moreover, as organizational decision makers consider these potential multilevel inputs, they should be aware that what is best for one level may harm or hamper what is best at another level. To illustrate, creativity at the individual level may best be served by allowing individuals time to explore and consider potential outcomes. Allowing employees such "extra" time, however, may hamper organizational bottom line figures—at least initially. This point highlights the aforementioned portfolio approach to innovation planning, which maximizes the possibility that an organization will have a fairly consistent output of innovation—provided multiple projects are engaged in over time. In sum, the following propositions appear warranted:

Proposition 25. Project portfolios, guided by an overall theme, will aid in the planning and, thus, in the innovation process.

Proposition 26: Planning of such projects will best be served by considering potential multilevel impacts.

Proposition 27: When planning for multiple projects and considering potential multilevel impacts, decision makers should be prepared for multilevel paradoxes where what is best at one level may not be best at another.

Training and Enhancing Cognitive Processes

The above discussion of cognitive creative processes should suffice to make a basic point: understanding the cognitive process model is critical to enhancing organizational innovation. If this point is granted, a new question then comes to fore: how can such processes be improved? Or, put directly—can such processes be trained? A recent meta-analysis by Scott, Leritz, and Mumford[19] answers this question by reviewing over seventy studies on creativity training. The results revealed, rather convincingly, that (a) training overall improves creativity, and (b) training the cognitive processes discussed thus far produces the strongest, most consistent improvements in creative performance. The authors suggest that the obtained support for the eight-process model is likely because such training provides strategies for working with knowledge that is already available. Thus, in light of recent meta-analytic efforts the following proposition appears relevant:

Proposition 28: *The processes comprising the eight-stage approach can be improved through training, resulting in substantial and consistent increases in creative performance.*

CONCLUSION

We began our discussion by highlighting the importance of creative cognition to organizational innovation. To reiterate this discussion, before an organization can implement new ideas, it must first obtain such new ideas. Thus, the generation of original, useful concepts stands as a critical initial step in obtaining a competitive advantage through innovation. Further, by understanding the processes involved in idea generation, as well as the important antecedents and influences of these factors, an important step toward organizational success and performance is taken.

To better understand how ideas are generated, an eight-process model of creative thought was presented. This model has been supported in numerous studies and provides researchers and practitioners with a concrete framework for understanding how innovation begins. This model was then viewed in relation to a host of related factors, including personality, ability, knowledge, errors, multilevel perspectives, and training. The results of such efforts, we hope, should provide the reader with not only an understanding of the eight-process model, but also relevant antecedents and outcomes derived from its use. To further provide the reader with direct, applicable tools to enhance innovation, each proposition is paired with a direct application in Table 9.1. The table serves to summarize the propositions spread throughout the chapter but also to demonstrate potential applications derived from their consideration. Such applications are not exhaustive, as there are numerous ways to make applied use of the stated propositions. They do stand, however, as an adequate starting point for enhancing idea generation in an organization. In fact, a review of these applications reveals a few important points. Thus, we conclude with a summary of these observations in the hopes of providing one final set of general recommendations for increasing creative idea generation in the workplace.

Proposition Application

As noted, a review of the proposition applications reveals several notable observations. First, it is clear that idea generation is a time-consuming and resource-intensive activity. Though some would believe that ideas come in "flashes" or quick bursts, in reality, high-quality, original ideas are in fact

TABLE 9.1. Application of Chapter Propositions

	Proposition		Application
1	Creativity is best understood as a process—or series of interconnected stages—rather than a singular mystical or spiritual activity.	1	Creative idea generation must be given substantial time to occur.
2	Creativity appears to involve a dynamic process pattern, whereby individuals may shift between generating and exploring ideas at multiple points in time.	2	Projects should not be ended prematurely if ideas that once appeared "fleshed out" return to an earlier, more generative (less concrete) stage.
3	Identifying and understanding the nature of the problem at hand is critical to creative performance.	3	Individuals and teams should spend substantial time and energy clarifying the aim and goals of the project.
4	Searching for and gathering information relevant to the situation at hand is critical to creative performance.	4	Resources should be dedicated specifically to information gathering. Such resources may include support staff as well as time from upper-level team members.
5	The selection of the most relevant concepts in a given situation is critical to the generation of new, original ideas.	5	Time should be dedicated to thinking, considering, and discussing the most important concepts, as well as removing from discussion unimportant or unnecessary ideas.
6	When a situation requires the combination of concepts that are similar to what was done in previous experiences, such experience and similarity will guide the combination process.	6	Past experiences as well as similarities among concepts should be elicited and pointed out explicitly during project development meetings.
7	When a situation requires the combination of concepts that share little in common with previously combined concepts and each other, abstract frameworks such as metaphors may aid in conceptual combination.	7	If a project appears somewhat unwieldy and there is little discussion structure regarding what should be done in future project stages, the use of guiding concepts such as metaphors may prove beneficial.
8	Once concepts have been combined, conceptually, it is necessary to formally generate workable, concrete ideas.	8	Deciding what ideas to combine is only a partial solution—the task of creating workable ideas is just as, and potentially more, critical to innovation.

9	The evaluation of ideas, or consideration of potential outcomes and resources necessary to produce such outcomes, is a critical aspect of creative performance.	9	Because the obtainment of a workable, concrete idea is a tempting place to end the creative process, a conscious effort (e.g., dedicated meeting times) must be made to carefully and critically consider such ideas.
10	Planning for idea implementation is a process critical to creative achievement.	10	Multiple meetings with multiple stakeholders should be set aside for planning implementation efforts.
11	The monitoring of the implementation of creative ideas is an important part of the creative process—largely due to feedback and subsequent adjustment mechanisms.	11	Once ideas have been implemented, one or more individuals must be explicitly charged with monitoring the progress of the implemented idea. Such individuals or teams should then have the capacity to make recommendations to those with the authority to make changes, or have the capability to make requisite changes directly.
12	Having the capacity, or ability, to frame problems in several alternative, creative ways is related to creative performance.	12	To successfully innovate, a number of employees should be selected for, and team composition comprised of, individuals with creative ability.
13	Fit between one's personality and creative problem solving situation will result in enhanced creative output.	13	Project team composition should take into account the personality of those involved and with an emphasis on creating fit between them and the project requirements.
14	Past experiences are important to conceptual combination and idea generation—but only if they are supplemented with additional knowledge structures such as schematic or associational.	14	When generating new ideas, encourage the discussion of previous experiences. In addition, however, ask questions such as "What else might these ideas relate to?" or "What are the big ideas we're working with here?"
15	When evaluating very new or novel ideas, it is critical to carefully consider such ideas with regard to potentially new, and unforeseen, positive outcomes.	15	The evaluation of creative ideas requires a certain novelty in and of itself. Evaluators must make conscious attempts to think of "unseen" uses and benefits of a given idea.
16	When evaluating creative ideas, be aware that potentially beneficial ideas are often dismissed due to an overweighing of perceived risk.	16	During evaluation meetings, it should be announced that any new idea is risky and that a dedication to innovation requires calculated risk.

TABLE 9.1 (*CONTINUED*)

	Proposition		Application
17	When evaluating new, original ideas, experts are largely beneficial—but should be paired with less expert individuals to reduce forecasting errors.	17	It is nearly always beneficial to include experts on a team or project—but others with less expertise or expertise in other areas will strongly compliment such expertise.
18	Training in causal analysis—or providing individuals with the cognitive tools for understanding what factors impact or cause desired outcomes—is beneficial to idea generation.	18	Training in causal analysis will benefit organizational innovation.
19	Personal involvement in a problem tends to increase the quality and originality of idea generation.	19	When forecasting ideas, ask questions such as "How might this idea impact your family or friends?" to induce personal involvement in idea generation and evaluation.
20	Creative processes, despite their individual level origins, must be considered in light of other multi-level influences.	20	An organization must have innovation support at all levels for idea generation to be maximally beneficial.
21	The use of teams for creative idea generation will likely result in team members arriving at differing creative process stages at different times.	21	Making team members aware that they may differentially arrive at the various creative process stages will reduce the conflict that may occur as a result of such differences.
22	The team-based approach to innovation is likely to result in a longer time frame than individual-level idea generation.	22	Team-based projects will require more time to generate new ideas and must be afforded such time for innovation to be successful.
23	Team composition may play an important role in creative idea generation—with greater creativity occurring in expertise-diverse teams.	23	Project teams should be comprised of varying types and levels of expertise.
24	Planning, despite being an individual-level phenomenon, both impacts and is impacted by a host of team-, organization-, and environmental-level factors.	24	Planning for innovation requires support from all organizational levels and contingencies.
25	Project portfolios guided by an overall theme will aid in the planning and, thus, in the innovation process.	25	Organizations should pursue multiple projects that share a common guiding strategy or theme.

26	Planning of such projects will best be served by considering potential multi-level impacts.	26	During the planning stages, time should be set aside to consider all potential impacts—particularly those occurring at multiple levels.
27	When planning for multiple projects and considering potential multi-level impacts, decision makers should be prepared for multi-level paradoxes where what is best at one level may not be best at another.	27	Innovation is not a "clean" task and may require short-term sacrifice at various levels for the benefit of another level. Such sacrifice should ultimately result in benefits for the entire organization.
28	The processes comprising the eight-stage approach can be improved through training, resulting in substantial and consistent increases in creative performance.	28	Training the cognitive process model, by providing a framework for applying past knowledge and experience, will result in increased creativity.

derived from substantial effort and time. Multiple meetings, considerations, and iterations are necessary for highly creative ideas to be derived. On a related note, then, is the second observation, which is that an organization must be fully dedicated to innovation if innovation is to occur. Employees must be provided both the time and resources necessary to generate new ideas. Further, this support must occur over a relatively lengthy time frame. In addition, an organization must be committed to seeing ideas through, even if such ideas oscillate between generation and evaluation before becoming fully realized, workable products or processes. Moreover, because innovative ideas are inherently novel and different, they may be met with some discomfort by those evaluating their utility. An organization must create and facilitate a working environment that supports the generation, review, and consideration of new—potentially risky—ideas. The third observation, seemingly paradoxically stated, is that idea generation does not end with the generation of an idea. A review of the eight-stage process model reveals that once concepts have been combined (i.e., idea generation), there are numerous stages an idea must subsequently pass through before it can be fully useful to an organization. Moreover, there exists a possibility that an idea may never be truly "finished" but exists rather in a state of continuous innovative improvement. Fourth, a review of the propositions reveals that teams play a particularly critical role in the idea generation process. Though it is relatively clear how teams are necessary to implement creative ideas, it has been somewhat less clear with regard to the impact of team composition on initial idea generation. What one team member says may impact, positively or negatively, the ideas generated by another team member. Moreover, the use of teams inherently means that idea generation will require somewhat more time than individual idea generation—reiterating, again, the importance of an organization's dedication to the support of innovation. Fifth, and similar to the fourth observation, is that idea generation is a multilevel phenomenon. Though ideas are ultimately derived from individuals, a host of inputs occurs at the team-, organization-, and environmental levels. By considering, altering, and adapting to such influences, a notable advantage is gained. Sixth, there exist concrete, obtainable training programs that can enhance creative idea generation. Thus, tools are currently available to directly enhance the generation of new ideas and should be taken advantage of. Seventh, and finally, expertise is a necessary component of idea generation. However, caution is warranted with such a blanket statement—under some circumstances, expertise may result in overconfidence and may act as a detriment to innovation. Thus, it is better stated that experts, when paired with individuals of lesser expertise or expertise in differing areas, will prove to be a critical component of idea generation and innovation.

In sum, the generation of new ideas is a difficult, time-consuming activity that must be engaged in if an organization seeks to be truly innovative. By fully understanding the processes involved in idea generation, however, an important first step is taken. Further, by facilitating and supporting each stage, as well as being dedicated to long-term innovation, an organization will be able to obtain the competitive advantage provided by being the first to put forth an original product or process. It is our hope that this chapter will aid in the facilitation of these goals.

NOTES

1. Dess, Gregory G. 2000. Changing roles: Leadership in the 21st century. *Organizational Dynamics* 28: 18–34.

2. Kuczmarski, Thomas D. 2003. What is innovation? And why aren't companies doing more of it? *Journal of Consumer Marketing* 20: 536–541.

3. Mumford, Michael D. and Samuel T. Hunter. 2005. Innovation in organizations: A multi-level perspective on creativity. In *Research in Multi-level Issues: Volume IV.* Edited by Fred Dansereau & Francis J. Yammarino. Oxford, England: Elsevier.

4. Taggar, Simon, Lorne Sulsky, and Heather MacDonald. In press. Sub-system configuration: A model of strategy, context, and human resource management alignment. In *Pathways to outstanding leadership: A comparative analysis of charismatic, ideological and pragmatic leadership.* Edited by Michael D. Mumford. Mahwah, NJ: Erlbaum Press.

5. Guilford, J. P. 1950. Creativity. American Psychologist 5: 444–454.

6. Basudur, Min, George B. Graen, and Stephen G. Green. 1982. Training in creative problem solving: Effects on ideation and problem finding and solving in an industrial research organization. *Organizational Behavior and Human Performance* 30: 41–70.

7. Parnes, Sidney J. and Roth B. Noller. 1972. Applied creativity: The creative studies project: II. Results of the two year program. *Journal of Creative Behavior* 6: 164–186.

8. Marcy, Rich T. and Michael D. Mumford. In press. Social innovation: Enhancing creative performance through causal analysis. *Creativity Research Journal.*

9. Hunter, Samuel T., Katrina Bedell, and Michael D. Mumford. In press. Climate and Creativity: A Meta–Analysis. *Creativity Research Journal.*

10. Sternberg, Robert J. and Todd I. Lubart. 1999. The concept of creativity: prospects and paradigms. In *Handbook of creativity.* Edited by Robert J. Sternberg. Cambridge, England: Cambridge University Press.

11. Wallas, Graham. 1926. *The art of thought.* London: J. Cape.

12. Amabile, Teresa M. 1996. *Creativity in context: Update to "The social psychology of creativity."* Boulder, CO: Westview Press.

13. Lubart, Todd I. 2001. Models of the creative process: Past, present, and future. *Creativity Research Journal* 13: 295–308.

14. Finke, Ronald A., Thomas B. Ward, and Steven M. Smith. 1992. *Creative cognition: Theory, research, and applications.* Cambridge, MA: MIT Press.

15. Mumford, Michael D. et al. 1991. Process analytic models of creative capacities. *Creativity Research Journal* 4: 91–122.

16. Mumford, Michael D., Norman G. Peterson, and Ruth A. Childs. 1999. Basic and cross-functional skills. In *An occupational information system for the 21st century: The development of O*NET.* Edited by Norman G. Peterson et al. Washington, DC: American Psychological Association.

17. Dewey, John. 1910. *How we think.* New York: Heath.

18. Reiter-Palmon, Roni, Anne E. Herman, and Francis Yammarino. In press. Creativity and cognitive processes: Multi-level linkages between individual and team cognition. In *Pathways to outstanding leadership: A comparative analysis of charismatic, ideological, and pragmatic leadership.* Edited by Michael D. Mumford. Mahwah, NJ: Erlbaum Press.

19. Scott, Ginamarie M., Lyle E. Leritz, and Michael D. Mumford. 2004. The effectiveness of creativity training: A meta-analysis. *Creativity Research Journal* 16: 361-388.

20. Mumford, Michael D. et al. 1996. Process-based measures of creative problem-solving skills: I. Problem construction. *Creativity Research Journal* 9: 63–76.

21. Mumford, Michael D. and Sigrid B. Gustafson. 1988. Creativity syndrome: Integration, application, and innovation. *Psychological Bulletin* 103: 27–43.

22. Hoover, Steven M. and John F. Feldhusen. 1990. The scientific hypothesis formulation ability of gifted ninth-grade students. *Journal of Educational Psychology* 84: 838–848.

23. Redmond, Matthew R., Michael D. Mumford, and Richard Teach. 1993. Putting creativity to work: Effects of leader behavior on subordinate creativity. *Organizational Behavior and Human Decision Processes* 55: 120–151.

24. Mumford, Michael D., Wayne A. Baughman et al. 1996. Process-based measures of creative problem-solving skills: II. Information encoding. *Creativity Research Journal* 9: 77–88.

25. Mumford, Michael D., Elizabeth P. Supinski et al. 1996. Process-based measures of creative problem-solving skills: III. Category selection. *Creativity Research Journal* 9: 395–406.

26. Mumford, Michael D., Wayne A. Baughman et al. 1997. Process-based measures of creative problem-solving skills: IV. Category combination. Creativity Research Journal 10: 59–71.

27. Basadur, Min, Mark A. Runco, and Luis A. Vega. 2000. Understanding how creative thinking skills, attitudes, and behaviors work together: A causal process model. *Journal of Creative Behavior* 34: 77–100.

28. Dailey, Lesley and Michael D. Mumford. In press. Evaluative aspects of creative thought: Errors in appraising the implications of new ideas. *Creativity Research Journal*.

29. Runco, Mark A. and Ivonne Chand. 1994. Problem finding, evaluative thinking, and creativity. In *Problem finding, problem solving, and creativity*. Edited by Mark A. Runco. Norwood, NJ: Ablex.

30. Lonergan, Devin C., Ginamarie M. Scott, and Michael D. Mumford. 2004. Evaluative aspects of creative thought: Effects of idea appraisal and revision standards. *Creativity Research Journal* 16: 231–246.

31. Mumford, Michael D., Devin C. Lonergan, and Ginamarie M. Scott. 2002. Evaluating creative ideas: Processes, standards, and context. *Inquiry: Critical Thinking across the Disciplines* 22: 21–30.

32. Mumford, Michael D., Katrina Bedell, and Samuel Hunter. In press. Planning for innovation: A multi-level perspective. In *Research in multi-level issues: Vol. VII.* Oxford, England: Elsevier.

33. Reiter-Palmon, Roni et al. 1997. Problem construction and creativity: The role of ability, cue consistency, and active processing. *Creativity Research Journal* 10: 9–23.

34. Reiter-Palmon, Roni, Michael D. Mumford, and K. Victoria Threlfall. 1998. Solving everyday problems creatively: The role of problem construction and personality type. *Creativity Research Journal* 11: 187–197.

35. Licuanan, Brian, Lesley R. Dailey, and Michael D. Mumford. In press. Idea evaluation: Error in evaluating highly original ideas. *Creativity Research Journal*.

36. Blair, Cassandra, and Michael D. Mumford. In press. Errors in idea evaluation: Preference for the unoriginal? *Journal of Creative Behavior*.

37. Dailey, Lesley and Michael D. Mumford. In press. Evaluative aspects of creative thought: Errors in appraising the implications of new ideas. *Creativity Research Journal*.

38. Dudeck, Steven Z. and Remi Cote. 1994. Problem finding revisited. In *Problem finding, problem solving, and creativity*. Edited by M. A. Runco. Norwood, NJ: Abler.

39. Dunbar, Kevin. 1995. How do scientists really reason: Scientific reasoning in real-world laboratories. In *The nature of insight*. Edited by Robert J. Sternberg and Janet E. Davidson. Cambridge, MA: MIT Press.

40. Henderson, Sheila J. 2004. Product inventors and creativity: The fine dimensions of enjoyment. *Creativity Research Journal* 16: 293–312.

41. Kaufman, James C. 2002. Dissecting the golden goose: Components of studying creative writers. *Creativity Research Journal* 14: 27–40.

42. Mace, Mary Ann and Thomas B. Ward. 2002. Modeling the creative process: A grounded theory analysis of creativity in the domain of art making. *Creativity Research Journal* 14: 179–192.

43. Mumford, Michael D. 2002. Social innovation: Ten cases from Benjamin Franklin. *Creativity Research Journal* 14: 253–266.

44. Mumford, Michael D. and Peter Moertl. 2003. Cases of social innovation: Lessons from two innovations in the 20th century. *Creativity Research Journal* 14: 261–266.

45. Frankwick, Gary L., Beth A. Walker, and James C. Ward. 1994. Belief structures in conflict: Mapping a strategic marketing decision. *Journal of Business Research* 31: 183–195.

10

Designing Rewards to Enhance Innovation

TONY DAVILA

R ewards—both social and economic—are powerful drivers of human behavior. But often, when talking about innovation, they are disregarded as if ignoring them makes their relevance go away. Badly designed rewards will inhibit the positive effects of other organizational design variables. For instance, at a telecom company, a customer service representative designed a software package that allowed her to increase productivity by a factor of ten. When her supervisors found out, she was punished for not following defined procedures. A person at a software firm decided to develop software that would be a great enhancement for the main product. Management acknowledged that it was a great idea but only gave a token amount of funding to the effort. In addition, developing her idea was added on top of her already demanding other performance objectives. In both cases, the implicit rewards that these managers got for their ideas clearly indicated that certain innovations were not welcome.

Having no explicit rewards for innovation does not mean that there are no rewards—as the prior examples illustrate—rather, it may mean that the wrong rewards are in place. Moreover, not all types of innovation require the same type of rewards; much to the contrary, they differ to a large extent. Figure 10.1 describes the characteristics of incremental versus radical innovations as two

This chapter is based on ideas developed in the book by Davila, Epstein, and Shelton, "Making Innovation Work," Wharton School Press (2005).

Incremental	Radical
Enhances current business model	May destroy a significant part of the current business model
Strong support from organization	Weak support from a significant part of the current organization
Embedded in day-to-day operations	Protected from day-to-day operations
Innovation structure within current structure	Innovation structure parallel to current structure
Detailed innovation process, little customization at the project level	Innovation process broadly defined, highly customized for each project

FIGURE 10.1. The Two Generic Innovations

extremes of the innovation continuum—while all innovations fall somewhere in between these extremes, these two generic types of innovation are useful to develop the arguments in the chapter.[1]

Incremental innovation advances the current business model through improvements such as better product performance, higher quality, or better customer service. In most organizations, incremental innovation is highly valued because it enhances the competitive positioning of the firm without significantly changing the internal power structure or the industry dynamics (at least in the short term). It is embedded in daily processes such as total quality management, customer relationship management, or new product development. Efforts to have incremental innovations are supported by top management, planned, deployed through routines, and monitored.

Radical innovation presents a very different landscape. If successful, it reshapes to a large extent the power structure within the company and the rules of the game in an industry.[2] It is not about advancing the current business model, but about coming up with a different business model. iTunes from Apple is not an enhancement of an existing business model, but a radical new way of delivering music to the end consumer. Salesforce.com is not about improving the CRM (Customer Relationship Management) software but about redefining how CRM is used and paid for. Radical innovation is riskier, infrequent, unexpected, and, because it challenges the existing definition of the business, does not naturally fit in the existing processes. Rather, the existing organization will have a tendency to reject it as disrupting the existing flows. If radical innovation is forced to fit into processes adapted to the current business model (as if it were an incremental innovation), it is very likely to fail (or become an incremental innovation). Managing radical innovation requires parallel designs, including very different reward mechanisms.

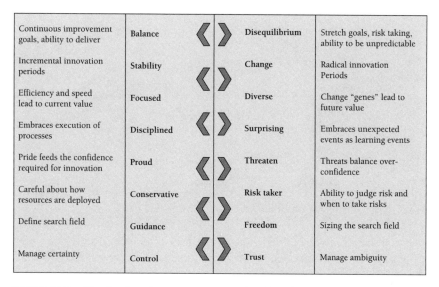

Continuous improvement goals, ability to deliver	Balance		Disequilibrium	Stretch goals, risk taking, ability to be unpredictable
Incremental innovation periods	Stability		Change	Radical innovation Periods
Efficiency and speed lead to current value	Focused		Diverse	Change "genes" lead to future value
Embraces execution of processes	Disciplined		Surprising	Embraces unexpected events as learning events
Pride feeds the confidence required for innovation	Proud		Threaten	Threats balance over-confidence
Careful about how resources are deployed	Conservative		Risk taker	Ability to judge risk and when to take risks
Define search field	Guidance		Freedom	Sizing the search field
Manage certainty	Control		Trust	Manage ambiguity

FIGURE 10.2. The Tensions between Incremental and Radical Innovation

Figure 10.2 illustrates the tensions that need to be managed to create innovation. Innovation requires balancing processes, stability, focus, and discipline to obtain the most value from the innovations of the firm. At the same time, it needs being out of balance, change, diversity, and surprises to be exposed to ideas that will drive future value. Innovation requires a company proud of its achievements, careful with how resources are deployed, but at the same time a company that needs to feel the need to explore and to invest resources in hunches and experiments. Innovation requires broad strokes outlining the direction of the company to align its members, as well as control to make information available for establishing discussions around opportunities. At the same time, its members need freedom to explore and top management's trust that they will work in line with the objectives of the company.

THE REQUISITES FOR INNOVATION

Other chapters in this book explore different aspects of organizational design. This chapter takes the team as the unit of analysis to understand the design of rewards for different types of innovation.

The motivation of team members is an important part in making innovation happen, and rewards have a large impact on it; but motivation also depends on (and influences) the resources available to the team, the interaction of team members among them, with other people in the organization and with people outside the organization, and their stock and flow of knowledge. Even the best reward system will be useless if resources are too scarce, the

FIGURE 10.3.   The Requisites of Innovation

team is inward looking, or their knowledge base is limited. In the same way, adequate resources, networks of interaction, and knowledge will be useless if team members feel that they will not be rewarded appropriately.[3] Figure 10.3 outlines these four levers.

RESOURCES

The first lever of innovation is the availability of resources. The lack of resources is often mentioned as one of the most important limitations for individuals and teams to be innovative.[4] However, the opposite—having too many resources—is not the solution either. 3M is well known for its policy of allowing its people to devote 15 percent of their time to explore their own ideas. Innovation requires slack in resources, but not too much.

As important as the number of resources is their mix. Figure 10.4 describes the four main types of resources required for innovation. The first type of resources is what is termed "freedom"—the time and money to look for ideas, test them, and translate them into value. A research team in a European medical devices company spent five years looking for a material to design a special type of clips used in brain surgery to temporarily close blood vessels. Regular clips cannot be used if during surgery an imaging procedure using magnetic fields is required—these clips respond to these fields and can move during the imaging procedure and create a life-threatening situation. During these five years, the CEO was always supportive of the effort—even if results took longer than expected—and gave the team the time and money to get the project to success. Support from top management and freedom were more important to the motivation of the team than any economic reward that they could have received.

The second type of resources is labeled "complementary assets." Seldom do innovations depend on just one type of assets; rather, they often bring together different technologies, or they need complementary business processes

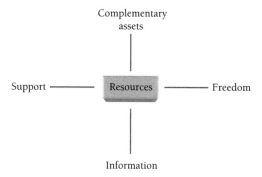

FIGURE 10.4. The Components of Resources

to be successfully deployed. Logitech, the world leader in computer peripherals, has taken the remote control market by storm—capturing more than 30 percent of the market in less than one year—through the acquisition of a small start-up with great technology and by leveraging Logitech's assets—from its brand name, marketing expertise, manufacturing capabilities, and engineering know-how—to grow the innovation fast and to success. In this case, business assets played a key role as complements to the technology. Pharmaceutical companies are teaming up with biotechnology start-up companies to have access to technologies that complement their internal R&D processes. For an innovation team to be successful, it must realize that it cannot do all by itself and must identify the complementary assets that it and the company will need to provide it with access to these complementary assets.[5]

The third type of resources is not tangible, as the prior two are; it is an intangible resource that makes or breaks innovation. The European team developing the brain surgery clip emphasized not only the importance of freedom but the support that it received from the CEO throughout the project. The importance of a culture that supports innovation is often mentioned as a key ingredient.[6] And culture becomes reality through the day-to-day interactions among people and the example set by supervisors. If these interactions and examples reward risk taking (regardless of the end result), creativity, questioning the status quo, experimentation, and advancing new ideas, the culture will crystallize to support innovation.

The final resource that needs to be available is information; again, it is an intangible resource, but one that needs tangible investments in technology. Information technology has made sharing information much simpler than it used to be. A large software company developed an intranet where the expertise of each person in the company was coded. The objective was to make specific knowledge that the company already had available to every person. Informal networks—an approach that misses large pockets of knowledge—were complemented with a powerful formal network. Large consulting firms make "engagement histories" available through the company's intranet to leverage existing knowledge as much as possible. Knowledge management technology lies behind these resources. Information technology has also made it possible to tap into the talent of people around the world. Today, it is common to have projects distributed among different locations that coordinate their efforts through IT. Information coming from the outside is also critical—from integrated information systems with suppliers to advanced market research techniques.

These four types of resources—freedom, tangible assets, support, and information—are seldom considered when analyzing rewards; but the best reward system will fail if the deployment of resources is wrong.

INTERACTION

The second lever for innovation is to design the organization in such a way that people get enough exposure to different mindsets to generate promising ideas and to develop innovations as robust to value capture as possible (see Figure 10.5).

Ideas, not only the ones that are typically considered to be the seed of an innovation, but also the flow of ideas that shape a project until it is translated into value, require people to be within streams where different views flow. These views are about how to make a business model succeed, different technologies, and different opinions about where markets are moving. Resources will fall in an empty box if they cannot be filled with quality.

The first aspect of interaction is the need for it. Challenging goals are often a trigger of this need to search. Sony's founder was continuously challenging his managers to come up with radical innovations—if VCRs could be produced at a cost of several thousand dollars, he wanted to have one for a few hundred dollars; if there were only black-and-white televisions he wanted a color one—and affordable. The idea of stretch goals—aiming at goals that require a

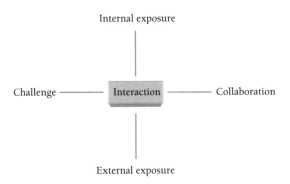

FIGURE 10.5. The Components of Interaction

different way of thinking about the business model to achieve them—captures this approach to challenging people.[7]

Stretch goals are more appropriate when motivating radical innovation. Incremental innovation relies on more realistic goals—having a new toy ready for the Christmas season, designing a digital camera with a specific target cost,[8] or designing a particular chip manufacturing machine with a clear technical goal in mind.[9]

In the same way, goals for radical innovation are broader and qualitative— "developing a cure for AIDS," "creating a viable business model for photovoltaic energy generation that does not rely on government subsidies," or "eradicating poverty from country X"—while goals for incremental innovation are more specific and place more emphasis on quantitative objectives—"reducing the cost of production by 10 percent," "improving customer satisfaction to 80 percent."

Finally, goals for radical innovation emphasize success—what new world the innovation is aiming at and how it will be different once the innovation is deployed. Incremental innovation is about what needs to be done to make the effort worthwhile—it describes minimum thresholds that, if missed, make the investment unattractive. Figure 10.6 summarizes the discussion on target setting.

Interaction is also enhanced through structures that maximize internal exposure to other functions. In new product development, the performance advantage of cross-functional teams over function-specific teams is widely accepted.[10] British Petroleum has created a structure to bring people from different geographies and business units together through the concept of "peer assists," where business units lend people in their organization with certain knowledge to another business unit facing a specific problem where this expertise is required.[11]

External exposure has become crucial in an environment where the talent and knowledge required to innovate seldom reside within a single organization. Conferences and trade shows are important vehicles to scout for new ideas. Red Herring, the leading media company on the business of technology, organizes conferences where venture capitalists, corporate ventures, entrepreneurs,

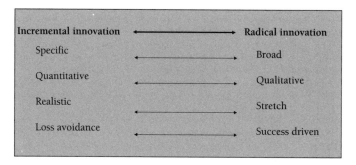

FIGURE 10.6. Objectives for Incremental and Radical Innovation

and technology companies come together to make deals happen. The technology behind Logitech's most radical product, the IO Pen—a pen that records what is written on each page regardless of the sequence in which it was written and then can be downloaded into a computer—was spotted at a trade show and addresses a very different problem.

The last aspect of interaction is collaboration—established agreements with external partners to deploy innovation. This collaboration ranges from having an Internet platform to share technology problems for individuals outside the company to propose solutions—a collaboration tool that Eli Lilly is using—to more traditional organizational designs—from strategic partnerships to joint ventures.[12]

KNOWLEDGE

The third lever to think about is the stock and flow of knowledge in the team (see Figure 10.7). To take advantage of availability of resources and the interaction with different mental models, innovation teams need to have depth of expertise. When Intel moved from being a memory company to its very successful microprocessor strategy, its deep understanding of silicon technology was a key ingredient in making the transition. Depth of expertise is required to identify new opportunities, not only technology opportunities, but also opportunities to redefine a business model. Often, it is people with a few years of experience in an industry who identify new business models—it has been true in industries such as telecommunications or health care. Depth of expertise is also key to interaction. It allows the team to assess the value of partnering with an outside party and integrate external technologies into the project. It also makes the team attractive to external parties—which simplifies the process of scanning the environment to identify opportunities or worthy partners.

Depth of expertise comes together with breadth of expertise. Cross-functional teams are intended to bring the required breadth. Problems in business are difficult not because of the complexity of the issues examined—physics or ethics

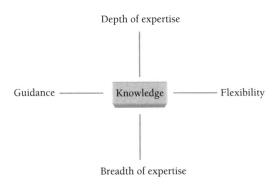

FIGURE 10.7. The Components of Knowledge

present much tougher problems—but because very different types of expertise come into play—something that does not happen to the same extent in other disciplines. This breadth may be required at the technology level—consider the technologies required to design a mobile phone—but is needed mostly at the business level—engineering management, marketing, manufacturing, financing, quality control, etc. Successful innovation combines T-type expertise with depth in a particular discipline, but breadth large enough to be able to interact with external parties with adequate understanding of the issues at hand.

Knowledge also requires flexibility; this is the ability to accept that there is valuable knowledge to be acquired from the outside. Flexibility captures the idea of being amenable to external influences. Successful teams run the risk of thinking that nothing outside them is as good as what they do. The not-invented-here syndrome illustrates this problem—nothing from outside will be as good as what the team does. A company had rejected acquiring a smaller competitor because the technology behind its main product was not as good as the technology of the larger company. When a new CEO took over the company, he decided to acquire the competitor—it was not technology that he was buying, but a superior market position in a particular product market. As the prior concepts have detailed, flexibility only flourishes with adequate expertise, adequate interactions with the external world, enough resources, and well-designed rewards systems. What is the value of being flexible when there is no expertise to judge the value of opportunities? When interactions are scarce?

Finally, knowledge requires guidance. The knowledge out in the world is immense, with no guidance; each person on a team and each team in a company will explore according to their own intuition. The result of knowledge with no guidance is likely to be wasted resources and disparate ideas that generate confrontation rather than discussion. British Petroleum is very clear about where it wants to go: "We are in *only four* businesses: oil and gas exploration and production; refining and marketing; petrochemicals; and photovoltaics, or solar." General Electric's policy of being number one or two in the industry also provides guidance on which opportunities are worth exploring.[13] Giving guidance of where the company wants to go in terms of innovation is the task of top management—it needs to decide and communicate where ideas will be welcome and what will happen to ideas that are outside the boundaries.

MOTIVATION

Resources, interactions, and knowledge are important to design reward systems in innovation (see Figure 10.8). But motivation is the closest of the four levers in Figure 10.1.

Sometimes discussions about reward systems are limited to economic incentives—as if money (or the expectation of future money) was all that mattered.[14] But as the CEO of a start-up company put it: "One thing that I have

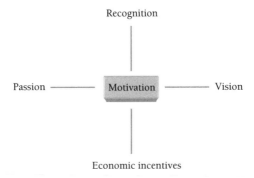

FIGURE 10.8. The Components of Motivation

learned over these years about technology people is that money is important, but food is extremely important."[15] Economic incentives are an important part of motivation, and often companies link bonuses to meeting project deadlines. Incentives are designed before a project starts—for example, linking 10 percent of the salary to meeting project objectives. Philips, the Dutch consumer electronics multinational, links the bonus of its product development teams to meeting release date targets. However, putting too much weight on these incentives has been shown to be detrimental to performance.[16] The next section elaborates on how to design incentive systems.

But rewards do not necessarily have to be either economic or defined before the project starts. Recognition is a reward that occurs after the results of the projects are observed. Usually, recognition is based on subjective evaluation. It may be an economic reward, such as a bonus, but often recognition includes tokens that have little economic value but large significance to people—a casual conversation where the CEO praises the work, the satisfaction of the team leader, a team trip to a hockey game, assigning the team to a more challenging project. The European team working on the brain surgery clip valued the words of support from the CEO more than any economic reward that could come out of the project. However, recognition has to be fair—giving a token reward for a very large success can be interpreted as considering the team ignorant of its accomplishments and being taken advantage of.

Often people engage in an innovation not because of what they expect to get, but because they love the challenge. They do it for passion—or what is known in the academic literature as intrinsic motivation. They are self-motivated, and putting emphasis on external rewards (such as economic incentives) may be detrimental because it attenuates this motivation. The R&D manager of a major car company described his engineers as motivated by their strong interest in car technologies and seeing their innovations as parts of the new models.

Another source of motivation is the vision. It is very different to work for enhancing shareholder wealth than it is to work to "save lives," as described in a hospital mission statement "for the reconstruction of Japan," as Sony described its mission after World War II. People are more likely to take risks and pursue ideas if the overall purpose of the organization is not simply to generate money but to make a difference in the world.

DESIGNING REWARDS FOR INNOVATION

Incremental and radical innovation require different reward systems. A structured, formula-based reward system with an emphasis on incentive systems is better fitted for incremental innovation. Incremental innovation is about solving a well-defined problem—increasing efficiency, improving quality, reducing product cost, or improving customer service—with shorter-term results and smaller impact on the organization. It is relatively easier to measure performance and to describe expected performance before the project starts. Incremental innovation projects can be planned, monitored through specific milestones, and evaluated against targets—think about stage-gate processes in new product development, where expected performance is planned for each gate and evaluated at the gate.[17] Cash-based incentives linked with performance through formula are more appropriate for this type of innovation.

As projects incorporate a more significant element of radical innovation, reward systems emphasize recognition and incentive systems based on long-term mechanisms (stock-based incentive systems) and subjective evaluation. Radical innovation works on less structured problems, the spark of creativity is more unpredictable, and objectives are fuzzier and are constantly reevaluated as new information becomes available. Radical innovation is about exploring new territory, trying alternatives, changing goals, rapidly adapting to new findings. Using specific goals, with cash-based incentives based on meeting these goals,

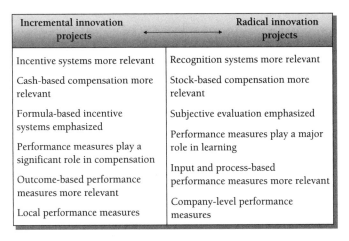

Incremental innovation projects	⟷	Radical innovation projects
Incentive systems more relevant		Recognition systems more relevant
Cash-based compensation more relevant		Stock-based compensation more relevant
Formula-based incentive systems emphasized		Subjective evaluation emphasized
Performance measures play a significant role in compensation		Performance measures play a major role in learning
Outcome-based performance measures more relevant		Input and process-based performance measures more relevant
Local performance measures		Company-level performance measures

FIGURE 10.9. Rewards in Incremental and Radical Innovation

would shift attention to meeting the targets that trigger the incentive.[18] Formula-based incentives are hard to use in the radical innovation arena because the value generated is unknown until after the fact. Recognition is better suited for radical innovation. It allows linking the rewards to the effort deployed, to the value of the innovation, and to results that were unpredictable. Once the project is done, managers have to feel rewarded for putting forth the effort and taking the risk even if the project was not successful; they must feel that they receive a fair share of the value generated from the project if it is successful. Stock-based incentives are better suited for radical innovation—they are not necessarily associated with particular targets, and they are tightly linked to the creation of value. Figure 10.9 summarizes this discussion.

A FRAMEWORK FOR INCENTIVE DESIGN

Figure 10.10 presents a framework for designing incentive systems. An incentive system has to reinforce the innovation strategy whether it is at the level of the company or the innovation project. The previous section has discussed the different needs of incremental and radical innovations. Strategies also affect incentive systems' design. Nikon, the Japanese camera manufacturer, sets very clear target costs for its cameras—product profitability is highly dependent on product costs. In contrast, Applied Materials, the leader in integrated circuits' production equipment, works at the edge of particle physics with tight deadlines imposed by its main customers. Product cost during product development has a secondary role, with product performance and time to market dominating the development strategy.

The innovation strategy guides the selection of the performance measures that will be used in designing the contract. Strategies where cost plays an important role, such as Nikon, emphasize cost-related measures. At the business-unit level, performance measures will depend on the business model for innovation—from

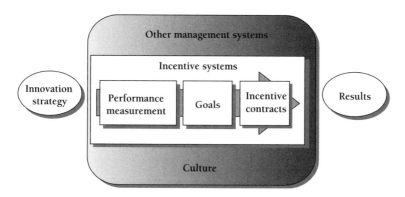

FIGURE 10.10. Designing Incentive Systems

inputs to processes, outputs, and outcomes. The design of performance measurement systems is detailed in another chapter in this series.[19]

Incentives are designed against performance targets and linked to incentives through contracts. From an incentive design perspective, three characteristics of measures and contracts are relevant to discuss: objective versus subjective, team versus individual, and relative versus absolute.

Subjective versus Objective

An important design decision is how to combine subjectivity and objectivity. Subjectivity may come through subjective performance measures or contracts that provide some room for subjectivity.

A significant advantage of subjectivity is that it allows incorporating information other than what is explicitly included in objective measures. It can adjust the "hard" numbers with additional information not necessarily reflected in the measurement system. A contract based on an explicit formula with explicit weights on objective performance measures cannot adjust for unexpected events. For instance, it cannot adjust for the negative impact of the unexpected bankruptcy of a key supplier of technology. In contrast, a subjective performance evaluation can account for it and reward the team more fairly.

Another limitation of objective measures is that they need to trade off completeness versus controllability. The more dimensions of a team's effort captured in objective measures (that is, the more complete the performance measurement system), the less controllable factors are also included. Think about measuring the performance of a CEO. Profits are more controllable than stock price; but they fail in capturing the actions of the CEO that increase future profits. Stock price captures the actions that increase both current profits and future ones, but it includes many more uncontrollable factors, such as interest rates, economy-wide factors, or the "mood" of the market.

Subjective evaluation is superior to objective evaluation in certain aspects. It can include information not foreseen before the project started, it can include observations of how the team worked and behaved, it can take into account efforts and actions that are hard to quantify in objective measures, it can adjust evaluation for uncontrollable events, and it can change the weights of the different dimensions of the innovation effort as their relevance evolves over time. But subjective evaluation has also its own limitations. It depends very much on the ability of the person making the subjective evaluation. If this person has the respect of subordinates, has collected information throughout the innovation effort, has the right incentives, and can be trusted to provide a fair evaluation, then subjective evaluation will work. But often this is not the case. Building reputation takes time, and often people will be in a position to evaluate much earlier than their reputation allows them. All of us think of ourselves as being better than we are—within a group, more than 50 percent of the people will assign themselves to the top 50 percent. So it is likely that subordinates will be unhappy with not-so-positive evaluations. When subjective evaluation is used, there is often "grade inflation" because the person evaluating has no incentives to provide negative feedback.

Companies use a mix of subjective and objective performance evaluation; but in designing incentive system, it is important to keep in mind these criteria to decide how to weigh these two types of evaluations.

Team versus Individual

Innovation projects are team efforts with a common objective of translating ideas into value. As such, it makes sense to have some incentives common to all team members. But some incentives should also be determined at the individual level. Certain individuals are key contributors with ideas, effort, and teamwork; as such, they need to have individual rewards. Without an individual component, the system can be perceived as unfair, thus leading to underperformance.[20]

Individual rewards are also important to avoid "free-riders"—people who do not carry their fair amount of work. A manager described his experience thus: "I was working more than fifteen hours a day most of the time, seven days a week, I was doing the analysis of every single project performance; I quit because I thought it was unfair to do all the work and then everybody getting the praise." The team leader needs to be empowered to replace members who are not performing to the standards of the team—a person who does not do his fair amount of work, whether because of lack of effort or lack of skills, may drag the performance of the whole team.

Objective measures are relatively easy at the team level—whether a new product was released on time, with the right product cost and specifications. Objective measures are more difficult at the individual level; then, subjective evaluation is needed. In Johnson and Johnson's medical devices division, members of product development teams worked on several projects at the same time as well as working for their function; individual performance evaluation was done based on the evaluation of each person who supervised the individual in his different tasks. Another alternative is to use 360-degree evaluation to average out idiosyncratic opinions.

Some companies use profit sharing or gain sharing mechanisms. These mechanisms encourage collaboration throughout the company and not only at the team level. However, their incentive effect decreases as the company becomes larger. It may even be the case that an excellent team may end up with no compensation because the rest of the company did poorly. This problem is also common when using stock-based compensation. In large companies, stock awards have no economic incentive effect, and their effect is limited to feeling part of the group. But if a team does very well and the stock poorly, the team may feel some solidarity with its coworkers, but it will also feel unfairly rewarded.

Gain sharing links incentives to the value of the innovation for as long as the innovation is creating value. Gain sharing often leads to rewards over several years—as long as the effort is creating value. While gain sharing measures what matters, this is value; long time horizons have the drawback that as time passes, efforts other than that of the team affect value—for instance, the effort of the salespeople in pushing the new product. Over time, other events impact the gains and the initial effort is diluted among these other events.

Relative versus Absolute

Targeted performance can be defined relative to the performance of other projects or initiatives—either inside or outside the organization. For instance, the CEO may be rewarded not on stock performance but on stock performance relative to other companies in the industry. Quality performance can be benchmarked against other companies. Relative goals have the advantage of being more tangible compared to absolute goals that can be perceived as "made up." Why should sales growth be 10 percent rather than 8 percent or 12 percent? In contrast, goals can be set relative to industry growth and stated as targeted sales growth is 2 percent higher than the industry average. When Mobil introduced a new measurement system, it used performance goals relative to competitors. ROCE (return on capital employed) and EPS (earnings per share) were measured against the top seven competitors; nonfinancial measures were linked to Mobil's ranking in the industry.

Relative performance within a company should be used with care because it creates competition rather than cooperation. It should be used if there are other organizational forces that support cooperation. The problems of the Latin American division of a large software company illustrate this argument. The division top position was granted to the country manager with the best record—creating competition among countries. While competition was healthy at the national level, countries were not cooperating and the division was losing deals that involved cross-national customers. All sales were booked to the country where the final sale was made and none to the countries that had helped. Countries other than the one where the sale was booked had no incentive to help in cross-national deals.

CONTRACT DESIGN

The last aspect of the incentive systems design is the design of the incentive contract. In addition to the discussion on subjective and objective, team and individual, and relative and absolute, four additional considerations are relevant to the design of contracts: expected level of pay, shape and slope of the performance-pay relationship, timing, and delivery of the pay.

Expected Level of Pay

The expected level of pay is the "market price" of a job. Compensation consulting firms have tables for industries and regions that help in identifying these prices. Of course, the particular compensation of a person will depend on the unique characteristics of the job and the person and on how the pay-for-performance is structured. Moreover, some companies choose to have an expected above-the-industry average in an effort to attract and retain talent.

Pay-for-Performance Relationship

The expected level of pay is relatively easy to find out. The pay-for-performance relationship is more specific to each firm. A variety of shapes exist—almost as many as there are firms and jobs in the market. In some cases the bonus is staged in three levels—no bonus for subpar performance, 15 percent for par performance, and 30 percent of salary for above-par performance. This structure was used at CitiBank's retail branches in the late nineties.

In other cases, the relationship between pay and performance is linear with performance measures, but with a floor (for which the bonus is zero) and a ceiling. The floor is intended to protect against very negative performance due to uncontrollable factors. The ceiling is intended to avoid rewarding for luck. A division of a pharmaceutical firm was the leader in a market; the market had another large player and a myriad of smaller ones. Competition between the two main players kept margins low. But the setting changed in a particular year. The FDA found problems in the manufacturing facility of the main competitor and closed it. The division was left as the dominant player, a position that it used to increase margins. Profit for the year increased 400 percent (the following year, things were expected to go back to normal after the competitor solved the problem or with the entry of new players attracted by the healthy margins). Without an upper ceiling, the division manager would have gotten an impressive bonus (350 percent of his salary, compared with the usual 30 percent)—partly because of his ability to put a competitor out of business, but mainly because of factors over which he had no control (the quality at the competitor's plant).

In still other cases, the relationship is linear all the way, and a "bank" account is used to accumulate bonuses in good years (above a certain threshold) and to debit negative bonuses in bad years.

Step changes are inferior to smooth linear relationships. A linear relationship rewards and penalizes proportionally to the performance, providing a constant incentive to improve performance. The CitiBank bonus system had two steps—from zero to fifteen percent and from fifteen to thirty percent of salary. A system with a floor and a ceiling has two kinks, at the floor and at the ceiling. In the presence of steps or kinks, a manager who knows that his performance won't get into the linear part of the bonus (or knows that it will get beyond the ceiling) may decide to limit his effort. Smooth relationships avoid these incentives to limit effort.

In addition to the shape, the slope of the relationship is another relevant parameter. Steeper relationships create more incentives to meet goals. But too-steep incentives may work against the intended effect because they may lead to risk-averse decisions. Researchers in basic science seldom work under steep incentive schemes because they are supposed to work with tough problems where risks are part of finding the solution. Rather, research contracts are cost plus—where a client such as the government reimburses the costs that the team incurs in the project. The objective is for these teams to focus on experimenting and trying new approaches (most of which will not work) to find the solution, rather than focusing on meeting targets for getting bonuses. Steep slopes also focus the manager's attention too much on the performance dimensions included in the formula at the expense of other relevant issues. If these performance dimensions are not complete, they may lead to problems. A medical devices start-up company had been acquired by a large pharmaceutical company. Part of the payment for the start-up was based on sales and profits over the following three years. The entrepreneurs decided to offer a very nice bonus to every single person in the company if sales and profit goals were met. The sales and profits goals for the first year were met—people had reacted to the incentives. But in their effort to meet the goals, product quality and service deteriorated to a level where the FDA had to intervene.

Timing

The third characteristic of the contract is timing. First, retention of key employees can be enhanced through deferred and long-term compensation. Stock options and restricted stock are clear examples of timing issues because the person cannot fully cash them for an extended period of time—usually five years. Second, for radical innovation projects, the full value of the innovation may not materialize for an extended period of time. Therefore, an incentive mechanism that takes into account the long-term is more adequate. Again, stock options and restricted stock fulfill this role. The use of these securities is common in venture-backed start-up firms—they save cash, but more importantly, they reward managers for their ability to generate value over a time horizon of several years.

Bonus payments can also be based on future performance. For instance, the bonus associated with a process improvement innovation project may be a percentage of the cost savings that the company realizes over time. This timing works better to reward for value creation and to retain employees.

Delivery of Compensation

Cash is the most common way of delivering incentives (through bonuses). Cash incentives are better suited for rewarding performance that can be readily measured, such as the performance of incremental innovation projects. Cash is also favored in larger firms where alternative mechanisms—usually stock-related—have less incentive power. Giving stock of a large firm provides little incentive, as the performance of the stock depends only to a very small extent on a particular innovation project.

Stock-based incentives are better suited for smaller firms—where the impact of an innovation is likely to have a large effect on the performance of the firm—and for radical innovations—which are supposed to change to a large extent a market and take longer to fully be translated into value. In larger firms, stock-based compensation for radical innovation is based on stock of the new entity being created around the innovation. In addition to cash and stock-related economic incentives, there is a large spectrum of other types of incentives—from prizes to promotions or perks. In most cases, these alternative mechanisms can be easily translated into cash. Their use is often based on the social or psychological aspects of the incentive. For instance, receiving a prize for achieving a particular goal carries not only the economic value, but the social value of being recognized within the organization as having received the prize and the psychological value of having been awarded the prize. Sometimes, companies use these prizes to provide lower economic incentives, with the expectation that the social and psychological values will work as substitutes. This approach to lower expenses has to be used with care unless the prize has a very large significance and reputation within the firm. Otherwise, people will see through it and the prize will be perceived as negative rather than positive.

CONCLUSION

Rewards help to balance the essential tasks of creativity and value capture and provide a crucial link between the innovation strategy and performance. But rewards alone won't do the work. When thinking about designing rewards, it is important to consider whether the overall environment is adequate to stimulate the generation of ideas and their translation into value. In this chapter, the innovation environment has been analyzed through four different perspectives—resources, interactions, knowledge, and motivation. Understanding these four levers is required for rewards to be effective.

NOTES

1. Innovation has multiple dimensions, and the incremental/radical dimension is just one of them. For a more in-depth discussion on dimensions of innovation, see Gatignon, H., Tushman, M. L., Smith, W., & Anderson, P. 2002. A structural approach

to assessing innovation: Construct development of innovation locus, type, and characteristics. *Management Science* 48 (9): 1103–1122.

2. Radical innovation can define very different business models. Some authors have argued that only start-up firms can deliver such a level of innovation, and that large firms should not try radical innovation but instead purchase promising start-ups. See Markides, C. 1998. Strategic innovation in established companies. *Sloan Management Review* 39 (3): 31–42.

3. On creativity in organizations, see Csikszentmihalyi, M. 1996. *Creativity: Flow and the psychology of discovery and invention.* New York: HarperCollins. Also see Jennifer George and Jin Zhou in this edited book.

4. On the importance of resources, see Amabile, T. M. 1997. Motivating creativity in organizations: On doing what you love and loving what you do. *California Management Review,* 40 (1): 39–58.

5. The inward looking of certain teams (and even companies) is referred to as the Not-Invented-Here (NIH) syndrome.

6. For the importance of culture, see Tushman, M. L. & O'Reilly III, C. A. 1997. *Winning through innovation: A practical guide to leading organizational change and renewal.* Boston: Harvard Business School Press. See also in this edited book chapters by Flamholtz and Kannan-Narasimhan and Manzoni.

7. For an analysis on the use of stretch goals, see Epstein, M. J. and Manzoni, J. F. 2001. Conflicting roles of budgets: Beyond trade-offs towards reconciliation. *Working paper, Rice University and INSEAD.*

8. For an analysis of target costing, see Koga, Kentaro, and Antonio Davila (1999) "What is the role of performance goals in product development? A Study of Japanese camera manufacturers" in Michael A. Hitt, Patricia Gorman Clifford, Robert D. Nixon and Kevin P. Coyne, editors *Dynamic strategic resources: development, diffusion and integration.*

9. For an analysis of cost management in product development, see Davila, Antonio, and Marc Wouters. 2004. Designing cost-competitive technology products: Improving product development through cost management, *Accounting Horizons.*

10. On the importance of cross-functional teams, see Clark, K. and Fujimoto, T. 1991. *Product development performance.* Boston: Harvard Business School Press; or Brown, S. L. and Eisenhardt, K. M. 1995. Product development: Past research, present findings, and future directions. *Academy of Management Review* 20: 343–378.

11. For more information on how BP structured its learning processes, see Andris Berzins, Joel Podolny, and John Roberts. (1998) British petroleum (B): Focus on learning. Graduate School of Business, Stanford University, case # IB-16B.

12. For an analysis of strategic alliances, see Arino, A., de la Torre, J., and Ring, P. S. 2001. Relational quality: Managing trust in corporate alliances. *California Management Review* 44(1): 109–132.

13. For a more in-depth elaboration of boundary systems, see Simons, R. 1995. *Levers of control: How managers use innovative control systems to drive strategic renewal.* Boston: Harvard Business School Press.

14. The rise to prominence of economics (and microeconomics in particular) has increased this partial view of human motivation. While economics does not assume that

money is the only motivator (actors maximize utility), often and for the sake of argument, utility is simplified to wealth. But this assumption is forgotten and the concept of the "economic man" who only cares about wealth is what is left (Simons and Mintzberg).

15. This comment is easily extended to academics. Just promise free lunch as part of a research seminar and the turnout and level of commitment rise significantly.

16. For a study on the effect of incentives on new product development project performance, see Davila, A. 2003. Short-term economic incentives in new product development. *Research Policy* 32: 1397–1420.

17. For a more detailed analysis of stage-gate, see McGrath, M. D. 1995. *Product strategy for high-technology companies*. New York: Richard Irwin, Inc.

18. For the dangers of overemphasizing incentives, see Teresa M. Amabile, Motivating creativity in organizations: On doing what you love and loving what you do, *California Management Review* 40, no. 1 (1997): 39–58; Mihaly Csikszentmihalyi, *Creativity: Flow and the psychology of discovery and invention* (New York: Harper Collins, 1996).

19. Nikon's product strategy also involves time-to-market, product performance, quality, etc. The performance measurement system highlights all these performance dimensions. For a more detailed discussion on performance measurement systems, see chapters by Epstein and Corrales and Etiennot in this book series or Davila, Epstein, and Shelton. 2005. *Making innovation work*, Wharton School Press.

20. An academic study reports evidence indicating that the evaluation of individual team members and individual reward based on position and status are correlated to a higher satisfaction among team members as opposed to a generic team reward for all members. Survey referenced in Shikhar Sarin and Vijay Mahajan, The Effect of reward structures on performance of cross-functional product development teams, *Journal of Marketing* 65 (2001): 35–53.

Index

NOTE: Page numbers ending in f indicate figures; numbers ending in t indicate tables.

About the Editors and Contributors

Tony Davila is a faculty member at IESE Business School, University of Navarra, and the Graduate School of Business at Stanford University, where he specializes in performance measurement and control systems for innovation management. He consults for large companies and Silicon Valley start-ups and has published in leading journals, including *Research Policy* and the *Harvard Business Review.* With Marc J. Epstein and Robert Shelton, he is co-author of *Making Innovation Work.*

Marc J. Epstein is Distinguished Research Professor of Management, Jones Graduate School of Management, Rice University, and was recently visiting professor and Hansjoerg Wyss Visiting Scholar in Social Enterprise at the Harvard Business School. A specialist in corporate strategy, governance, performance management, and corporate social responsibility, he is the author or co-author of over 100 academic and professional papers and more than a dozen books, including *Counting What Counts, Measuring Corporate Environmental Performance, Making Innovation Work* (with Tony Davila and Robert Shelton), and *Implementing E-Commerce Strategies* (Praeger, 2004), and co-editor and contributor to the multi-volume set *The Accountable Corporation* (Praeger, 2005). A senior consultant to leading corporations and governments for over twenty-five years, he currently serves as editor-in-chief of the journal *Advances in Management Accounting.*

Robert Shelton is principal at PRTM Management Consultants. He advises executives in a wide variety of industries and speaks on issues of innovation and business strategy to corporate, government, and university audiences around the world. He previously served as managing director at Navigant Consulting, vice president and managing director with Arthur D. Little, and managing director of the Technology Management Practice at SRI International, and his work has been cited in such publications as the *Wall Street Journal* and CNN Financial News and has been broadcast on NPR. With Marc J. Epstein and Tony Davila, he is co-author of *Making Innovation Work.*

Katrina E. Bedell-Avers is a doctoral student in industrial/organizational psychology at the University of Oklahoma. Her major research interests include outstanding leadership, planning for innovation, and creativity.

James E. Carter is a director in the energy practice of Navigant Consulting, Inc. He has conducted creativity and assertiveness seminars for a number of commercial enterprises. As a vice president for several service companies, Mr. Carter established and nurtured creative cultures in organizations as large as 500, achieving significant improvements in productivity, profitability, and morale. He holds degrees in engineering, business, and law; has been admitted to the bar; and is a licensed professional engineer.

Terry Dartnall is senior lecturer in the School of Information and Communication Technology at Griffith University, Brisbane, Australia. He has held fellowships at Otago University, the Australian National University, and Sussex University, and senior positions at Adelaide University and the National University of Singapore. He is interested in the foundations of artificial intelligence (AI) and cognitive science, and in human and machine creativity. He has chaired international conferences on AI and creativity, served on many editorial boards, and been an advisor to the National Science Foundation. He is a recipient of the prize for Best Contribution to Cognitive Science in Australasia. He is editor of *Creativity, Cognition, and Knowledge* (Praeger, 2002); also a fiction writer, his short story collection, *The Ladder at the Bottom of the World*, was published as an ebook in 2006.

Eric G. Flamholtz is president of Management Systems Consulting Corporation, which he co-founded in 1978. He is also professor at UCLA's Anderson School of Management and has served previously on the faculties of Columbia University and the University of Michigan. He is a member of the Board of Directors of 99 Cents Only Stores, a NYSE company. While earning his doctorate at the University of Michigan, he worked as a researcher for Rensis Likert at the Institute for Social Research.

Tamara L. Friedrich is a doctoral student in industrial/organizational psychology at the University of Oklahoma. Her major research interests include creativity, the management of innovation, and leadership.

Jennifer M. George is the Mary Gibbs Jones Professor of Management and professor of psychology in the Jesse H. Jones Graduate School of Management, Rice University. She has published many articles in leading journals such as the *Academy of Management Journal, Academy of Management Review, Journal of Applied Psychology, Journal of Personality and Social Psychology, Organizational Behavior and Human Decision Processes,* and *Psychological Bulletin*. She is currently an associate editor for the *Journal of Applied Psychology* and serves on the editorial review boards of the *Academy of Management Review,*

Administrative Science Quarterly, Organizational Behavior and Human Decision Processes, International Journal of Selection and Assessment, and *Journal of Managerial Issues.* Her research interests include affect, mood, and emotion in the workplace, personality influences, groups and teams, creativity, pro-social behavior, values, work-life linkages, and stress and well-being.

Samuel T. Hunter is a Ph.D. candidate in industrial/organizational psychology at the University of Oklahoma. His major research interests include creative cognition, innovation management, and outstanding leadership.

Rangapriya Kannan-Narasimhan is a doctoral student in the human resources and organizational behavior department at the Anderson School of Management, UCLA. Her research interests include corporate entrepreneurship, organizational culture and cross-cultural psychology. She has co-authored articles on these topics that have been included in scholarly publications.

Michael D. Mumford is University Professor of industrial and organizational psychology, director for the Center for Applied Behavioral Studies, and professor of management at the University of Oklahoma where he directs the doctoral program in industrial and organizational psychology. Dr. Mumford has published more than 150 articles on creativity, leadership, planning, integrity, and job analysis and has recently been named a George Lynn Cross distinguished research professor. He is a fellow of the American Psychological Association (Divisions 3, 5, and 14), the American Psychological Society, and the Society for Industrial and Organizational Psychology. He serves on the editorial boards for *Creativity Research Journal, Journal of Creative Behavior,* and is currently the senior editor for *Leadership Quarterly.*

Nancy K. Napier is professor of international business and executive director of the Global Business Consortium at Boise State University, where she previously served as a former associate dean of the College of Business and Economies and chairman of the management department. Her articles on creativity and innovation, entrepreneurship, economic development, and organizational culture have appeared in such journals as the *Journal of Management Inquiry, Human Resource Management Journal, Human Resource Planning, Organization, Academy of Management Review, Journal of Management Studies,* and *Journal of International Business Studies.* She also hosts *Idaho Business Matters,* a weekday radio program on NPR News 91, and regularly attends and speaks at professional and academic conferences, including the European Group for Organizational Studies, the Western Academy of Management and National Academy of Management. Her books include: *Managing Relationships in Transition Economies* (with D. Thomas, Praeger, 2004), *Western Women Working in Japan* (with Sully Taylor, Quorum, 1995), and *Strategy and Human Resource Management* (with J. Butler and G. Ferris, Southwestern, 1991).

Dean Keith Simonton is Distinguished Professor of Psychology at the University of California, Davis. Besides nearly 300 articles and chapters, he has authored nine books: *Genius, Creativity, and Leadership* (Harvard, 1984), *Why Presidents Succeed* (Yale, 1987), *Scientific Genius* (Cambridge, 1988), *Psychology, Science, and History* (Yale, 1990), *Greatness* (Guilford, 1994), *Genius and Creativity* (Ablex, 1997), *Origins of Genius* (Oxford, 1999), *Great Psychologists and Their Times* (APA, 2002), and *Creativity in Science* (Cambridge, 2004). His honors include the William James Book Award, the Sir Francis Galton Award for Outstanding Contributions to the Study of Creativity, the Rudolf Arnheim Award for Outstanding Contributions to Psychology and the Arts, the George A. Miller Outstanding Article Award, the Theoretical Innovation Prize in Personality and Social Psychology, the Mensa Award for Excellence in Research, and the Robert S. Daniel Award for Four-Year College/University Teaching. He has also been elected Fellow of the American Association for the Advancement of Science, the American Psychological Association, the Association for Psychological Science, the American Association of Applied and Preventive Psychology, and the International Association of Empirical Aesthetics. He has served as editor of the *Journal of Creative Behavior* and as guest editor of *Leadership Quarterly* and *Review of General Psychology*. His research program concentrates on the cognitive, personality, developmental, and socio-cultural factors behind exceptional creativity, leadership, genius, talent, and aesthetics.

Jing Zhou is associate professor of management at the Jones Graduate School of Management, Rice University. Prior to joining Rice, she was associate professor of management and Mays Fellow in the management department at the Mays Business School at Texas A&M University. Her current research interests include contextual factors that promote or inhibit individual employees' and work teams' creativity and innovation. She has published in top journals in the field of management, such as *Academy of Management Journal*, *Journal of Applied Psychology*, *Journal of Management*, and *Personnel Psychology*. Currently, she serves on the editorial boards of several top journals in her field, including *Academy of Management Journal*, *Academy of Management Review*, *Journal of Applied Psychology*, and *Journal of Management*.